P9-CCY-982

Mary Taylor
Sidoti

(too many siblings! ...
Forgive ...)

On Persephone's Island

A Sicilian Journal

MARY TAYLOR SIMETI

NORTH POINT PRESS
San Francisco   1987

Copyright © 1986 by Mary Taylor Simeti
Drawings copyright © 1986 by Maria Vica Costarelli

First published by Alfred A. Knopf
Reprinted by arrangement

Grateful acknowledgment is made to the following
for permission to reprint previously published
material:
Penguin Books Ltd. Excerpt from *The Peloponnesian
War* by Thucydides, translated by Rex Warner
(Penguin Classics, 1954). Copyright © Rex Warner,
1954. Reprinted by permission of Penguin Books
Ltd., London.
Sellerio Editore. Excerpt from *Delle cose di Sicilia*,
Vol. I, edited by Leonardo Sciascia. © Sellerio
Editore, Palermo, 1980.

Printed in the United States of America
Library of Congress Catalogue Card
Number: 86-62840
ISBN: 0-86547-282-3
SECOND PRINTING

Cover design by David Bullen

North Point Press
850 Talbot Avenue
Berkeley, California
94706

FOR TONINO

Scatter, now, some glory on this island, which
    the lord of Olympus,
Zeus, gave Persephone and bowed his head to
    assent, the pride of the blossoming earth,

Sicily, the rich, to control under towering cities
    opulent;
Kronion granted her also
a people in love with brazen warfare,
horsemen; a people garlanded over and again
    with the golden leaves of olive
Olympian.

                    Pindar, *First Nemean Ode*

On Persephone's Island

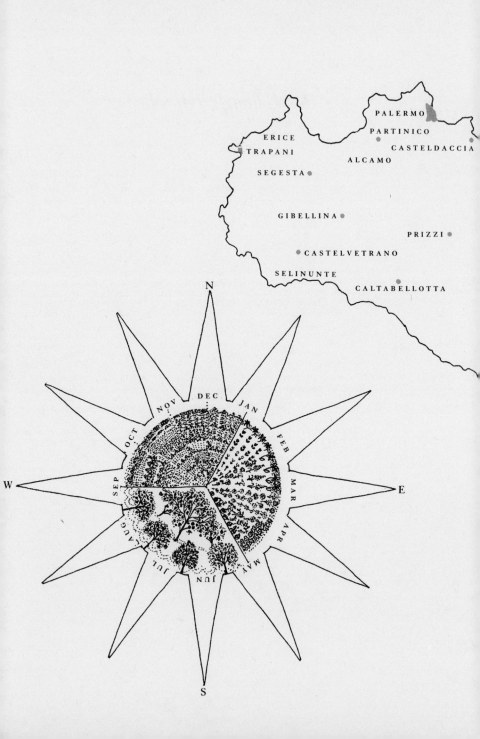

PALERMO

PARTINICO

CASTELDACCIA

ERICE

TRAPANI

ALCAMO

SEGESTA

GIBELLINA

PRIZZI

CASTELVETRANO

SELINUNTE

CALTABELLOTTA

N

NOV DEC JAN

OCT FEB

SEP MAR

W E

AUG APR

JUL MAY

JUN

S

Prologue—October 1962

❧ Like most young Americans traveling abroad in the early sixties, I arrived in Sicily with an excessive number of suitcases, considerable ignorance, and a great many warnings. In college I had studied the Sicilian Middle Ages, and over the summer I had read about Sicilian poverty in the writings of Danilo Dolci, the social reformer at whose center for community development I hoped to volunteer. This kernel of fact, meager as it was, had been fleshed out by the cautionary tales of friends and acquaintances, both at home and in the north of Italy, who all considered me courageous, if not downright foolish, to set off by myself for an island of dazzling sun and bright colors where bandits and mafiosi lurked in the shadows and where the rest of the population was proud and reserved, distrustful of foreigners, and sure to misinterpret the presence of a young girl alone.

But from the window of the train that was bearing me south to Palermo the only color to be seen was gray: gray storm clouds piled up against gray mountains, gray olive trees tossing up the silver undersides of their leaves to the wind, and a gray sea tossing up silver foam onto gray rocks and beaches as the train threaded its way through the necklace of tunnels and coves strung out along the coasts of Calabria and northern Sicily.

My mother was living in Florence at that time, and it was there that I boarded the train in the middle of the night. Living on my own in a Sicilian village was not what my mother had had in mind when she offered me a year in Italy to celebrate my graduation from Radcliffe, and as she saw me into my compartment she was obviously hard put to be both encouraging and liberal minded, and yet with the same breath remind me to be careful about the men, the Mafia, the drinking water, and all the other things that would no doubt come back to her as soon as the train pulled out of the station.

On her graduation trip in 1924 she and her college roommate had left the boat at Naples and taken a train across southern Italy to Bari. They were the only women on the train, and the soldiers who shared their compartment spent the whole trip comparing my mother's ankles to those of her friend by measuring them between thumb and forefinger. Yet I did not recognize in her story my own age, my own curiosity, my own train ride south, since I was still too young to believe that she might ever have had any experience relevant to mine. So I hushed her up and settled my suitcases as quickly as I could, anxious not to disturb my fellow travelers who were already sleeping in their bunks. The Florence stop was not a long one, and soon we were moving, my mother waving forlornly in the yellow light of the station platform as the darkness swallowed us up.

It was not a restful night. I was too excited to do more than doze, and two of my fellow travelers turned out to be under three and equally excited, so I was glad when the train pulled into Naples in the uncertain light of a gray dawn, and I could abandon any pretense of sleep and introduce myself to the Sicilian family whose compartment I was sharing. My Italian was only just adequate and I was quite unaccustomed to the Sicilian accent, but I managed to understand that they had emigrated to Milan in search of work some years before and were returning to Palermo for a visit. I also managed to explain that I was traveling alone, via Palermo, to the town of Partinico, where I intended to live by myself and to work for the next year or two.

They were horrified. Throughout the morning, as we wove our way slowly down the Calabrian coast, they alternated between pressing me with large rolls and thick slices of salame from their shopping bag of provisions, and reiterating their surprise and indignation that a young American girl should choose—nay— should be allowed to wander off into the wilds of Sicily with no family to protect her. There was no censure, only commiseration. Surely my mother was out of her mind.

By the time the train had backed and filled itself, first on, then off the ferry that carried us across the Straits of Messina, it was early afternoon, but the heavy rain that shut out the landscape made it seem still later. Another passenger joined us at Messina, a man in his thirties who stared at me steadily from behind his dark glasses.

His gaze was, however, a minor discomfort. What I could not avoid was the fact that I had wired the Dolci Center asking to be met at the Palermo station at two-thirty, yet as the train rolled on it was becoming increasingly apparent that we couldn't possibly arrive anywhere near that hour. At last I broke the silence that had fallen upon the compartment since the man in dark glasses had joined us, and asked if we were far from Palermo. It turned out that we still had most of Sicily to cross, that the scheduled arrival time was two hours later than I had been told in Florence, and furthermore the man in dark glasses, who worked for the railroad, claimed that the train was already an hour behind schedule. As the afternoon wore on and the sky got darker and darker, it became clearer and clearer that there would be no one waiting for me at the Palermo station.

I was somewhat of an anachronism even for 1962: most of my traveling had been done with my family, and in almost the same style in which my mother had traveled in 1924—not a step taken without the blessings of Wagon-Lits Cook. Confident of being met in Palermo, I had neglected to plan beyond my arrival there. I had no idea in which direction Partinico lay or how I could get there on my own. Neither, it turned out, did my fellow passengers, who were all true Palermitani and considered anything that lay beyond as unworthy of civilized interest. They supposed that there was a bus to Partinico, but when and from where it might depart, nobody knew.

The compartment took my plight to heart, discussing the pros and cons of the various possible solutions with what I was discovering to be a true Mediterranean love and enthusiasm for other people's problems. And, unfortunately for my already shattered peace of mind, with the true Mediterranean sense of melodrama: it seemed that wherever I might turn, a fate worse than death awaited me. I suggested a hotel. "A young girl alone?!" The couple insisted that I go with them to their parents' house, but with visions of sleeping six to a bed I assured them that that was quite impossible. The man in dark glasses then promised that the minute we arrived he would go off to find out about the bus, and it was on that note of dramatic suspense that the train finally emerged from the darkening rain into the relative cheer of the Palermo station.

Vast numbers of relatives were waiting to welcome home the young family, and, reluctantly accepting my last grateful but firm refusal of their offers of hospitality, they climbed down to be wrapped up and carried off in a cloud of tears, cries, and resounding kisses.

I had brought with me all and more than I needed for a year's stay and could not take a step without assistance. But the man in dark glasses helped me to assemble my luggage on the station platform and went off in search of a bus schedule. The astonishingly large crowd that had been waiting for the train had by this time captured and borne off its prey, and the platform was almost empty except for the railway workers. Perched on a large pile of suitcases, I watched the man in dark glasses disappear into the station. I felt sure that I would never see him again, and twenty-four hours of travel and admonitions had so flattened me that I never stopped to think how strange it was that this should upset me. But in a few minutes he was back.

"The last bus left an hour ago. There is nothing to be done. I must drive you to Partinico in my car."

My better judgment didn't stand a chance. It wasn't until my suitcases and I were piled into a little Fiat and parked by a bar where the man in dark glasses was telephoning to his mamma that he would be late for supper, that the voice of *my* mamma could be heard above my desperation. Who was this man who was driving me off into the night? I was still debating whether I had time to get out and make a note of the number on the license plate without being caught in what would have been an excruciatingly embarrassing position when he came back and we were off.

The lights of the city dropped rapidly behind and below us, as the road we were following climbed steadily upward. It was almost completely dark now, but the headlights reflecting off the wet tar gave enough light for me to see that we were curving back and forth along the side of a mountain, sheer rock on my side of the road, sheer drop on the other. It was interesting, he'd never driven this road before, said he as we skidded briskly around the bends. Very, said I, bracing myself for the crash.

It seemed an endless journey, but it can't have been more than half an hour before we were in Partinico, asking directions to the Center, and I was wondering how I could be sufficiently polite and grateful while discouraging any follow-up on our acquaintance. The Center was still open, and when I and all my luggage were safely unloaded, the man in dark glasses shook my hand, waved aside my thanks, and drove off. I never saw him again, or had another chance to express my gratitude for what he had done for me.

I owe him much more than just a ride. By his disinterested generosity toward a foreigner in difficulty, the man in dark glasses stripped me of the prejudices instilled by the warnings of well-meaning friends and delivered me to Partinico with my honor and my belongings intact, my spirit cheered, and my mind free to discover Sicily for myself. Now, as twenty years later I attempt to draw a portrait of my destination, I can see that these two figures have stood sentinel throughout my journey: my mother, whose passionate curiosity for all that surrounded her was a legacy far more valuable to me than her warnings, and the nameless Sicilian whose chivalrous gesture was my introduction to the strong, impulsive soul of Sicily, a soul that reaches across and beyond all that is so distressing here and, like the island sun, warms and illumines even as it creates dark shadows.

I WINTER

In October the sowing of the wheat
begins, and November honors that which
lies beneath the ground awaiting
rebirth; the dead return in a ritual visit to
the living, just as the living celebrate
the cult of the dead, and the whole period
between the beginning of November
and Epiphany is a *tempus terribile*, in which
the gates to the Afterworld remain open.

Franco Cardini,
I giorni del sacro: il libro delle feste

THE ZISA, PALERMO

Chapter One

❧ November is a time of beginnings in the double calendar that we follow in our family. Our life here in Sicily is divided between the academic year, which requires our presence in Palermo—where my husband, Tonino, teaches agricultural economics at the university and where our children, Francesco and Natalia, go to school—and the agricultural year, which turns our attention to the vineyards and the olive groves at Bosco, the family farm thirty miles away. Here we take refuge as soon as school lets out for vacation, for a summer of farming after a winter of academic pursuits.

The grapes ripened late this year because of the exceptionally dry summer, so we commuted back and forth from the middle of September, when the schools opened, well into October. But we cannot manage that all year round: quite apart from the exorbitant price of gas here, no one lives on the land in this part of Sicily, we have no neighbors in wintertime, no friends for the children to see, and no guarantee of getting through the mud to the highway once the heavy rains begin.

Every so often the unpleasantness of urban life becomes too much for us and we talk of moving out permanently, but the problems this would create for the children are enormous, so each time we reconcile ourselves to continuing this split existence, at least until our younger child has finished high school.

We are sowing no wheat this year; the fields that last winter held the seed will lie fallow until spring, and October has been dedicated to equipping the children for the winter and to at least the pretense of catching up with the wear and tear on the Palermo apartment, despite our reluctance to invest time and money here when so much remains to be done at Bosco.

That done, I am free to descend to the tiny office on the ground floor of our apartment building where I have spent the last few winters reading about Sicily, research for a book of months that would trace the varying rhythms and calendars—archaic, agrarian, contemporary—that govern the passage of time on the island. But time takes over as I take up my pen; the day I start to write ushers in my twenty-first year in Sicily. What began twenty years ago as a brief visit, an interlude between college and graduate school, has been transformed by choice and circumstance into permanence. Right from the outset, then, the book of months becomes a journal, a chronicle of my Sicilian coming of age, in which these personal beginnings, mine and my family's, coincide with a new year in that classical calendar that provides the structure for my thoughts. For rural Sicily still belongs to Magna Graecia, her crops and her celebrations still echo those of the ancient Greeks, for whom

> the agricultural year fell into three main divisions, the autumn sowing season followed by the winter, the spring with its first blossoming of fruits and flowers, . . . and the early summer harvest . . . of grain and fruits [to which] was added with the coming of the vine the vintage and the gathering in of the later fruits. . . .
>
> Jane Ellen Harrison, *Prolegomena to the Study of Greek Religion*

❦ Sicily joins me in celebrating this alternative New Year's and welcomes November and the onset of winter with festivity. All Saints' Day is followed by All Souls' Day, officially known as the "Commemoration of the Defunct," but more familiarly called I Morti, "The Dead." "What are you doing over The Dead this year?" For years I have puzzled over I Morti, convinced that to understand why it is the most beloved of the Sicilian feast days would be to grasp some basic truth about the Sicilian character.

If the inner meaning still eludes me, the outer trappings entrance, since I Morti is to the Sicilian child what Christmas is to the American. During the night the dead come out of the convents and the cemeteries where they are buried and go about the town in procession, leaving behind them presents for those children who have been good and have remembered them in their prayers: hidden troves of elaborate toys, of marzipan and sugar statues.

Just at the time that the countryside turns in upon itself to nurse the dormant seeds and vines, Palermo blossoms forth in this artificial flowering of marzipan, a cornucopia of fruit and vegetables molded out of almond paste. Each pastry shop works hard to outdo its competitors in realism—spiny prickly pears with all their prickles, pomegranates bursting with seeds, roast chestnuts tinged with the bloom of ashes—until the shopwindows rival in miniature the variety and the color of the vegetable stalls in the marketplace.

Here marzipan is known as *pasta reale* or as *frutta di Martorana*, from the convent of the Martorana in Palermo, where the nuns excelled in the preparation of almond paste. It is said that once their mother superior, Sister Gertrude, wishing to celebrate the pastoral visit of the bishop, instructed the nuns to mold the paste into apples, peaches, pears, and oranges, which were then hung on the trees growing in the cloister garden. Strolling in the cloister before dinner with the mother superior, the bishop marveled to see so many different trees bearing fruit all in the same season. Still greater was his surprise when, at the dinner table, he bit into a bright red apple and discovered that it was made of almond paste.

Today it is still possible to play a practical joke with *pasta reale*, even if it would be difficult to invent one as enchanting as Sister Gertrude's: you can buy cakes of soap, sandwiches with the filling dribbling out, even complete meals served on paper plates. I once gave my children fried eggs and peas for supper, and it wasn't until they put their forks to it that they realized it was made of marzipan.

There is a pastry shop in the center of Palermo that used to elaborate on a different theme each year. Once they made marzipan seafood—fish of every size and species, clams and mussels, squid and shrimp, all displayed in the shopwindow on the flat wicker trays the fishmongers use, so lifelike as to make the pastry seeker think he had stopped in front of the wrong store. Another time, in an absolute triumph of patience and dexterity, they produced *semenza*, a window full of baskets of peanuts, hazelnuts, toasted chick-peas and pumpkin seeds, marzipan imitations sold in brown paper cones just like the real *semenza* the Sicilians buy at street-corner stalls to nibble on as they make their way up and down the main street on their evening stroll.

The same gay colors of the marzipan are used to decorate the *pupi di cena*, statues made from melted sugar poured into plaster molds, then painted and stuck with bits of silver paper. The shop windows or tiered street stands selling these *pupi* are dominated by the *paladino*, the knight in armor of the Sicilian puppet shows, most often mounted on horseback and brandishing a sword, a snippet of real ostrich plume cascading from his helmet. Next to him will stand a peasant girl balancing a basket of eggs on her hip, a ballerina or a carabiniere in full dress uniform, traditional figures that have recently been joined by Zorro, Superman, and Mickey Mouse.

The same store of marzipan fame used to make marvelous *pupi di cena*, each one individually sculptured and painted with the greatest attention to detail. The year I discovered this store one window was filled with sugar peasants, about fifteen inches high, each selling something different, with baskets of fish or fruit on their heads or jugs of wine and oil in hand. They were very expensive, so I bought only one, to give away as a present. In my ignorance I waited too long to buy one for myself, and when I went back a few years later the man who made them had retired, and the store had only run-of-the-mill knights to sell. I have a knight, a more authentic representative of the tradition and very beautiful in his crude and brilliant colors. But I regret those street vendors.

If the culinary delights of I Morti find their highest expression in Palermo, the smaller towns generate a more festive air. The main street of Alcamo, the town where my husband grew up, is lined with stalls: in addition to the usual (and this time genuine) *semenza* sellers, who have their wares spread out on barrows painted with the bright primary colors of Sicilian carts and strung with lights and paper garlands, there are the torrone vendors, their stall shelves groaning under the weight of vast trays of almonds and hazelnuts in caramelized sugar and spread with slices of the holiday version of torrone, hazelnuts smothered in tricolor nougat striped pea green, white, and shocking pink, a travesty of the Italian flag that is reminiscent of the election night scene in *The Leopard* and is so bilious in aspect as to have discouraged me from ever tasting it. It is nonetheless a gay addition to the holiday scene, as are the toy booths offering something for every pocketbook: elegant dolls ripple their long satiny skirts in the wind, bicycles and push-pedal cars sparkle next to soccer balls and plastic tea sets and compete with clusters of red plastic donkeys on blue wheels, a local version of the hobby horse that appears to be the most beloved—or most economical—of Sicilian toys: they are ubiquitous, propelled by stout little legs along every street and sticking up from every rubbish dump.

The flower sellers brandish bright masses of color, great bunches of yellow, white, bronze, and purple chrysanthemums, the flowers of the dead, which are destined to decorate the tombs. From both sides of the street the calls of the vendors vie for the attention of the endless stream of families enjoying the *passeggiata* and comparing the wares, dressed in their best and walking arm in arm, pushing baby carriages, cracking *semenza* and leaving a train of peanut shells behind them.

Even on a normal Sunday or at the end of a weekday afternoon the *passeggiata* is a solemn rite, the moment when business is transacted, social ties renewed, news spread, and public opinion formed, not to mention an important occasion for asserting one's economic status and ability to dress. Back and forth, arm in arm, the current of people flows along the Corso, diverted into small eddies as it passes the bars, swelling in front of the churches as new strollers come out from mass, impervious to the few fool-hardy drivers who attempt to fend the flood. The *passeggiata* has a morbid fascination: I think of how my husband and his friends, in their rebellious youth, could find nothing more nonconform-ing to do than to move to another street, where they walked up and down in solitary superiority. The poverty of alternatives, al-though much alleviated by the economic boom of the last twenty years, is still depressing to me, as is the idea of having to carry out the bulk of one's social relations under the careful scrutiny of the whole town. But my children, who have grown up in the an-onymity of a modern residential neighborhood in a big city, are intrigued by the *passeggiata;* when they were younger and we were in Alcamo of a Sunday, they would never refuse their father's in-vitation to "go as far as the piazza" and would come back wide-eyed with wonder at the number of people their father knew to stop and speak to.

Until a few years ago I Morti was a long holiday: the first of November was All Saints' Day; the second, All Souls' Day; and the fourth was a national holiday celebrating the end of the First World War, so the third crept quietly in to join the party, schools and offices closed for four days, and a bonus came whenever the four days fell on either side of a weekend. Then, in one of its periodic outbursts of efficiency, the Italian government decided to suppress a great many of the nation's twenty-odd national and religious holidays, or to make them into movable feasts that al-ways fall on Sunday, so now only the first of November is offi-cially recognized. Actually, as often happens, the government's efforts in this direction have had ridiculous side effects. All the middle and secondary school teachers in Italy now have four days' vacation, to spread out during the year as they choose, since the government cannot afford to pay them for the work they do on the four days that were formerly holidays. And most Sicilians, whose respect for the dictates of Rome has always been marginal, continue to enjoy I Morti at length.

Be it long or short, the holiday culminates in the visit to the cemetery. The women of the household make a preliminary trip to clean out the family chapel or spruce up the tombs, sweeping, dusting, throwing out dead flowers, and spreading a fresh cloth, rich with lace and embroidery, on the chapel altar. Everything must be clean and in order for the official visit, and a tomb that is neglected causes comment.

On the appointed day, traditionally November 2, the family assembles, arms laden with flowers, to pay their visit. While this is certainly a harrowing experience for those who have recently had a death in the family, on the whole the atmosphere of festivity spreads from the Corso to embrace the cemetery as well. Children play tag around the cemetery paths while the grown-ups, women to one side and men to another, stand around gossiping, pay visits back and forth between tombs and chapels, observe carefully the quantity and quality of the flowers at each sepulcher, pluck out a few blossoms from their own bunches to lay on the tombs of more distant relatives or friends.

In Partinico, in the years when I was first living in Sicily, the children from the local orphanage were brought to the cemetery to beg contributions for the orphanage funds. No decent funeral in Partinico was without the orphans: a double row of brown rain capes over blue smocks marching at the head of the funeral procession with a fat red-haired woman in attendance. Probably the trips to the cemetery on I Morti were an exciting change in routine for the children, as well as a profitable undertaking for the institution, since anyone would be an easy touch for an orphan on such an occasion. The children themselves did seem cheerful and unperturbed by their constant association with death, and even the funeral processions were rocked by surreptitious shoves and smothered giggles. Nonetheless to me these were scenes straight out of Dickens, and I would be happy to learn that the practice has been discontinued.

Sicilian history is a bitter and bloody succession of wars, conquests, pestilences, and famines. Small wonder, then, that the Sicilians have come to seek consolation and even to luxuriate in the funeral panoply. The coffins still journey in glass-sided carriages drawn by black horses with black plumes nodding on their harnesses, and even the motorized hearses often have large gilt angels weeping on the four corners of the roof. The funeral procession is headed by the priest, together with two or three altar boys; then come the wreaths of flowers, six feet high and bearing black ribbons with gilt letters announcing the names of their donors. A new custom, recently introduced at some funerals in Alcamo, demands that a small group of friends and relatives walk behind the wreath-bearers, carrying armfuls of flowers from which they tear off petals to strew before the coffin. (Although some onlookers derisively describe this, together with chewing gum and other dubious novelties, as an *americanata*, it is in fact a return to the customs of ancient Greece.) The hearse bears the coffin—carved wood for married adults; white for children, spinsters, and bachelors in tribute to their chastity—followed by the family, dressed in black and accompanied by the friends and relatives who bring up the rear of the procession.

A few years ago there was a clamorous case in the Palermo newspapers, when a young girl was severely beaten by her brothers because she hadn't cried in their father's funeral procession. Yet stranger than the need to feign grief where affection is lacking is the preoccupation with public opinion even among those who have nothing to hide. When her eldest son died, my mother-in-law was prostrated, and no one could have doubted the genuineness of her grief, and yet when we would manage to persuade her to come out for a drive so as to have some air and distraction, she would insist on leaving the house by the back door, lest someone should note these outings and take them as a sign of indifference.

Still strictly observed in most parts of Sicily, although in the big cities and among the middle class it has been much curtailed or even eliminated, mourning has many strange rules. The summer her son died, for example, my mother-in-law would not allow us to turn on the lamp in front of the summer house by the sea; if we wanted to enjoy the cool of the evening in the garden we had to do so in the dark. She herself was married, together with her sister, just a short time after her father's death. Her older brother, finding himself with two nubile but engaged sisters on his hands (their mother had died long before), was in a hurry to get them settled, but since they were in mourning, the double ceremony had to be held very simply, and at four o'clock in the morning.

I am fascinated to read, in a footnote to the Greek myths collected by Robert Graves, that the wearing of black for mourning was originally a message to the dead rather than to the living, a disguise adopted to escape being haunted by the ghost of the deceased. This connection with their most distant history has long since lost its original significance for most Sicilians, but I wonder if in the deepest recesses of the uneducated peasant mind it still lingers, a thread in the peculiar time warp that weaves so much of Sicily's ancient past to its present. Certainly the belief in spirits is still strong: my friend Gabriella, who teaches in a junior high school in one of Palermo's poorest neighborhoods, was instructed by her students to avoid clearing the supper table completely and to leave out some bread and wine overnight "for the spirits." Gabriella was very upset at her failure to dispel this superstition, and yet she occasionally finds herself saying *buon giorno* when she is the first one to come home at noon, greeting out loud the spirits of the empty house as her grandmother taught her to.

The Feast of the Dead always ends on a tragic note, as the newspapers publish accounts of the children who have been wounded or blinded by the BB guns or other weapons that the dead have ill-advisedly brought them. The statistics are always accompanied by articles signed by famous educators on how badly the Italians choose their children's toys, everyone clucks his disapproval, and the Sicilians settle down to the winter.

🌱 Actually winter is still far off at the beginning of November. The Sicilian climate is divided into wet, cold winters and hot, very dry summers; with the exception of a few brief rainstorms that sometimes come at the end of August in answer to the winegrowers' prayers, there is usually no rain from early April until mid-October. The October rains are heavy, often causing flooding and damage to the crops, since this is a land of extremes in weather as in many things, and an extreme drought follows more water per minute than one would have ever thought possible.

But the deluge brings Indian summer, here known as Saint Martin's summer in honor of the saint whose feast day falls on the eleventh of November. All over Italy in these days elementary school children are writing on the blackboard: *"Per San Martino, ogni mosto è vino."* For Saint Martin's Day all the must has finished fermenting and become new wine, ready for tasting, accompanied by the *biscotti di San Martino*, little round anise-flavored biscuits as hard as rocks, which appear in all the bakeries at this time. My husband, Tonino, spends hours in the wine cellar, testing, tasting, mixing, and squinting at the light through glasses of new wine, still slightly cloudy, which end up all over the kitchen, deathtraps for the last of the myriad tiny gnats that gather for the grape harvest and stay as long as the cold holds off.

Real summer has slid into Saint Martin's summer with only the slightest drop in temperature this year, and as we drive out to Bosco for the weekend, a brilliant sun lights up the landscape. The leaves turning yellow in the vineyards and dark red in the peach orchards are pale reminders of weekend drives in New England during my childhood. In Sicily the October rains, the crystalline air swept clean of heat haze by winds that bring a suggestion of cold, the smells of must and of roasting chestnuts are harbingers of a very different season. After the long dry summer in which only the stubborn vines and the citrus trees keep their color, when all the grass and the roadside weeds are scorched and withered and the light and dust together bleach the countryside monochrome, Sicily in November turns unexpectedly green. Grass springs up overnight along the roadsides and under the grapevines, which suddenly march across a carpet of *cavoliceddi*, a wild cousin of the mustard family whose intense, almost bitter flavor when boiled and tossed with oil is perfect company for Sicilian sausage spiced with fennel seed. The *giriteddi*, a wild variety of Swiss chard, also spring to new life, and soon we will see old men with sacks over their shoulders out in the fields and along the hedgerows, gathering wild greens to sell in the city markets, where they are still much appreciated despite the increasing industrialization of the urban palates.

The miracle of water repeats itself each autumn. Sicily is green, intensely and springishly green all winter long, green in the vineyards and the olive orchards where the grass grows wild, green in the vegetable gardens where lettuce, spinach, chard, and cabbages will flourish throughout the season, and green in my flower beds, where the weeds, kept under control in the summer by sheet composting and parsimonious watering, now leap into new vigor and battle their way through a foot of mulch. Last summer's petunias are still in bloom, and next spring's ranunculi and nasturtiums are already sprouting their first leaves. This is heady stuff for my northern blood, and my first steps when we arrive at Bosco each Saturday are toward the garden, to see what has come up. Autumn is a race: wait for the rains to soften up the earth for the plow, but make haste before it is too late to sow the vegetables that will keep us through the winter when the tomato vines, the peppers, and the eggplants have given up.

Sometimes I am tempted by the idea of a solar greenhouse, summer all year long, but then I envy the gardeners in my American gardening magazines, who can rest and plan and pore over seed catalogues in the winter months, while I must spend all my Sundays battling to keep up with a week's accumulation of weeds no matter how cold and rainy it may be.

This weekend I am in luck, with two days of sunshine and warmth, perfect for working the soil, softened now after a summer of dry rock-hardness but not yet waterlogged and congealed into heavy clay. I have with me a package of flower bulbs that has just arrived from Holland. Each year I add to my much-beloved collection of narcissus and daffodils, and this year I put in a large order of grape hyacinths, encouraged by the success of the ones I planted two years ago. But the latter have already sprouted all their leaves, and I am assailed by doubts that I am putting the new ones in too late. It is difficult to know where one is at on this island, perched on the edge of the subtropical.

As I work in my flower beds I can hear sounds of conversation and laughter, punctuated by whacking noises, which drift down to me from the olive grove. November is olive time, and the harvest has begun. The harvesters spread nets out under the trees, pick what they can reach from ladders, and beat the rest of the olives down by hitting the branches with canes. Even with the help of the nets it is backbreaking work; many of the olives were flung to the ground by the October storms, and the workers must gather them one by one as they crouch over the cold damp earth. Yet the olive harvest is one of the few occasions in the year when the women go out to work in the fields alongside the men; this unaccustomed company, in marked contrast to the normal routine of long and solitary hours behind plow or hoe, leavens the work, especially when the sunlight filters down through the branches and there is no wind to bite the groping fingers.

The olive harvest has a particular personal quality that the wine harvest has lost, now that most of the growers confer their grapes to the big cooperative wineries. Olive oil is the soul of Sicilian cooking; butter and other vegetable oils are a recent introduction, whereas olive oil has traditionally been used for everything: eaten raw on pasta, salads, and boiled vegetables; used to fry fish or sweet fritters and doughnuts; as a cure for squeaking hinges; or beaten up with lemon juice and rubbed into chapped hands.

I was startled and slightly revolted the first time I saw Tonino rub olive oil onto his skin, for somehow I had never quite focused in on the fact that the oil with which all those classical Greek athletes massaged themselves was the same that I was accustomed to eating on my salad. And yet it would appear that in antiquity, olive oil was prized above all for cosmetic purposes: Psalm 104 speaks of "wine that maketh glad the heart of man, and oil to make his face shine, and bread which strengtheneth man's heart." The oil from the sacred olive groves of Athene was perfumed with volatile oils and awarded to the victors in the Panathenaic contests.

It was the Greek colonizers who brought cuttings of cultivated olives with them to graft onto the wild oleasters of Sicily, and the Sicilian today preserves the greatest respect for this mainstay of his household and goes to great effort and expense to insure his family their year's supply of good, unadulterated oil, preferably grown on trees he knows and processed in a trustworthy press.

Small farmers usually have a few trees, enough for family needs, while even the bigger producers in this area, which does not specialize in olive growing, still operate very much at a personal level and sell their excess production to friends and relatives. It is common for peasants who own no olive trees to sharecrop someone else's, thus buying their annual supply with a few days' work, a habit that persists even when they have become prosperous enough to have acquired their own land.

It is not enough to know which trees your olive oil comes from, unless you also know where and how it has been pressed. Most presses are fairly small family affairs, with five or six men working the machinery, located in barns in the countryside or, more commonly nowadays, in warehouses on the edge of town. We have our own, a country press that was started by my husband's eldest brother, Stefano, shortly before his death, and has been kept going mostly through inertia and the good offices of a friend who is willing to run it for us: "This way I know what oil I'm getting."

The building is big and rambling, typical of the farmhouses around the Gulf of Castellammare, although "farmhouses" is a misleading term, since they are more like minor fortresses, a series of large one- or two-storied buildings with storage, stables, and workers' quarters on the ground floor, and the apartments of the padrone on the piano nobile above, with a balcony from which he could keep a watchful eye on the doings down below. In the course of time the buildings have reached out to embrace a court-yard from which a big gate with enormous iron doors heavy with irons and padlocks gives guarded access to the outside world. Both our house at Bosco and the house at Finocchio where the oil press is located follow this pattern. Finocchio, which is the bigger of the two, belonged to three brothers who divided it up among themselves, and the share that went to Tonino's grandfather and now belongs to his brother Turi includes the oil press on the ground floor and upstairs a tiny apartment, two rooms and an alcove for the bed, plus half the courtyard. The apartment, now completely abandoned, was never used except during the olive harvest: my in-laws would stay there in aid and comfort of Ste-fano while the press was running, and indeed my widowed mother-in-law gave up going out there for "the season" only when she turned eighty.

I had my unforgettable first view of Finocchio only a few days after I arrived in Sicily. The Dolci Center organized a sympo-sium on irrigation in a town on the southern coast of the island, and it was there that I met Tonino. (Only years after we were married did I learn that his presence there was neither profes-sional nor fortuitous: in a period in which Sicilian girls were still very strictly chaperoned, the foreign girls who came to the Cen-ter were hotly contended, and Tonino decided to get first crack, much to the chagrin of the Partinicotti, who lamented that Al-camo got more than its fair share.) Tonino had arranged with the friend who was giving us a ride home to be dropped off at Fi-nocchio, where we arrived at dusk only to find the great gate locked and bolted. Stefano had gone to Alcamo and had locked his par-ents in for safekeeping, which surprised nobody but me. It was apparently unremarkable that one should have to scale the wall to get home. I learned later that there were bandits operating in that area then, the "gang of Highway 113," and for the first few years that I knew Tonino we never traveled the road between Partinico and Alcamo without first emptying our pockets and hiding our cash in my bra.

The olive is a capricious tree: for every year that it bears a heavy load it takes a couple of years off to rest. In the lean years the press opens for only a short time, operating on and off as the meager harvest dribbles in. But in the good years it will open for I Morti and keep going until Christmas, often working round the clock. Finocchio is alive and humming then, the courtyard choked with tractors, cars, and trucks, with brown gunnysacks of olives piled up in the bins along the wall, and with groups of men, peasant and landowner alike dressed in rubber boots and *coppola*, the flat golf cap that in various tweeds (and black for mourning) is the most common note in any southern Italian street. It would be unthinkable for anyone to leave his olives at the press and go home until it was time to come and pick up the oil. The journey from tree to oil jar must be accomplished under the padrone's eye to insure that no olives are exchanged or subtracted, nothing added. And so while the olive sacks stand in line, their owners gossip, play a hand of *scopa*, stretch their legs along the dirt road that leads to the highway, or catch a nap in their cars.

They are attentive when their turn comes, however, adjusting with the utmost precision the great brass weights on the scale where the olives are weighed and following the olives around the big barn as they pass from machine to machine. The sacks are emptied onto rollers that separate out the bitter-tasting twigs and leaves and carry the olives through a spray of water and into a mill that gives them a first coarse chopping. From there they pass into an enormous steel bowl in which two giant stone wheels, perhaps five feet in diameter and two feet thick, revolve in opposite directions as they rotate in a hypnotic and inexorable dance that grinds the olives, pits and all, to a smooth paste. This is squeezed out in a glistening pale brown ribbon onto woven wire disks, which are piled one upon another on wheeled dollies, interspaced with heavy steel disks, and rolled into the presses where they are slowly compressed so that the juice runs out, like maple syrup running down the sides of a stack of pancakes. The juice goes from the presses through the centrifuge and comes out in a thin stream of cloudy green oil, ready to be funneled into plastic jugs and loaded into the cars.

The steady grinding of the great wheels, the whirr of the presses, and the clanking of the steel disks drown out all but the loudest conversations. An invisible brush has painted every surface, each machine, each wall tile and bench with a thin patina of oil, and the workmen place their feet warily on the slippery floor. The very air is permeated with the smell of the new oil, which clings to one's clothes and vies with the perfume of the jasmine vine on the courtyard wall. Strong and harsh and ever so slightly bitter, but with all the flavor and the color of the olive intact, Sicilian olive oil is a far cry from the pale insipid stuff that is exported to the States, and a slice of freshly baked Sicilian bread, sprinkled with oil and salt and preferably still hot from an oven that has been fired with almond shells, would beat ambrosia any day. To eat it with the first oil of the new crop assumes the solemnity of a ritual. One November my husband and I happened to drop by the house of a peasant who worked for us just as his wife was taking the week's supply of homemade bread out of the oven. She made us the present of a loaf; Tonino whipped off his sweater, wrapped it carefully around the bread, shoved me and the bread in the car, and made for Finocchio at breakneck speed to get to some new oil before the bread had cooled off.

It is satisfying to see that Francesco and Natalia, despite intimate acquaintance with potato chips, ice cream cones, and all the other enticements that their father's wartime childhood lacked, still have the greatest appreciation for these rituals. Francesco ends every meal, no matter how fancy or filling, with bread and oil, a sort of cork to insure that there are no air bubbles from which horrible hunger pangs might spring, and both children depend on bread and oil to get them from one meal to the next.

❧ The sun is quite low in the sky as I tuck the last of the bulbs under its cover of earth for a very brief sleep and spread the bed with mulch. I must hurry if I am to reach the olive grove before it gets too dark to distinguish the dark brown olives from the earth, and the peasants drive off to town for the night. Etiquette requires that I go to say hello, and although I am genuinely pleased to see the Pirrello family, this rather feudal mantle sits most uncomfortably on my American shoulders.

The nuances and contrasts that color our relations with the various peasants who work for us are a capsule history of Sicily in the last fifty years. The people who are picking our olives—they own no olives themselves and sharecrop a part of our olive grove rather than buy oil for family consumption—are all related to the three Pirrello brothers whose father was a sharecropper for Tonino's grandfather. They are tireless workers—at the grape harvest it is hard to find other people who are willing to work in the same crew with them and maintain their murderous rhythm—and have managed with great sacrifice and frugality to accumulate a certain capital: some of the land they cultivate now is their own, and each brother has transformed his small one-room house in Alcamo into a two- or three-storied building. Cicco still keeps a mule, but more out of habit than necessity, since he has a car now for going out from Alcamo to the fields to work, and Nito has a tractor.

Apart from harvesting the olives, they don't really do very much work for us anymore: as one by one the old vineyards on the property that had come into the Simeti family together with the Pirrellos as part of my mother-in-law's dowry ceased to produce, the sharecropping contract was abolished, and now the peasants work only on a daily wage basis, pruning and tying up the new vines on the land that now belongs to my brother-in-law.

Cicco, the eldest of the Pirrello brothers, is small and white haired, prematurely aged and bent by a lifetime of hoeing under the Sicilian sun and wind. Whenever I see him out of his element, seated at home during a visit or in church during a funeral, I am struck by his awkwardness in repose, his inability to relax in a chair, his very limbs expressing their impatience to be back at work. Nito once drove our tractor from one vineyard to another for us at the end of a long day of grape harvesting. A flat tire delayed us, and when we finally arrived to pick him up, we discovered that while he waited he had cut down all the weeds around a deserted barn, "just to pass the time."

Centuries' accumulation of work and technique and know-how is ending with these three brothers. They have several sons, none of whom wants to go on in agriculture. Emigration and the postwar Italian economic boom, which filtered down to Sicily only in the sixties and seventies, have emptied the countryside of labor, for the young men refuse the endless hours and thankless conditions under which their fathers labored. The few who remain command handsome salaries, and soon there will be only small farmers who do all their own work, most of it mechanized, helped out by family and friends at peak moments like the grape harvest, and large-scale capital-enterprise farmers who can afford to hire labor on a year-round, full-time basis. Tonino's race is dying out too; the middle-class farmer who is really just a small-scale absentee landlord has little place in Sicily's future, and Francesco and Natalia will face some difficult decisions when they inherit the farm.

Meanwhile Tonino and the Pirrello brothers move tentatively about amidst echoes of former relationships. Having known Tonino since he was a baby, the Pirrellos have always addressed him with the familiar *tu* form. He refused to do as his mother wished and ask that they give him the formal address when he assumed direction of the farm, and he often greets them half-jokingly in the same manner that they, out of habit ingrained by centuries of servitude but also courtliness, often greet him: *Baciamo le mani*— We kiss your hands. He feels guilty because he has neither the time nor the natural inclination to control and to discuss at length their work, but they tend to take this as a sign of neglect and indifference rather than as evidence of his trust.

Tonino at least grew up in a world in which this relationship was still natural. I have no such past to temper the awkwardness I feel in coming on them like the lady of the manor as they work, and the hoeing that seemed arduous while I was planting my bulbs now appears a capricious fancy, decorative and unproductive. Consider the lilies of the field, I tell myself as I approach the olive trees. The Pirrellos quickly allay my discomfort with the warmth of their greetings, their expressions of wonder at how tall the children have grown (Francesco overtook them all by the time he was twelve, and Natalia is headed in the same direction), and their concern for my mother-in-law's health. I navigate safely the perilous waters of their kinship, linking the right wife and children to each brother, and remain there picking and chatting with them until they decide to stop for the evening.

The next morning the children and I go down with baskets to the vineyard where the red grapes grow. Tonino planted this piece of land about ten years ago, experimenting with table olives interspersed with red-grape vines. Olive trees are slow growers, so it will be a long time before these trees are big enough to need all the land for themselves, and in the meantime the grapevines have come into full production. Bosco lies in an area that is famous for its white wine, the Bianco Alcamo D.O.C., and Sicily has never produced much red wine, so the choice of red grapes was a whim on Tonino's part anyway. In the beginning the vineyard produced only a small keg of very strong vinegar each season; we have a photograph of the children in bathing suits and rubber boots stamping on the first year's harvest, enough to fill a plastic baby bath. Once, in a moment of bitter disappointment, Tonino told the children that the vineyard was theirs—a rash move, since it now produces excellent wine—but fortunately they have never taken their proprietorship very seriously.

The grapes have long since been harvested, however, and it is the olive trees that demand our attention. There aren't very many olives, since some trees don't bear at all yet, but patient searching fills up two baskets with large olives ripened to a dark reddish purple that will turn black in the curing. The olives I picked early in October when they were still green were soaked in water and then put down with oregano and fennel seed in a brine salty enough to pass the universal test of floating an egg. These I will spread in fruit crates and sprinkle with coarse salt to make the bitter juice drain away and then, next Sunday, I will dry them off one by one and put them into jars to be covered with newly pressed oil.

Outside the kitchen door two quince trees grow, a reminder to me each time I look out that the jam season is not yet over. Each fall I struggle against the wind, the passersby, and the suspiciousness of my mother-in-law (she would much prefer me to pick them green and useless than to see some thief enjoy them ripe) to keep the big fuzzy quinces on the trees until they have properly ripened to a bright yellow. This year I have won, and the ripe quinces are transported to Palermo with us to be turned into jam and into *cotognata*, a thick paste that is dried in molds and then cut into slices, a favorite Sicilian sweet. One of the prettiest products of the Sicilian ceramic tradition are the *cotognata* molds, shallow pottery bowls with designs in relief on the bottom—fish, flowers, or a fancily decorated *M* for the Virgin Mary. I like them so much that I use the ones I have all year round as ashtrays, and my *cotognata* has the simple flat form of an ordinary dessert plate.

❧ Despite brief intervals of furious rainfall, Saint Martin's summer holds for the whole month: the morning crispness wilts in the sun, Francesco bundles up only to return at noon in a T-shirt, his discarded sweaters stuffed into his book bag. On the farm the end of November brings a moment of respite, with nothing to be harvested, fermented, or cured, so I propose a different weekend to end the month: Saturday in Palermo for the pleasure of the kids, old enough now to prefer the company of their peers to the pastoral delights of Bosco, and on Sunday a trip to the city of Enna.

Tonino has often been to Enna for professional reasons, but the rest of us have seen it only from the *autostrada* to Catania, perched high on a mountain that marks the very center of the island, the "navel of Sicily." So strategic a location has naturally been a temptation to the many succeeding waves of conquerors that have swept over the island, and Enna has been besieged and stormed many times, yet surprisingly enough its thirteenth-century castle has managed to survive being such a bone of contention and remains one of the biggest and best-preserved fortresses in Sicily.

If it is the castle and the drive through the sweeping wheat fields of the interior, so different from the vineyards and orchards of the coastal plain around Bosco, that I use as bait for the family, for me this trip is something of a pilgrimage. Enna is the ancient seat of the cult of Demeter, the corn goddess, patroness of agriculture and the good harvest, bestower of fertility, the Mother. Together with her daughter Persephone she held all Sicily, the most fertile of the Mediterranean islands, in her protection, and her shrine stood on the top of the mountain on Enna, overlooking the wheat fields and the flowering plain where Hades (or Dis) galloped his black horses as he bore off Persephone, known to the Romans as Proserpine, to be his queen in the Underworld.

> Near Enna walls there stands a Lake Pergusa is the name
> Cayster heareth not more songs of Swans than doth the same.
> A wood environs every side the water round about,
> And with his leaves as with a veil doth keep the Sun heat out.
> The boughs do yield a cool fresh Air: the moistness of the ground
> Yields sundry flowers: continual spring is all the year there found.
> While in this garden Proserpine was taking her pastime,
> In gathering either Violets blue, or Lillies white as Lime,
> And while of Maidenly desire she filled her Maund and Lap,
> Endeavoring to outgather her companions there. By hap
> Dis spied her: loved her: caught her up: and all at once well near:
> So hasty, hot, and swift a thing is Love, as may appear.

The Lady with a wailing voice afright did often call
Her Mother and her waiting Maids, but Mother most of all
And as she from the upper part her garment would have rent,
By chance she let her lap slip down, and out the flowers went.
And such a silly simpleness her childish age yet bears,
That even the very loss of them did move her more to tears.

Ovid, *The Metamorphoses*

Of all my early schooling I best remember the many happy
hours spent drawing scenes from the Greek myths as our teacher
read them aloud to us, and I still visualize the gods as they appeared in the drawings pinned up on my classroom walls. Given
this felicitous introduction to Greek civilization, it is odd that
during my subsequent career as a history major I should have
avoided any course in classical history. Indeed, I felt a distinct
aversion to all things Greek, which only now I see might be related to the truly horrendous view that Olympian mythology takes
of women. What was a young girl to make of such a bevy of first-
class bitches? However expurgated a version we were given, there
was little there to reconcile us to the role of wife and mother for
which the 1950s were so assiduously preparing us. Aphrodite was
a slut, Hera was a jealous shrew, and if Athena and Artemis, despite a rather nasty taste for revenge, came out middling well, the
price to pay was eternal virginity. Last came Pandora, to heap all
the world's ills on shoulders already bent under Eve's contribution. No wonder I developed a distaste for the Greeks.

One cannot, however, live twelve miles from the temple of
Segesta and remain immune to the power of the Greek world.
From finding passive pleasure in the contemplation of a classical
landscape, I have slowly progressed to searching out the Greek
sites and learning to listen to what they have to say to me. Sicily
is studded with classical sites: the solitary perfection of the temple at Segesta; the overrestored and overcrowded temples at Agrigento strung out along a crest of land against the sea; the tumbled
ruins of Selinunte; the giant altars and theaters of Syracuse. But
I have most often found myself drawn to the lesser, more ancient

sanctuaries that lie in the shadows of the magnificent monuments to Olympian deities, to the altars where the archaic cult of the Great Mother melded with the worship of the Olympian Demeter and her daughter, the Maiden, Kore, to become that of Persephone, Queen of the Dead, who holds in her hand the pomegranate as a promise of resurrection and rebirth. These underground, chthonic goddesses were worshiped in caves and at springs, at the Santuario Rupestre at Agrigento, where the fissures in the cliff behind the tiny temple gave up thousands of terracotta votive statues of Demeter and her daughter, and the floor of the temple precinct turns purple in April when tiny wild flags sprout between the stones, or in the lonely sanctuary of the Malaphorus, the Bearer of Fruits, across the river from the acropolis of Selinunte, where a cluster of poppies still dedicates the inner temple to the goddess.

At the same time, although I cannot point to any one initial moment of awareness, Persephone has begun to make herself felt in my life. Perhaps it was when I first read that she had been carried off from Sicily, or my pleasure in the old pomegranate tree that grows outside the gate at Bosco. Perhaps it was my growing interest in calendars: the story of Persephone's descent into the Underworld each winter and her return four months later with the spring was perhaps the earliest attempt to divide the year into seasons and to explain its rhythms.

At first I only joked about the seasonal pattern of my own life, Palermo the Hades from which I emerge each spring for a brief summer in the sun of Bosco; mythical affinities seemed more than slightly ridiculous in the prosaic context of my daily life. It was a chance encounter with the review of a children's book, a retelling of Greek myths with the intent of restoring to the Greek goddesses their archaic, pre-Hellenic dignity, that started me on a serious search for more and different information and led me to realize, as I hunted among the shelves of a feminist bookstore in New York last summer, that many American women are engaged in the same voyage of discovery on which I, independently, have embarked by mere geographical accident.

But I still have trouble taking myself seriously, especially when I look at the tall and graying forty-year-old in the mirror, of whom Junoesque is the very most I can say. Mindful of childhood drawings, of delicate nymphs in diaphanous garments, I am tempted to abandon the whole idea. At least it makes a good story, I tell myself, and, putting my tongue firmly in my cheek, I start off with the family for Enna to begin my search for Persephone.

The *autostrada* from Palermo to Catania runs east along the coast for about fifty miles before dipping south to cut through the center of the island. On this sunny Sunday morning we look out on a landscape remarkably different from our usual weekend fare on the western route to Bosco: the mountains are higher and more dramatic in their outlines, the transition from mountain to coastal plain is more abrupt, the river valleys cut more frequently and more deeply into the landscape. The soft mutations of green and yellow in the vineyards and olive orchards of the west here give way to the dark emerald of the lemon trees that blanket the plain, climb up and down the terraced valley walls, varying in hue only with the play of light and shade. The sun sparkles on the glossy lemon leaves just as it sparkles on the waves of a sea that is also darker here and more intense in color, while the roadsides are carpeted with deep-green acanthus plants. In the spring these will sprout tall spikes of pink-and-white flowers, similar to giant snapdragons, but now the spiky, curling leaves, as perfectly symmetrical on the plant as they are on a Corinthian capital, imitate only the green of the lemon trees.

The landscape changes abruptly as the highway turns south along the valley of the Hymera River and follows the base of the Madonie Mountains, which pose a formidable barrier between the wealthy coast and the barren interior. For a while yet the valley floor preserves the fertility of the coastal plain, its fields the soft blue-green of artichokes and cauliflower plants, but these soon give way to the wheat fields, the famous stands of grain that made Sicily the breadbasket of the Roman Empire. In an endless march they struggle up and down the hillsides, skirting the scarred troughs where erosion has raked away entire pieces of hill, skipping over the slopes too steep to plow, to the north climbing up to the cliffs of the Madonie, to the south disappearing over the crest and on to the next wave of hills. The concrete pillars of the highway viaduct striding along the rocky riverbed echo the infinite progression of the fields and are for long stretches the only sign, together with the careful contour plowing, of human passage. The arrows at the highway exits seem to point nowhere; only occasionally can one see a town crouched on a distant hilltop or a flock of sheep implying the presence of someone to herd and milk them.

In summertime the sun bleaches the stubble left after June's harvest to a blinding white-gold and grinds the earth to powder, but now this desolate landscape is softened by the rain and the plow, upholstered in a green velvet worn thin or even threadbare: the fallow fields are thick with grass; others, plowed early, are pale with the green tips of newly sprouted wheat; and in the most recently worked fields the fresh brown earth shows through completely. Here and there a tuft of orange or yellow where a tree begins to turn belies the green suggestion of spring.

Our destination, hovering high above the road, is entirely wrapped in cloud, and nothing is visible to indicate that we are nearing a large town. Enna is built on a narrow plateau that runs along the crest of a solitary mountain; the sides of the mountain drop away sharply, too steep for building, and the road that switchbacks up from the mountain runs through woods brilliant with autumn colors and carpeted with ferns, where only scattered rosemary bushes recall the Mediterranean.

The car enters the cloud, some walls appear, and we find ourselves in the town. The change from the sunny warmth of Palermo is hard to believe: a bitter wind shreds and agitates the mist that appeared compact when seen from below, and it buffets the car as we drive around the castle at the easternmost extremity of Enna's mountain, to where the Rock of Demeter is poised like an enormous boulder at the very edge of the cliff, over a drop of more than twelve hundred feet down to the plain below.

A narrow footpath brings us up and out onto the flat surface of the rock. This was the site of the shrine in which, according to Cicero, stood giant statues of Demeter and of Triptolemus, son of the king of Eleusis and only witness to Persephone's rape. Grateful for his revealing what had happened to her daughter, Demeter "supplied Triptolemus with seed-corn, a wooden plow, and a chariot drawn by serpents and sent him all over the world to teach mankind the art of agriculture." No sign of the temple remains, but the mist that blots out all evidence of later centuries, save the iron railings to which we cling, re-creates its numinous bulk, repopulates the fields below with white-draped figures, and suggests the tangible and welcome presence of the great goddess, surveying the crops from on high and bringing them to a safe harvest.

Only a few yards but more than a millennium away, the arched portal of the castle awaits us. It is an enormous structure, the outer walls of which were once girded by twenty towers. We pass through two vast courtyards, each large enough to camp an army, before gaining the smaller inner courtyard of the citadel, which gives access to the only remaining tower, the Torre Pisano.

The walls of this square tower, made of the same gray stone as the rest of the castle, rise up in sharp, clean lines for about three stories before ending in very simple crenellations. The austerity of the outline is softened by the ivy growing up the walls, as elsewhere in the courtyard the occasional shrub or rosebush suggests what medieval gardens once flourished here. The tower is fully restored, and we are able (and, in obedience to the law of ascending motion that governs travel with children, required) to climb up the narrow inner staircase and stand on the top for as long as we can resist the bite of the wind, staring out from between the crenellations and waiting for the wind to blow holes in the curtain of mist that hangs all around us. Occasionally the folds draw back and we can look down for a moment to the sunlit plain below, see Lake Pergusa sparkling in the distance, glimpse Etna, the great volcano that dominates eastern Sicily.

Perhaps it is the overly thorough restoration that has obliterated the character of this building, suitable for toy soldiers or for someone who has only read about castles. Whatever charm it may retain for us cannot compete with the discomfort inflicted by the wind, and although we are in better shape after a dish of pasta and a couple of glasses of wine, there is still no question of doing any leisurely exploration on foot, so we make our way toward Enna's southern gate, driving slowly through piazzas deserted during the Sunday siesta and peering down curving streets and ancient alleyways that would be inviting on a summer day.

As we drive down the southwestern flank of the mountain, the clouds lift and the island is spread out before us, wave on wave of hills flowing through the mists toward the sun, already low in the sky, a troubled sea of gold and lavender that stretches out to the horizon where the real sea, invisible, begins.

Lake Pergusa proves to be a bitter disappointment, a brilliant example of the Sicilians' best efforts to ruin their landscape. As is true of all the island's interior, the wooded hills and flowering meadows that once attracted Persephone have long since been sacrificed to Sicily's need to produce more and more grain, but here the subsequent erosion has given way to a more contemporary blight. The lake itself, hardly more than a large and stagnant pond with neither inlet nor outlet, lies in a gentle and recently reforested valley, which has been invaded by myriad summer villas in the same hideous architectural style—modern misallied to Mediterranean and generating flights of fancy—that desecrates the Sicilian coasts. All around the marshy shore runs a fancy track for car racing. It is a landscape neither Greek nor Sicilian, totally without character, and although we feel obliged, having come all this way, to make the drive around the lake, we are glad to be done with it.

The road leading back to the highway skirts the eastern end of the mountain. Demeter's rock hangs over us, golden against the finally blue sky, and to the east broods the dark purple cone of Etna, rising high above the intervening mountains and smoking leisurely in the setting sun. This is a moment such as I had hoped for, when the spine-tingling echo of the goddess's footsteps rings softly across the centuries.

The children doze as we drive back toward Palermo, and Tonino's thoughts have returned to his work. I am content to sit in silence, watching the changes that the waning light works on the countryside, at present pink, lavender, and russet where the morning showed green and yellow and brown. Sifting through the day now ending, I feel slightly cheated: for all that I had put tongue in cheek, I expected something more from this pilgrimage, some greater indulgence than a brief lifting of the clouds at the end of the day. I had imagined myself standing on Demeter's rock and looking down onto the shores of the lake, watching Persephone, sharing Demeter's moment of distraction and the horrible clutching of her bowels as she turns her gaze back and Persephone is no longer there.

That was not how it happened. There was no moment of distraction. Lake Pergusa is too far away for Demeter to have watched Persephone from her rock in any mortal fashion. Although the goddess does not seem overly generous of herself today, perhaps this fact of geography conveys a first message. Perhaps a mother *cannot* be present at her child's rite of passage, or offer her own wisdom and experience to ease the journey, and it is useless to resent one's own mother or to expect to succeed where she had failed.

And perhaps the weather that has so blighted the day is a reprimand. The cold winds and rain of Demeter's grief will darken Sicily as long as her daughter dwells below the earth. Go back to Palermo, then, attend to winter business, seek Persephone in the spring, when, attended by rites of propitiation and welcome, she returns to the land.

It is dark by the time we reach Palermo, and the city lights, man's most felicitous addition to the natural landscape, string a web between the high mountains to the south and the startling black forms of Monte Pellegrino and Aspra, the two promontories that rise straight from the sea to guard the port. The lights catch us and draw us back into the city.

Chapter Two

🌿 December is like an Italian fireworks show, a long string of minor festivities leading up to the *batteria grande*, the grand finale of Christmas and New Year's.

The first of these falls on the sixth, when San Nicola opens the procession of generous visitors from the Other World whose gifts, according to the Florentine historian Franco Cardini, represent the tie between autumn and winter, between death and fecundity, a procession that will culminate in January with the Epiphany. Feast but not vacation, Saint Nicholas is quite déclassé in Sicily, where from Santa Claus he has been reduced to tooth fairy. I was amused to meet this old friend in a new guise but had given little thought to the significance of his role until Francesco's first baby tooth became loose. The first in his kindergarten class to undergo this experience, he was totally unprepared for the alarming idea of losing a piece of himself and quite unconvinced by my assurances that a new tooth would grow to replace the loose one, whose every wiggle reduced him, barely five years old, to tears.

San Nicola rescued us by introducing Francesco to the market economy: the idea that someone would buy the tooth from him reconciled Francesco to his impending loss, and I realized for the first time the importance of this ubiquitous figure (who it is said appeared to the children of ancient Rome in the form of a ladybug) in whatever form he or she may assume. And San Nicola turned out to be a good guy, willing to credit a letter explaining that Francesco's first tooth had been swallowed with a mouthful of spaghetti, and with five shiny 100-lira pieces under his pillow Francesco thought he owned the world. (The innocence of the firstborn is never repeated: when Natalia's time came I was low on change and put a 500-lira bill under her pillow. She took one look and came raging into our room: "You didn't give me enough!")

Two days after San Nicola comes the Feast of the Immaculate Conception. Immune to the government's efficiency campaign, the Virgin brings us the gift of a holiday, which we choose to spend in town, sleeping late in the morning and wandering about the old city in the afternoon to watch Palermo celebrate.

Sicily is a fun-house mirror in which Italy can behold her national traits and faults distorted and exaggerated. The urban landscape of Palermo reflects the sack of Rome, but here the old "historic center," with its four *mandamenti* that date from before the Arab occupation in the ninth century (the area was inhabited in the Paleolithic period and colonized by the Phoenicians at least as early as the seventh century B.C.), has been left more tragically to its own devices, and such restoring and renovating as have transformed the popular neighborhoods of Trastevere in Rome or Santa Croce in Florence into high-priced and fashionable residential areas are in Palermo only just beginning.

The Palermo *mandamenti* are hodgepodge warrens of tiny streets and crumbling baroque palaces, balconies dripping with plants and intersections blocked by heaps of uncollected garbage, sculptured portals giving onto stately courtyards filled with motor scooters and piles of old crates and cardboard cartons, blacksmiths' shops and tinmongers, carpenters and upholsterers, street markets spilling over with fish and vegetables of all imaginable colors, great sides of beef, entrails and heads of slaughtered animals hanging on iron meat hooks and oozing blood and flies. The darkest, most malodorous alleyway has some small treasure, a portal, a window, a flowering shrine, to reveal, and the somberness of the rotting gray facades is mitigated by the fluttering wash stretched out across the narrow streets or slung from balcony to balcony, by the lengths of colored canvas threaded through the ironwork of the balcony railings to protect the ankles of the ladies sitting there from indiscreet glances and to give a modicum of privacy to this much-used, much-loved extension of the cramped quarters within, and by the swarming, swooping, chittering, and shrieking flocks of children that are to be found here at all hours and in all weather.

The money to rebuild the old city has been appropriated for years, plans and counterplans have been drawn up, but the pie is too big and the task of dividing it among parties, factions, and Mafia has so far stymied the local government. Every so often a house falls down in the middle of the night, burying alive the inhabitants as they sleep, or the police evacuate at gunpoint a building that threatens to crumble, obliging the families to sleep in trucks or camp out on the steps of the town hall for weeks until the mayor manages to find them some place to go. Newspaper articles and public indignation flare up briefly, until some new scandal diverts them—there is no lack of fuel here—and each year a little more of the area disintegrates beyond any hope of restoration. But the neighborhood is colorful and cruel and courageous in the sheer obstinacy of its endurance and in the imagination and inventiveness with which it manages to survive, and it is here that one must go, keeping a very firm grip on one's purse, to discover the charm and the fascination of Palermo.

For the Palermitani the Feast of the Immaculate Conception has had great importance ever since 1624, when the city government vowed to pay an annual tribute of 100 ounces of silver coins to the Virgin Mary in thanksgiving for her help in liberating the city from plague. This vow has been honored through the centuries with a solemn procession, in which all the municipal authorities participate, headed by the viceroy or the regent or by whoever represented whatever foreign power was presiding over Sicily at the moment. Nowadays it is the archbishop and the mayor and the prefect who follow the silver statue of the Madonna as it is carried through the streets.

We leave the car on the outskirts of the old city and wander up through the narrow streets until we reach the wide Via Roma just as the procession is passing, the big statue preceded by the town band, by groups of children and members of the various confraternities carrying candles. The Madonna herself, banked with flowers and standing on a wheeled wooden cart pushed by some of her more hefty devotees, is followed by the officials and then by a big group of the faithful and the curious.

There is no doubt that a somber business suit, no matter how well cut, makes for a dreary procession. I would much rather have watched the procession described by Arthur John Strutt, an English gentleman who in the 1830s made and then wrote *A Pedestrian Tour in Calabria and Sicily* (what other kind of tour could he have made with such a name!):

> At four o'clock I went to the palace of the Duke, situated in the *Strada di Cassaro*, the whole length of which the *Immacolata* performs, on her way from the church of St. Francesco, her habitual residence, to the *Matrice* or cathedral, whither she goes to spend a week; at the end of which period, should her peculiar servants, the monks of St. Francesco, fail to come and fetch her back again, with all due pomp, she will infallibly be claimed and detained by the monks of the *Matrice*. There is, however, I should apprehend, but little fear of their being forgetful on so important an occasion.
>
> The first symptoms of the procession were torches, fifteen or twenty feet high, made of dried reeds, which were carried flaring up the street, and followed by peasants playing on bagpipes, tambourines and castagnets. The bagpipes are very large, the great pipe being three or four feet long; some of them are of handsome black wood, with silver keys. The tambourines, on the contrary, are very small, and made entirely without parchment, being merely hoops with jangles; they are grasped in the right hand, and played by being rapped, in time, upon the left wrist and forearm. After these rustic musicians came a confraternity of Penitents, bareheaded and barefooted, with cords around their necks, and crowns of thorns on their heads; accompanied and enlivened, nevertheless, by bagpipes, tambourines and castagnets. Next came a confraternity of Gentlemen Sweepers, dressed in black, and bareheaded; their hair nicely curled and their tucked up trousers displaying bare legs and feet. These gentlemen had new brooms in their hands, with which they swept and prepared the street for the coming of the *Immacolata;* a precaution by no means unnecessary here, if she wishes to walk without soiling her feet. Then another confraternity, furnished with baskets of herbs and flowers, strewed the street thus newly swept, and were followed by a body

of white Penitentiaries, with white shoes and white-hooded masks. Then came a band of black monks; then a band of bourgeois, with silver bannerets; then different confraternities and congregations; and then the city volunteers with their band, and a most curious cavalry corps they were. A very handsome panoply of gold brocade followed, under which walked the church dignitaries, with their archbishop carrying the host; and immediately after, with her altar and wax lights complete, came the Immaculate Statue, carried bodily along, by sixty supporters, and accompanied by sixty more in the same uniform, to relieve guard. Directly following the statue, a candle in one hand, his cocked hat in the other, walked his Excellency General Tschudy, Governor-general of Sicily, and actually performing the office of Viceroy of the kingdom. Behind him walked, uncovered, the Prefect or Provost, the nobles, counsellors, senators, and other public personages; followed by a regiment of guards and dragoons; while the state carriages of the governors, senators, and other grand people brought up the rear. The grated balconies belonging to the nuns were crowded, and the thought of the contrast which the gay world below afforded to their own dull cloisters, would have been enough to make me quite melancholy had I had time to indulge in it.

The Duke having regaled his company with those delicious pistacchio ices, for which Palermo is justly famous, and which in spite of its being December are a real luxury, nay almost a necessary article in this climate, we took our leave.

I console myself with the thought that Mr. Strutt didn't get to see what is now the high point of the afternoon, when the procession reaches Piazza San Domenico, at the center of which stands a tall column surmounted by a statue of the Madonna. The gates of the railing that encircles the base of the column have been opened for the occasion, and the marble steps are carpeted with little bouquets of flowers, mostly simple offerings of wild iris, the small purple ones, once sacred to the Eumenides, that bloom throughout Sicily in December, wrapped in tinfoil and placed on the stone or tucked into the ironwork. Just outside the railing the Fire Department has parked its biggest and shiniest hook and ladder, with the ladder raised up to reach the top of the column.

The procession drifts into the piazza, squeezing up against the crowd, which is jostling for a good view and arguing with the policemen who are trying to clear a space for the statue and for the dignitaries. When all have elbowed their way in, a handsome and *sportivo* officer in the elegant dress uniform of the carabinieri climbs briskly up the ladder, bearing an enormous wreath from which flutters a tricolor ribbon of red, white, and green. It is a gusty day and the ladder sways back and forth against the column. A hush falls over the piazza as we all watch open-mouthed while the carabiniere hangs the wreath at the foot of the statue. There is a protracted moment of suspense as a big gust of wind sways him backward before he has the wreath exactly in place, and then as he waits until the wind dies down enough to allow him to click his heels and salute the Virgin in proper military style—Look, Ma, no hands! Our hero finally descends to the cheering of the crowd, and the procession resumes its march.

Ready, like the Duke's guests, for a snack, we decide not to follow for the moment, but to cut across to Piazza Venezia, to the Benedictine convent, where the nuns make the best cannoli in Sicily. Cannoli are the best known of Sicilian sweets, tubes of fried pastry filled with ricotta cheese that has been mixed with sugar and bits of chocolate and candied citrus peel. They require a light hand: filled too soon or with too much sugar, they become soggy and cloying. The ones made by the Benedictine sisters are crisp and delicious, filled while you wait.

The convent is a dreary building much like the one described by Mr. Strutt, with iron grills on all the windows. The door giving on to Piazza Venezia opens onto a narrow room crowded with people queuing up at the far end, in front of a small grilled window through which one shouts one's orders to the lay workers, who deal with the public so that the sisters need not break their vow of silence. Under the window is a revolving tray in which one places one's money, and which is then wheeled around to offer the pastry in exchange. We line up to wait our turn and I watch with amusement the strange mixture of people who fill the room: a clutch of bearded students, a family whose carefully pressed but threadbare clothes belie the sacrifice that buying this holiday treat involves, an elderly couple well but inconspicuously dressed, a slatternly woman in felt slippers and a shapeless long-sleeved jersey dress on which is almost visible the outline of the apron she took off before popping around the corner to the convent. It is a sampling of the neighborhood. The same jumble of architectural classes—hovels cheek by jowl with palaces—is reflected in the inhabitants. The desperately poor may share a courtyard with well-to-do middle-class couples who are reluctant to leave the neighborhood where their families have lived for generations, while students and New Left ménages have tunneled into the rabbit warren of apartments, attracted by the combination of charm and cheap rents. And occasionally an open window in a baroque facade will permit a glimpse of aristocratic splendor, albeit somewhat moth-eaten, that has managed to survive into the twentieth century.

Our turn comes finally, and gripping our cannoli we push out into the street, to continue our walk through the twilight and nibble on the crisp crust, savoring the sweet ricotta and brushing off the powdered sugar that the wind is blowing down onto our coats. From the Via Venezia we turn on to the Via Maqueda and pass the Quattro Canti di Città, the four corners of the city, each corner decorated with a fountain in which a pagan lady representing one of the four seasons is chaperoned by one of the four virgin saints who are the patronesses of the four *mandamenti* of old Palermo.

This intersection marks the very heart of the city, the meeting point of the two main roads of the Roman camp, the center of the Arab town where the Corso (*Càssaro* in Sicilian dialect, from the Arabic *Al-Qasr*, "the fortress") led up from the fortified port to the castle that later became the Royal Palace. This division of the city into four quarters that meet at the Quattro Canti is still very much felt by the residents: until recently there was little intermarriage among them, and the differences in dialect and accent are significant enough to reveal to the discerning ear which *mandamento* the speaker was born in.

To the southeast lies the Kalsa, with Saint Agatha as its patroness. Site of the old Arab citadel, El-Halisah ("the Elect"), and traditionally inhabited by sailors and fishermen, this neighborhood was badly damaged by American bombing in World War II, and much of it is truly squalid, although some of Palermo's loveliest treasures are hidden in its winding alleys and garbage-littered squares.

To the northeast is the quarter we are coming from, now called San Pietro but once known as the Amalfitana after the merchants and traders from the maritime republic who had their offices there. Saint Ninfa is its patroness, while Saint Cristina watches over the southwestern *mandamento*, the Albergheria, which once belonged to the officials of the Norman court who crowded their residences around the Royal Palace.

We turn west on the Corso, passing the fountain with the statue of Saint Oliva, headed for her quarter, the Capo. I have suggested that we combine the last bites of cannoli with a look at the apse of the cathedral, whose great neoclassic dome, perched uncomfortably on a Norman base, dominates the city. This massive bastion is a status symbol, a monument to the power of its builder, the archbishop of Palermo, who erected it in 1185, to the greater glory of God and to remind the people of Palermo—and the king in his palace across the piazza—of the strength of the reactionary feudal nobility of whom he was the leader. This archbishop was called Gualtiero Offamiglio, a name that sounds peculiar to the ear of the Italian speaker until one learns that he was an Englishman and that his name is the best the Sicilians could do with "Walter of the Mill."

The cathedral has been much altered over the centuries, and only the eastern exterior gives a good idea of what the original Norman construction looked like. Even here a little mental barbering is necessary, lopping off the tops of the towers and plucking away the dome, in order to savor the solid geometric forms of Arabic architecture and the rich Norman decoration of black and white marble inlays that wind their way about the blind arches of yellowish stone.

It is almost dark now, and we begin to feel cold, but I cannot go near the cathedral without giving a brief greeting to Emperor Frederick II of Swabia and his mother, Constance, who lie buried within. If it was Frederick who brought me to southern Italy and revealed the charms of the Mezzogiorno to me as I searched for college thesis material, passing years and a raised consciousness have shifted my allegiance to Constance, the last Hauteville, heir to the Norman kingdom, who was married off to the German Emperor Henry VI, and after ten years of barrenness became pregnant at forty. Traveling south through Italy, Constance had reached the town of Jesi in the Marche when the labor pains began; she ordered that a tent be set up in the public square, and there she gave birth before witnesses, to show the world that the tiny Frederick was the legitimate heir to the Kingdom of the Two Sicilies.

There are four tombs, imposing red porphyry caskets borne by crouching lions, somber and elegant, incongruous in the pastel neoclassic interior that houses them. There are always a few bunches of flowers and a faded wreath in front of Frederick's tomb, placed there by German tourists, and even a few blossoms laid before that of Henry VI, the much-hated "flail from the north." But the Sicilians do not remember their own: no flowers for Roger II, the most brilliant of the Norman kings, or for his daughter Constance. I am, as always, deeply moved by these tombs, and I repeat to myself my old promise to bring some flowers someday for Constance; better still, someday I shall write her story.

The children are complaining that the wind has whetted their ever-ready appetites and that the cannoli were only a teaser. We must keep to the character of our day: we will go eat *pani cu' la meusa* at San Francesco. *Pani cu' la meusa* is to Palermo more or less what the hot dog is to America, a much-loved and economical snack or supper. *Meusa* is *milza*, beef spleen that is first boiled and then sliced very, very thin and sautéed in rendered lard. It is served in a *foccaccia*, a roll that looks like a cross between pita bread and a hamburger bun, together with a slab of ricotta and some grated *caciocavallo*, a sharper, saltier cheese. It is a greasy, messy treat, which is probably part of its charm, and truly delicious to anyone who has a taste for innards.

The place to go in Palermo for *pani cu' la meusa* is the Antica Foccacceria di San Francesco, in the heart of the Kalsa, which has been serving the best in the city since 1834. Its decor was last renovated at the beginning of this century: the storefront still has the same bow windows decorated in beaten tin, now thickened by innumerable coats of red paint; the original marble-topped tables still cluster on their cast-iron legs around the huge wood stove. This magnificent beast, also of cast iron and eight feet wide or more, has been converted to bottled gas, but its brassware gleams, including the rail around the bottom, a footrest for the customers who wait their turn as the cook stirs, drains, and lifts the *milza* onto the *foccaccia* with beautiful rolling flicks of the wrist, a constant sinuous motion that recalls the way an experienced *pizzaiuolo* will maneuver the long-handled pizza shovel in and out of the oven.

The original owners are still keeping an eye on the cook, two brothers smiling down from the sepia-tinted photograph that hangs on the back wall, their bowler hats pushed back jauntily, their waxed mustachios curling gaily, and their gold watch chains sparkling across their well-rounded bellies. The old lady presiding over the cash register—a daughter? a granddaughter?—is no period piece, however; her sharp eye reflects good business sense as well as pride in her family tradition.

The Focacceria is crowded tonight, and we are lucky to get ours before the *focacce* run out. Outside the piazza is filling up with people and we suddenly realize why: the Madonna, who has been trotting around Palermo all afternoon in procession, is coming home to rest in the church across the way. The church of Saint Francis is a lovely thirteenth-century building that was restored to its medieval simplicity after the bombing of the Second World War. Its stark, unadorned facade is broken only by a beautiful rose window and a simply carved doorway reached by a short flight of steps that runs the breadth of the facade. A wooden ramp leading over the steps has been erected for the occasion.

All the clientele of the Focacceria, licking their fingers and wiping their chins with the inadequate squares of tissue paper that pass as napkins in most Italian bars, push out to join the crowd that is pouring into the piazza and gathering around the statue of the Madonna that has halted in front of the church door. The great wooden doors open wide, revealing ribbed columns that rise in the flickering candlelight, their arches lost in the shadows. A hush settles on the piazza, the blue-smocked workers who have wheeled the Madonna round the town tense to the ready.

"*Uno, due, tre—VIA!*" The workmen give a great heave and charge up the ramp, pushing the statue before them, urged on by the crowd. The Madonna sways perilously on the rise, appears to genuflect as she dips over the top, and glides smoothly down the nave. The piazza cheers and claps. Palermo has fulfilled its vow once again.

🌿 The Palermitani have no sooner recovered from the Immacolata than they have to prepare for Saint Lucy, whose feast falls on the thirteenth of December. It was a surprise to discover not only that the Saint Lucy who appears crowned with a wreath of candles in Scandinavian households and the Santa Lucia whose Neapolitan praises I had sung with great gusto in my grade school years were one and the same—the patroness of light and sight whose feast day was celebrated, according to the Gregorian calendar, on the longest night of the year—but that Saint Lucy was in fact a Sicilian, an early Christian martyr from Syracuse.

Legend has it that Lucy was assiduously courted by a pagan for the beauty of her eyes, and so she plucked her eyes out and sent them to her suitor. She is always depicted holding her eyes on a plate, and she is much beloved of the Sicilians, both because she was a fellow islander and because they, like most Mediterranean peoples, have always been afflicted with eye diseases. The beaten silver ovals with lacy edges and a pair of eyes cut out of the middle, so that they look like a fancy carnival mask, are still among the votive offerings most commonly encountered in Sicilian shrines.

As far as I know, there is only one place left in Palermo where these offerings are still manufactured, and it is one of the most intriguing shops I have ever visited, a tiny place on the Via dei Bambinai, just behind Piazza San Domenico. The top half of the door is opened to display on the left a glass case in which the silver ex-votos hang, thin sheets of metal that have been hammered over molds into the shape of the part of the body that has been cured by saintly intervention: besides eyes there are noses, hands, breasts, buttocks, bellies, feet, and then X-ray views showing lungs, kidneys, intestines. For less specific ills, one can have the whole human figure, man, woman, or child. Then there are the animals that have been cured: cows, horses, donkeys, pigs, and sheep. Only animals of a certain economic importance are portrayed, perhaps because the saints cannot afford to waste miracles on mere pets.

On the other side of the door, dismembered dolls sway in the breeze, pink plastic legs or chubby torsos with gaping holes at the neck and shoulders. They are a new and cheaper version of the old pink wax ex-votos that were sometimes parts of the body, more often whole dolls dressed carefully as the Christ Child.

The shop itself is very small, the back cut off by a curtain and a ladder leading to the wooden loft, and it is crammed with ancient pedal-operated sewing machines and cartons full of doll parts. It smells of mold and mice and worse, and every so often there is a startling burst of noise and motion, as a pigeon flaps up from underfoot to perch on the edge of the loft and glare at the intruders.

The presiding gnome is a woman of uncertain age, less than five feet tall, whose pasty skin and shrunken figure speak of a childhood spent in the damp dark alleys of the Cala, of too much pasta and too little protein. She and her brother have inherited this business: she learned the art of making wax statues from her mother, while the brother carries on the molding of the silver ex-votos, with a sideline in repairs bequeathed by their father, who was a repairman for the Singer Sewing Machine Company. They love to chat, and their life history comes tumbling out amidst the flapping of pigeon wings and the cries of children scrapping in the street outside. It takes no great urging for the brother to open a drawer full of doll legs, bits and pieces of velvet, and other flotsam and fish out a plastic photograph album filled with pictures of the statues they have made and of others that have been brought to them for restoration from as far away as London. It turns out that this odd pair are among the only people in the world who know how to restore wax votives, and they proudly show off the "before and after" photographs: an exquisite scene of the Last Supper belonging to an aristocratic Palermo family, a Holy Family signed by the wife of Serpotta, the famous Sicilian stuccoist who worked at the end of the eighteenth century. They assure the visitor, perhaps in answer to a look of puzzlement, that they have a *laboratorio* down the street where they do the restoring. Certainly it is hard to imagine such fragile treasures surviving a stay in the shop itself.

Aside from offering ex-votos to Saint Lucy in return for her help, the Palermitani also honor her feast day by abstaining from eating anything made from wheat flour, which means no pasta and no bread, the two mainstays of the normal Sicilian diet. They replace these with rice, cooked either in a risotto or as *arancine*, "little oranges," rice croquettes stuffed with chopped meat and chicken giblets stewed with peas and tomato sauce and fried to a deep golden orange, or they eat *panelli*, seasoned chick-pea flour that is boiled to a paste, cooled, sliced, and fried. *Panelli* are, as far as I know, the only dish in all of Italian cooking that requires chick-pea flour, and they are made only in Sicily, no doubt a legacy from the Arabs. The Sicilians normally eat the hot *panelli* in a roll, which they buy on the street corner from vendors who do their frying over bottled gas in the back of their Vespa vans or even in donkey-drawn carts. But on Saint Lucy's Day, of course, the *panelli* are eaten without the rolls.

Dinner ends with a dish of *cuccìa*, a sweet pudding made of whole-wheat berries that have been soaked and boiled, then mixed with a sort of blancmange and seasoned with cinnamon, sugar, and chocolate shavings. There are many different explanations for the custom of eating *cuccìa* and barring the use of wheat flour on Saint Lucy's Day. Most commonly it is said that Palermo was once suffering from a terrible famine (not an unusual occurrence across the centuries); the granaries were all empty and the population starving. Delivery came on Saint Lucy's Day with the arrival of grain-laden ships in the harbor, and the famished people cooked up the grain without waiting to see it go through the mills.

I have been interested to read that the Greeks made something similar, a dish called *panspermìa* that was prepared for the feasts of the Thargelion and the Pyanepsia, the coming and the going of the summer sun. It was a mixture of all different seeds that were boiled over a slow fire, a method of cooking that symbolized the proper balance between heat and humidity, between sun and rain, needed to ripen the fruits of the earth. I don't know that there is any real tie between *panspermìa* and *cuccìa*, other than the fact that, like many ritual dishes including *cuccìa*, *panspermìa* is probably nicer to read about than to eat.

❧ The time has come to celebrate a private feast, a sunny weekend after ten days of rain. On Saturday we drive out to Bosco, hurrying to catch the last of the sun, as the afternoons are very short now and by five it is dark. The rain will surely have rendered the lower road impassable, so we circle around to the upper road, much longer and bumpier, and stop to admire the last of the wild cyclamen blooming thick where the road dips down into a little valley and is muddied even in summer by some underground spring. The pale pink flowers uncurl like tongues of faint fire against the dark, shiny, white-veined leaves and glow beneath the shadow of the wild honeysuckle, whose branches are heavy with berries, arranged symmetrically on the leaves like a tiered centerpiece of persimmons grown specially for the table of a dolls' house.

Tonino drives on ahead, eager to check on his casks and cisterns, to make sure that all is well with the wine and that no untimely fermentation has taken place. The children and I decide to walk the last half mile and take a census of the possible Christmas decorations growing along the banks of the road, an ever-changing corridor of shrubs and wildflowers, sometimes high enough to cut off all view on either side, at times thinning out to show us the magnificent backdrop of the Gulf of Castellammare.

The gulf is a deep bay, closed in on either side by mountains and bordered to the south by gentle hills that run down perpendicularly toward the sea until they flatten into a narrow coastal plain. The dirt road we are walking on follows the crest of one of these hills: to the west we can see Alcamo lying at the foot of its solitary mountain, a small afterthought, mantled with pine woods and crowned with an Arab watchtower, next a gap where soon the sun will set, and then the barren, eroded mountains of Castellammare, leading out to Capo San Vito, the northwesternmost tip of Sicily, marked by a lighthouse that will presently begin to twinkle in the distance. We are walking toward the sea, which glitters in the clear air, free of the heat haze that in the summer months smudges sea and sky horizonless. To the east is Partinico, my first Sicilian home, and beyond it Montelepre and the mountain hideouts of Salvatore Giuliano and his bandits, and then the high and lunar landscape of the mountains that separate us from Palermo.

We have arrived at the olive grove that marks the beginning of our property. The trees are old ones, with marvelously gnarled trunks, and the children stop to stroke the moss that grows up the northern side, shriveled in summer, luxuriant now after the rains. Fascinated by this suggestion of more northern climates, of lush green lawns she sees only in pictures, Natalia is always bringing home pieces of moss to raise in plates.

The road winds through to the other side of the olive grove and the house comes into view, two hundred yards away across a field that slopes down to the valley to the west where the bulk of our vineyards lie. To the right of the road a thin strip of vineyard marks the limit of our property: the eastern valley, more abrupt and mysterious somehow in its shaded olive groves, was sold to pay the inheritance taxes when Tonino's grandfather died, together with a wing of the house that backs onto the *cantina* where our wine casks are kept. This sale remains a great thorn in our flank, even though the farmers who bought it, the Blunda family, come here rarely, and then show a tact and discretion unusual in a land whose language lacks a word for privacy.

This is the best view of Bosco—one is far enough away to have some feel of the size and to see the play of the different roofs as they slip and slide their way around the courtyard, and now that the mulberry trees are bare of leaves, there is a clear view of the big arched window at the end of the living room, a converted wine cellar that once housed double rows of huge wooden casks, and of the high stone arch with its semicircle of wrought-iron rays above the wooden gate leading into the courtyard. Beyond the gate, on the far side of the courtyard, the windows are dark and shuttered still, but the white walls and the red tile roofs glow in the late-afternoon sun. The land dips suddenly behind the house, so that seen from here the sea and the sky are its only backdrop.

I am told that Bosco is beautiful to any eye, but to mine it is much more. When my husband's eldest brother died, just eighteen months after we were married, all our dreams of a nomadic life of development work in the Third World faded, for we found ourselves responsible for two elderly and semi-invalid parents whose only means of support was a farm that turned out to be unproductive and debt-ridden. Somehow it never occurred to us that there might be any alternative to accepting these responsibilities as they fell, but for me they were passive responsibilities, emptying rather than filling up my life and aggravating a chronic state of aimlessness. In America great things had always been expected of me: I came from a distinguished family, I had had a distinguished academic record in my own right (as a freshman in college I had even been given an honorary scholarship to reward the promise I had shown), but somehow I had never discovered where all this promise was supposed to carry me. In Sicily I sought the space in which to sort out my own expectations from all the others, and I found myself with almost more space than I could cope with: alone for most of the day with nothing to do, no place to go, no relevant qualifications, I was unable to lay my hands on any of the famous "inner resources" that I had been led to believe would take the drudgery and the boredom out of housewifery, and I was terrified of being forced to admit there might be even a shred of truth in the dire prophecies my mother had made about married life in Sicily.

On weekends the obligations of farm and family called us to Alcamo, where, while Tonino stalked the piazza in search of the people he needed to talk to, I sat in my in-laws' house, cold and bored and childishly resentful of the moth-eaten dreariness of my surroundings, of the uncomfortable chairs and inadequate lighting, of the atmosphere heavy with age, ill health, and mourning. Tonino's parents were anxious to do their duty toward their daughter-in-law, even though she was an unknown foreigner with neither property nor profession, and they received me with an uncomprehending yet affectionate generosity that I did my best to reciprocate. The disparity between their lives, which had begun at the end of the nineteenth century in the same small Sicilian town where they were now drawing slowly and painfully to a close, and my youth in metropolitan, mid-twentieth-century America, was enormous: I was an enigma to my in-laws, and inasmuch as they embodied Tonino's background, too different from my own—or so I had been warned—for our marriage ever to be successful, my in-laws were a threat to me. Building a bridge of kindness and comprehension was slow and difficult work.

It was a bleak period of which I remember very little. If I had picked unpromising terrain on which to find myself, I was very lucky in my choice of a companion. Easygoing and tolerant to an extreme, Tonino has never shown the slightest need to visit his own insecurities on other people, or the slightest inclination to take over anyone else's helm—not even in the rare but sticky moments when I would almost have welcomed a little paternalistic intervention. He always seemed entirely confident that I knew who I was and what I was doing, and this fiction buoyed me up for as long as it took for me to grow some confidence of my own.

The turning point came in 1968. An earthquake knocked the farmhouse at Bosco down and permitted us to rebuild it with government help, and two months later the first of our children was born. The house grew side by side with the children, first on paper and finally, in 1975, in stone and cement. Just as having children here has made me more than a mere expatriate and given me a stake in the future of Sicilian society, so the work I put into Bosco has won me, I feel, the right to put down roots. What began as a burden became a blessing as I scraped and varnished and dug and planted, a visible, tangible explanation of my life here—both for the Sicilians, for whom all the usual labels, such as name, accent, clothes, or college degree, are in my case illegible, and for the Americans, myself at times included, who wonder what on earth someone like me is doing in Sicily.

Right now the house is set in a wintry landscape: the mulberries, the pomegranate, the pears and plums have mostly shed their leaves, although the almond trees seem to be keeping theirs much longer than is usual, perhaps to enjoy the rain after such a terribly dry summer. The oleander bushes, tall as trees, are scraggly and lifeless. And then there is the palm, growing in all directions, intent on sprouting as many tufts of fronds as it can possibly squeeze onto its circumference, instead of concentrating on just one as proper palms do. This tiresome rarity is, as always, a mess, a green and living symbol of the eternal chaos that attends people like us who try to do too many things at once. And I never did get around to pruning it this summer—I could do it this weekend, before the birds start to nest again.

Pruning the palm is a tricky job; I still haven't discovered the best tools for the task and invariably end up so full of scratches that I am embarrassed to return to city life. The first time I ever tackled it I found a belt of machine-gun bullets hidden in the tangle of dead branches and new sprouts: after World War II

Tonino's second brother, Turi, discovered an abandoned German munitions depot and would bring home all sorts of cartridges and bullets to play with and explode, much to the horror of the family. This belt had no doubt been confiscated and hidden in the palm. I presume that what I prune these days is all newer, postwar growth, but nonetheless I proceed gingerly.

Across the last half of the field a row of cypresses accompanies the road, planted about five years ago as a windbreak for the land where someday I plan to have a flourishing vegetable garden, today represented by a dozen artichoke plants, some scattered clumps of Swiss chard, and the canes, tilting at crazy angles, that held up last summer's string beans. I suppose Tonino and I had Tuscan landscapes in mind when we planted the cypresses, but the extremes of the Sicilian climate have wrought their usual havoc on our ordered imagining; each cypress has grown to a different pattern, some tall and thin, some fat and squat, some curled over at the top like a candle in the summer sun. And then there is the gap: it was just a year ago that we arrived for the Christmas vacation to discover that the biggest and most shapely of the cypresses was gone; all that was left of it was a large hole in the ground.

Tonino always becomes just a little bit more "Sicilian" as soon as he sets foot at Bosco, assuming an air of suspicious surveillance that takes the form of frequent binocular or telescopic inspections of the surroundings and a critical, pessimistic interest in what each neighbor or passerby is up to. In this instance there was a marked squaring of the shoulders, and the next day he set off "to have a look around." He found the cypress on his first try, planted in front of the local shepherd's house and garlanded with tinsel and colored lights. After extremely delicate negotiations, both parties accepted the convention that this was a boyish prank on the part of the shepherd's youngest son, and it was agreed that the tree would come home in the new year. And so it did, accompanied by a large fresh pecorino cheese and a basket of ricotta, but two transplantings in an unusually dry winter were too much for the cypress, and this summer we sawed it up for firewood.

The sight of Bosco fills me with peace and the sense of my great good fortune in having been granted such a place to put down roots, but I often wonder if I will ever be able to savor this feeling unalloyed by the anxiety of having so much to plant, prune, harvest, sew, paint, sand, restore, wash, clean. Will I ever catch up enough to be able to slow down to a gentle hum of activity, to enjoy sitting and looking, or walking for the sake of walking, without the excuse of something to pick? Surely not until we live here all year round, and probably not even then; perhaps this frantic pace is an attempt to assuage my guilt at having so much in a land where so many still have so little.

As I pass the first of the flower beds I pause without thinking to pull up a handful of weeds: the crocuses are showing their tips and the nasturtiums are in flower. In two weeks the weeds have gotten a dangerous head start, totally undiscouraged by six inches of mulch, and I must get cracking on that palm, the cobbled pavement will have disappeared under the grass that is covering everything with a thick green quilt, the last of the olives must be wiped off and put under oil. My pace quickens, the moment of contemplation passes, and I am home.

We are well into December now, and Palermo is seized by the Christmas spirit, a fever that in truth comes both tardily and uneasily here. There is little left of the old rituals, of the blind singers who used to wander about the streets of the old city at night singing novenas, or of the families who would pack their Christmas supper into a basket and take it to church with them, turning the long vigil before midnight mass into a gay and boisterous picnic. (The ecclesiastical authorities took a dim view of this custom, and the first of the many edicts unsuccessfully prohibiting it dates from 1399.)

The wax figures of the Christ Child that were once produced in vast numbers in Via dei Bambinai, tiny babies cradled inside a waxen fruit, a lemon, a prickly pear, or a pine cone, have disappeared, and although it is still possible to find *mustazzòla*, flat brown cookies with lighter-colored dough molded in the form of the Baby Jesus lying on top, or the *buccellato*, ring-shaped pastries filled with figs and almonds, the bars and pastry shops give the place of honor to the panettone manufactured by Messrs. Motta and Alemagna to the north, acclaimed by endless TV commercials as the most sacred of Italian Christmas traditions.

Christmas in Sicily has been limited both by tradition and by poverty to a family feast, observed by going to midnight mass, by eating copious meals and spending evenings at bingo and card games, and has always ranked well below I Morti or the feast day of the local patron saint. Newfound prosperity and the consumer society have combined to erect a fancy superstructure on this archaic foundation, but although most families now have a Christmas tree next to, or even in place of, the old *presepio* or crèche (and in Palermo the middle class gamble furiously from the Immacolata to Epiphany), still the rituals to support these novelties are lacking. Even the exchange of presents has been adapted to maintain that most delicate and intricate balance of favors, prestige, and string pulling that governs every aspect of Sicilian life. Christmas has become the occasion for capturing the attention of a doctor or a lawyer, repaying a local politician for a favor, insuring a good grade at school or the chance of a job for one's son.

The merchants do their best, of course. Christmas music is piped through the department stores, lights are strung across the big shopping streets, sidewalk stands glitter with tinsel and plastic ornaments, creating an atmosphere similar to that of Christmas in an American city, if in a lower key. Palermo traffic, ever a chaotic race in which only the fittest survive, gives up any pretense of order or reason, and the streetlights serve only to indicate the densest concentrations of honking cars and swearing motorists, piled up against each other in the middle of the intersection, gridlock in fact and on principle.

To save my nerves I take the bus downtown to do some

Christmas shopping, and I get off at the Quattro Canti. My route takes me down the Via Maqueda and past Piazza Pretoria, a handsome square in front of the city hall that is filled by an out-sized baroque fountain alive and wriggling with nymphs, tritons, river gods, and other such aquatic fancies, including a naked lady lying alongside a beast half horse and half sea serpent. The Palermitani claim she represents a Neapolitan queen whose sexual tastes were said to run to horses, and they call this the fountain of shame. The city hall next to it is a lovely building, with a palm-filled courtyard and a handsome stone stairway leading up to the mayor's office, an enormous gilt, brocaded, and chandeliered room with tall windows overlooking the piazza. At one end of all this magnificence, the mayor sits behind a huge marble-topped table, reigning over incredible inefficiency and rampant corruption. I have spent so much time in the piazza with delegations from my children's schools, waiting to be admitted to the august presence in order to petition for chairs or water or janitors or whatever other basic necessity was lacking, that I can no longer pass by here without a sense of disgust and discouragement. Shame indeed!

This is the very heart of the Palermo Baroque, so it is a shock to the eye to turn the corner behind city hall and come upon the red domes and cubic form of San Cataldo and the graceful columns of the belltower of the Martorana behind it, an island of Norman gaiety and restraint in a heavy sea of gray stone.

San Cataldo, a small chapel belonging to the Order of the Knights of the Holy Sepulcher, has been restored to its original Norman simplicity, while the church behind it has suffered the opposite fate and is much altered by baroque additions. Known as the Martorana because it was donated in the fifteenth century to the nearby convent of marzipan fame, its true name is Santa Maria dell'Ammiraglio, for it was built in 1143 by Admiral George of Antioch, principal adviser of King Roger II.

There is a brilliant and moving description of this church, its history and its mosaics, in John Julius Norwich's *Kingdom in the Sun*, but the description to which I most often return is in the diary of Ibn Jubayr, a Spanish Moor who visited the church eight hundred Christmases ago when he was shipwrecked off Sicily on his return from a pilgrimage to Mecca:

> Of the things belonging to the infidels, one of the most remarkable which we encountered was that called the Church of the Antiochite. We visited it on the Day of the Nativity, which is a solemn feast day for the Christians, and found it filled with a great gathering of men and women. This is a building to which no description can do justice, beyond question the most beautiful monument in the world. Its inner walls are all golden, lined with colored marbles the likes of which have never been seen before, inlaid with mosaics in gold and bordered with green mosaic garlands. Above this a row of windows with golden panes blind one with their light and arouse in one's soul sentiments from which we pray that Allah may protect us. We were told that the founder of this church, from whom it takes its name, spent many hundredweights of gold on it. He was the vizier of the grandfather of the present polytheistic king. This church has a bell-tower with columns of different-colored marbles; each story is supported by a colonnade, hence it is known as the Belltower of the Columns, and is one of the most marvelous constructions one could hope to see—may Allah by his favor and his generous handiwork soon nobilitate it with the call of the *muezzin.*
>
> The Christian women of this city seem Muslim in appearance: they speak Arabic fluently and wear capes and veils like our women. On the feast day they appeared dressed in silken robes embroidered in gold, and wrapped themselves in splendid mantles and colored veils, and walked in golden slippers. They proceeded toward their churches, or better still their dens, adorned with all the ornaments of Muslim women, with jewels, with paints, and with perfumes. And, to make a literary joke, we remembered the verse of the poet:
>
> "He who one day enters a church, will come upon antelopes and gazelles."

Ibn Jubayr, "Viaggio in Sicilia," in *Delle cose di Sicilia*

I decide to allow myself a moment's distraction from my shopping, but the only beasts I encounter upon entering the church are a small crowd of wedding guests awaiting the arrival of the bride. Like all the Norman churches, the Martorana is a very popular place to be married in, and it is rare to visit it without butting in on a wedding. As I take a rapid tour of the mosaics above the altar, I find myself listening to the conversation of a group of women, relatives perhaps, who are checking that all is in order before the ceremony begins. It is an amazing sequence of horror stories—brides struck dead on the wedding night, honeymooning couples killed in car accidents, betrayal and revenge—quite similar in tone to what women used to tell me about endless labor and difficult deliveries when I was pregnant for the first time. Their voices rise and fall in the dim light like a litany, and I suddenly wonder if such conversations are not in themselves a ceremony, a ritual of aversion meant to placate the Kindly Ones.

The last stop on my shopping list brings me back to Piazza Venezia: the cannoli we ate there last week and the excuse of Christmas presents have inspired me to order one of the masterpieces of the nuns' pastry production, about which I have read the most enticing descriptions. I must choose between two. The first, known as Il Trionfo della Gola, the "Triumph of Greed," is a cone-shaped cake, made of layers of almond paste, sponge, blancmange, and *zuccata*—the preserves made of a zucchinilike squash that fill the center of many Sicilian pastries—all enveloped in a coating of pistachio paste, highly colored and decorated and so sweet that a spoonful or two must be all that anyone not born in Sicily can manage. If it is the name that appeals to me above all in this cake, the other confection promises to hide behind its more prosaic title of Grappola d'Uva a treat for the eye as well as the tongue. I decide to order this, the "Bunch of Grapes," and negotiate through the grill for a two-kilo bunch to be picked up the next day. It will not be cheap, but I have been thinking about this bunch of grapes for three years, and I fear that if I lose any more time, it will end up like the sugar statues I arrived too late to buy. At the end of the eighteenth century there were many convents in Palermo producing pastries, but in 1866, after the advent of Garibaldi and the unification of Italy, when the vast terrains belonging to the religious orders were confiscated and many groups dispersed, the number slowly began to shrink, and now only these Benedictine nuns in Piazza Venezia still support themselves in this manner. Indeed, the younger nuns apparently have chosen more socially committed activities, and the tradition is carried on by only eight of the older sisters and will, I suppose, die with them.

The Bunch of Grapes, when I go to pick it up the next day, will be all and more than I imagined, a life-size cluster, perhaps twelve inches long, eight inches wide and five high, each grape fashioned individually from pale green paste, with two veined and curling leaves of darker green paste resting at the top, where a green paste branch pokes out; small green tendrils curl about the fruit, which is dusted with a silver bloom. It has all the rococo opulence of eighteenth-century Palermo, a dish straight out of *The Leopard*, well worth the princely sum I am paying for it.

Fortunately it is destined for friends with whom we always exchange presents over supper, so I will get a taste of it too. (Otherwise, I fear, they wouldn't be getting it—greed triumphs easily where I'm concerned.) As the grapes, made of an almond and pistachio paste just sweet enough that you can eat many more than you ever intended to, are plucked away one by one they reveal the base, a thin layer of paste wrapped about the most delicate *zuccata* preserves mixed with chopped pistachio nuts and flavored with cinnamon. The sugar and spice are dosed with such exquisite restraint as to suggest celestial intervention: surely this is nothing less than a Christian rendering of ambrosia!

❧ The bus trip home from the center is endless, and as I look out on hundreds of drivers snared in an enormous trap of their own making, I am visited by a flash of fellow feeling. Pre-Christmas panic grips me, I feel overwhelmed by the elaborate traditions I have imported from America. In the early years of my marriage, the tree, the *presepio*, the gala Christmas Eve dinner were a statement of identity, an attempt to expatriate the Christmases of my childhood, in which each act, each moment, and each mouthful repeated themselves year after year, and a dam against the desolation of Christmas Day spent with my in-laws, whose only concession to the feast day was an unusually elaborate dish of pasta, and cannoli for dessert.

Then Christmas became an antidote to the boredom and isolation of bringing up small children in a strange city: by making all my presents by hand and baking triple batches of gingerbread men, toll house cookies, and sesame cakes I could occupy a good three months. As the children have grown older and I have made more sense out of my life here, an inverse process has begun, and we are now down to one batch of gingerbread men, made together with the children, and mostly purchased presents. The Christmas Eve dinner perseveres: I first made it for myself and for my two English friends who, like me, most felt their rootlessness at Christmastime, then for our children, and for a few Sicilian friends who have become addicted to this Anglo-Saxon celebration. The group varies a bit from year to year, but the kernel struggles faithfully through the mud to Bosco each Christmas Eve.

Around about the twentieth of December this responsibility becomes a terrible weight on my shoulders, and I begin to resent living in a world where rite and tradition are becoming ever more a private affair that has fallen squarely into the woman's lap. I have been reading about the Greek Pyanepsia, the autumn festival dedicated to Apollo, departing god of summer, which included a sort of public Christmas tree, an olive or bay branch decorated with purple and white wool, hung about with all sorts of autumn fruits, with cakes and small jars of honey, wine, and oil. How grand to be a Greek and have it all taken care of for me, or even to be enough of a Palermitana to leave it all to the dead, or to get my kicks in July from the Festino, the big festival in honor of Saint Rosalia.

Vacation starts late this year, which means I must be extra-organized, dedicating the preceding weekend to removing three months' accumulation of dust and cobwebs, and remembering everything that has to go out to Bosco with us, for there will be no time for afterthoughts. The inside of my head is papered with lists.

Thursday the twenty-third finally arrives, school is over, Christmas greetings have been delivered to teachers and to the friends we won't see until our return in the New Year, and we load the car and the van with suitcases and packages, with cartons of food and bags of carefully wrapped presents that the kids can't keep from pinching and poking, trying to see labels and guess contents.

Our tree also gets loaded on the van: a branch from an umbrella pine, six-foot and bushy, a peculiar lopsided Sicilian version of a proper fir, but very ecological. The Regional Forestry Service does its annual pruning in mid-December and distributes the best branches for use as Christmas trees, so whatever we lack in aesthetics is more than compensated for by the knowledge that we have not further damaged this already too treeless land. Tucked in around the tree are Francesco's violin, Natalia's hamster (thank heavens Francesco has given up on raising escargots), the dog, the cat (in a different vehicle from the hamster), book bags for vacation homework, the Christmas cards I haven't finished writing, an eccentric assortment of beasts and bundles that the piazza finds very amusing.

A final stop at the nursing home to pick up my mother-in-law, and we are off. The last ten days before Christmas are always anxiety-ridden: will it rain so much that our guests won't be able to get through? They now come equipped with galoshes, and there was a year when it was necessary for them to leave their cars down at the bottom of the hill and stagger up on foot. Since this year the lower road is still out of commission, we have passed out maps of the upper road, but even that will be chancy in the last stretch, as we discover when we skid and slither across the field from the olive trees to the house.

This will be our seventh Christmas at Bosco; each year a little changed, with a detail added and another abolished, our ritual has assumed a new, more rustic character. In Palermo it was my one elegant production of the year: an adult meal eaten late on Christmas Eve with the best china and silverware dusted off for the occasion, requiring frenzied cooking, cleaning, and decorating, during which I became almost catatonic and the children were "kept out from under" until the last possible moment. Bosco has changed all that, and even if the burden of the cooking and cleaning still falls on me, everyone participates in the preparations, which have become part of the festivities.

Being at Bosco has also introduced us to what in seven years has become one of our favorite tasks: the search for Christmas greenery to decorate the house. We must choose a moment when the house is already clean, not so long before Christmas that the leaves will wilt or dry, but before the twenty-fourth, when all my efforts go toward food. This year leaves us no choice: we must unload the cars in haste as soon as we arrive in order to accomplish our mission before dark. Armed with gardening gloves—so much of Sicilian vegetation is thorny or prickly that to bring it home in armfuls presents problems—and heavy jackets, warm hats, and pruning shears, the children and I start back up the road.

Tradition requires us to go as far as the third fork, the better part of a mile, without picking, just scouting, and then to turn and come back down, gathering as we go. Our greenery is not that with which my ancestors decked their halls: holly grows only in the mountains in Sicily, and the umbrella pines are too rare and too precious, not to mention too tall, to think of cutting off any boughs. But we do very well, for our hedgerows are full of *pungitopo*, "mousepricklers," a member of the asparagus family with sharp gray-green leaves and big red berries that the Italians use for Christmas decorating, and then there are great tangles of smilax, with bunches of small scarlet berries that keep their color for weeks, if only one has the patience to extricate them from the tearing, grasping tendrils. Smilax is a lovely vine, and in Sicily it keeps its shiny heart-shaped leaves all winter so that the berry clusters stand out against dark green. Each year I promise myself to return in the spring to dig up some shoots to plant near the house, and each year I forget.

On the hawthorn trees, spring's small bouquets of white flowers give way to big berries, the size of small crab apples, which turn bright crimson in September and cling cheerfully to the bare branches all winter long. Another plant, a vine whose name I do not know, produces large clusters of juicy red berries spilling down one leafless tendril. It seems to prefer the most overgrown and inaccessible spots in which it is almost impossible to unwind the stem from the dry branch it has chosen as support without knocking off all the berries, but the final prize is a brilliant garland of fruit.

We hunt for variety in the texture and the color of the foliage: wispy branches of asparagus fern; dark spears of *tuvàro*, a form of heather with tiny needlelike leaves and clusters of flowers that have dried from their September purple to a wintry brown; the gray-greens of the lentisk, the rockrose, and the false rosemary. Our burdens are becoming unwieldy, Natalia begins to complain about the thorns, and even Happy, our Dalmatian, has tired of chasing up and down the track and is trotting on ahead. The children have decided that enough is enough and march homeward, while I linger to pick a few wild iris, a small offering for the kitchen shelf (to keep the Eumenides kindly tomorrow), and then to stop at the lemon tree outside the gate. The beautiful glossy lemon leaves, pea green when they are new, dark emerald when mature, give breadth and generosity to the austerity of the wild plants. Tangerines and oranges are often sold here with a few leaves attached, a living gauge of how fresh they are, and a greater temptation to the buyer than anything a Madison Avenue packaging expert could devise.

Tonino, long since returned from his expedition to the citrus grove with two baskets filled with oranges, grapefruit, and tangerines, has tea waiting for us and a fire burning brightly. Warmed inside and out, we start to decorate the house. The major decisions have long since been made: the *presepio* goes in the *palmento*, a raised platform about ten feet by six in the corner of the kitchen, where once the grapes were trodden. It has a low stone wall at the front pierced by a carved marble spout from which the must once flowed, a massive pillar on its outmost corner, and a wall on the side where we have cut a doorway and steps so we can use it as a pantry. Its shelves are filled with bottles of wine and tomato sauce, jars of jam and olives, canned tomatoes, pickles, chutneys, relishes, the fruit of my summer's labor, which make a multicolored backdrop for the *presepio*. This in itself is a miniature melting pot: the central figures, brought by my mother from Portugal, are set up on the bottom shelf of a Florentine *ceppo*, a three-tiered wooden pyramid topped by a gilt pine cone and lit by candles. We place the *ceppo* on a large cloth-covered crate, level with the front wall of the *palmento*, and wreath it with green leaves, berries, and pine cones, while oranges and lemons nestle in more leaves on the upper shelves. French *santons*, a Portuguese brass band, some Italian *presepio* figures that belonged to Tonino's family—one selling oranges, another sharpening knives, still another making ricotta—all throng through branches and berry clusters along the top of the wall in joyful if motley procession.

When the *presepio* is finished we combine leafy branches with berried ones in enormous bunches for the living room, whose raftered wooden roof, two stories high, dwarfs anything but the most massive furniture, the most voluminous compositions. Green garlands go along the top of the tiled kitchen fireplace, and on the shelf near the door little branches from the lemon tree make a gleaming green forest for the Portuguese "Flight into Egypt" figures.

Fresh candles are placed in the candle holders and a few branches set in water to keep fresh for tomorrow's dinner table. Each step is discussed to verify that everything is as it was last year. The possibility of changing, a new place to hang the Swedish straw wreath or a different position for the tree, is suggested just for the pleasure of flirting with danger, then rejected in that total respect for rite and continuity that my children demand of Christmas.

Finally we bring in the tree and set it in a bucket weighted with stones and filled with water. When the children were small I did the tree myself, an oeuvre of symmetry and balance. As they grew and wanted to participate, it was a struggle for me to relinquish my monopoly, to accept their help without trying to control it, to sacrifice symmetry for Christmas spirit, and what should have been an act of love risked becoming a war of nerves. It was the moving of Christmas to Bosco that brought me to my senses: now we prepare the tree, put on the lights, add the shiny garlands, and then put out on a table all the boxes of ornaments—balls and wooden snowflakes, Indian fish and Swedish Santas, Thai dragons and glass mushrooms from Germany. The decorating is done by everyone on Christmas Eve: the lower boughs, which the youngest can reach, are always groaning under the weight of ornaments while the upper branches go bare, the wooden snowflakes create a small blizzard on the lower left side, and Swedish Santas congregate to the right. But I shall repress the urge to indulge in a little surreptitious redistribution as I go in and out between living room drinks and kitchen pans and shall say how beautiful it is. And so it will be.

By now I know exactly when I have to cook what: the menu for Christmas Eve has been the same since 1965. Cheese biscuits with our *aperitivo*, then roast turkey stuffed with apples, raisins, and rice, giblet gravy, whipped sweet potatoes, peas and mushrooms, cranberry sauce. Plum pudding and hard sauce polish us off. A more un-Sicilian meal it would be difficult to devise, but what was originally a nostalgia kick for expatriates has become balm for the Sicilian souls as well. The plum pudding comes out from England every summer in Jane's suitcase, so the only difficult item is cranberry sauce: friends and foresight must be enlisted to make sure that we have some each Christmas. I have contemplated trying to grow cranberries at Bosco but am forced to admit that a Sicilian hilltop is a long way from a New Jersey cranberry bog.

By the afternoon of the twenty-fourth, everything that can be cooked ahead is ready, the turkey is stuffed and sewn and awaits its appointment with the oven, which has been determined after long consultations with *Joy of Cooking* and complicated conversions from pounds to kilos and Fahrenheit to Centigrade. This is the only part of the preparations that I cannot remember from year to year, perhaps because it is the lightning rod for all my anxieties. Having the turkey done at the right moment belongs to the same category as catching airplanes and is invariably rendered more tricky by the cylinder of bottled gas running out in the midst of it all, thus throwing all my elaborate calculations askew.

When we have gone to look out the window at least two dozen times, and twilight has darkened the road outside the kitchen door, we see at last the twinkle of headlights on the bare branches of the quince bushes, and the first car arrives, soon followed by the others. We are seventeen in all this year, and range in age from four to eighty-three. I was delighted when the youngest guest made his entry a few years ago to restore that sense of unblemished wonder that the older children have outgrown. The eldest, my mother-in-law, contributes another sort of wonder: she has been present at this Christmas Eve dinner for twelve years now, ever since her husband died, and she still thinks that I am absolutely out of my mind—all this work and buying of food and presents to spend Christmas with people who aren't even distantly related is more than her Sicilian upbringing can encompass.

Tree decorating, table setting, last-minute gravy making—a three-ring circus is under way, and the confusion borders on chaos. I send up a silent prayer that there are no balls among the presents heaped under the tree: the wide open spaces of the living room are an irresistible invitation to a soccer game, and past years have taught me that it is very hard to refrain from trying out a new ball.

It is always amazing, if flattering, that a meal that takes so long to prepare can be over so soon, but it is, and the children are eager to get at the presents and impatient with the grown-ups who linger over coffee. Lassitude and the love of teasing conspire to draw out the coffee until it is clear that no one can survive any longer, and we leave the kitchen and its brightly blazing fireplace to pass through the big arch into the living room, which this year is finally warm and welcoming, thanks to the newly installed cast-iron stove.

I too have been waiting for this moment: my part is finished, Christmas can carry on under its own steam from here on out. Tomorrow's rites are family ones, the children's stockings, panettone for breakfast, and the opening of family presents. The following day my brother-in-law and niece will arrive from Milan, and a friend will come from Rome with her small son. Before I know it the vacation will be over, and it will be time to load the cars again. But right now it is all before me, and I savor the moment as I savor the first sip from the bottle of Grand Marnier that Pam brings me every year.

Chapter Three

🌿 "Everybody in Italy eats *zampone* and lentils on New Year's Eve—why can't we?"

Francesco suddenly declared that he wanted the traditions of his Italian blood respected too, so before leaving Palermo I bought a *zampone*, a large sausage of chopped pork stuffed into a hollowed-out pig's foot.

It's no sacrifice on my part, for I have no New Year's traditions of my own to perpetuate. As I grew older, my childhood resentment at being excluded from an adult celebration evolved, through adolescent anxiety about how and with whom I would be invited to spend the evening, into distaste for gaiety on command. My beginnings have always been autumnal; the return to the city and to school with new books and new faces when I was a student, then new rhythms and new freedoms with the children out all morning when I became a mother. The grape harvest culminates our year of work and hope, the October rains mark a new cycle in the agricultural round. The longer I stay at Bosco, the more I am attuned to this calendar and the less I care about January first.

For the moment, at least, everyone is content to make New Year's a family affair. We eat our lentils, their coinlike shape a promise of affluence in the year to come, and pick at the *zampone*, which is *not* destined to become a tradition (we are all rather revolted by the cloven hoof lying on the platter in a pool of grease), play *tombola*, and at midnight open a bottle of champagne and a chocolate-covered panettone, imported food for an imported feast.

The *tombola*, Italian bingo, is at least an authentic tradition, the favorite Sicilian pastime during the Christmas holidays. The evenings spent at *tombola* with cousins, uncles, and aunts are possibly Tonino's only real Christmas memories, and we use the old family set, the number cards with their Art Deco borders torn and faded from years of play. Each number has its own name— "Nineteen, San Giuseppuzzo!"—in a complicated iconography of pagan and Christian symbolism, and between my requests for information about this, the shouting required by my mother-in-law's deafness, and the excitement of the youngest generation, we manage to produce the requisite noise and cheer. Muted gaiety at midnight, the cork pops satisfactorily, and we are happily off to bed. As we close the outer door for the night, everyone piles out despite the cold to admire the full moon piercing the crystalline sky with a promise of frost.

New Year's Day is glorious, as good an omen for 1983 as one could hope for. A cloudless and unbelievably blue sky has allowed the sun to heat the air, even while the gray veil of frost still lingers on the grass and the flower beds. Tonino and I are unable to stay in bed on what is the first really beautiful day of the vacation, and with sun warming our backs we set to cleaning up the courtyard.

Some ten yards square, the courtyard is bordered to the north and west by the main house. To the east and south are low, one-story·buildings that once housed the stable, the chapel, and the sharecropper's quarters; after the '68 earthquake they had to be completely rebuilt, together with most of the main house, and they now contain a small apartment for guests and an all-purpose laundry, carpentry, and storage room. We were careful not to disturb the original paving of the courtyard, a grid of cobblestoned squares crisscrossed by rows of rectangular stone slabs worn smooth by at least a century's worth of boots and hoofs. But this, the courtyard's most distinctive feature, is hidden now by a thick growth of dandelions, nettles, clover, and crabgrass. There are even two clumps of chives: for years I have been trying unsuccessfully to grow chives from seed, and my only luck has been this spill, accidental and inconvenient.

Tonino resumes hostilities in his war on crabgrass while I arm myself with pruning shears. I love to prune, although it is instinct and impulse rather than scientific knowledge that guide me in this affectionate aggression, akin to peeling sunburned backs or squeezing blackheads. I start to the right of the gate and gradually work my way around the courtyard, stooping over the vases to cut back the geraniums, which grow to enormous bushes in this climate and flower all year round, then reaching up to tame the vines with which we are trying to subdue the summer glare of sunlight on stucco. There are all sorts: jasmine, bougainvillea, wisteria, Virginia creeper, clematis, and still other vines whose names I have never discovered. Around the big carved stone washtub in the center grow more geraniums, two small pines, and a tiny kumquat tree, a present from Gabriella, its miniature oranges just turning yellow.

Along the western side of the courtyard runs a covered porch where we eat or swing in a hammock in the summertime, now filled with firewood and the dwindling pile of winter melons, and strewn with mud-encrusted rubber boots. Two massive columns hold up the porch roof, and at the foot of each sits a carved stone tub, once used to catch the must as it was pressed out of the grapes in the *palmento*, now spilling over with foliage.

Watching the courtyard's slow metamorphosis from the chalky desert of our first summer at Bosco, when the builders were still at work, to the soothing and leafy haven it is now, has given me much satisfaction, but if I am proud of my own handiwork in bringing this about, my greatest delight is in three plants that are none of my own doing, but gifts from the gods.

Opposite the porch, in front of the guesthouse door, a grapevine has emerged, growing unnoticed until its trunk had hardened into wood, curling up and over the faucet and reaching to the roof, blessing of Dionysus on our vineyards and our wine making. In front of the stone tub at the left-hand column of the porch, a wild olive has sprouted, sacred to Athena, goddess of wisdom, of order, and of creativity. Next to the other tub a pomegranate tree, shooting up from ancient roots, is now a good four feet tall and will soon add its shade against the summer sun and, in time, bear the red fruit of Persephone.

It is colder inside than out, and Tonino has put a large log of olive wood on the kitchen fire. It is not at all unusual for us to burn olive wood, since our trees were given a major pruning a year ago, but today it is particularly satisfying to watch this thick trunk blazing, a point of conjunction between two calendars. During the vacation I have been browsing through *The Greek Myths* of Robert Graves and have just discovered a different Greek calendar, based on thirteen lunar months, a calendar of very ancient and very sacred origins, in which each month was represented by a tree. Twigs, each standing for the first letter of its tree's name, could be used as a secret alphabet for conveying sacred messages. The vowels were represented by twigs from the trees sacred to the solstices and the equinoxes; the winter solstice, for example, was the fir or the palm (depending on the climate, I suppose— perhaps next year we should use a palm for our Christmas tree!). Originally reserved to the priestesses of the moon in archaic Greece, this alphabet was later used by Druids and spread as far as Ireland.

The first month of the tree calendar, which began on December 24, two days after the winter solstice, has as its symbol the oleaster, the same wild olive that is growing in the courtyard, which the Greeks believed would drive away the evil spirits. The cultivated olive does not breed true but must be grafted onto the oleaster with cuttings that were originally brought from Libya to Greece, and from there to Sicily. Here the Greek colonists set out their olive groves and built shrines to Aristaeus, son of Apollo and Cyrene, who spread the arts of beekeeping, cheese making, and olive grafting as he wandered around the Mediterranean.

Olives no longer have a place in the contemporary New Year. Modern Italy appears to run on a fiscal calendar, divided into twelve months plus the *tredicesima*, the "thirteenth," an extra month's salary guaranteed to all Italian workers as a sort of Christmas bonus and a good filler for the newspapers, which get a lot of copy each year out of speculation as to how the Italians will spend their *tredicesima.* Each month ends with *il ventisette*, the twenty-seventh day of the month, when the monthly salaries are paid. To have *il ventisette* is the greatest aspiration, the symbol of a person who is *sistemato*, "settled" into a stable job with a guaranteed monthly wage. Major observances fall in November, when an advance payment on income tax is due, and at the end of May with the final accounting. Other minor taxes on cars, driving licenses, etc., punctuate the year, which comes to a standstill in August, the vacation month, when factories close, business activities cease, and the cities empty.

A calendar based on the seasons, on sowing and harvesting, on death and rebirth, is irrelevant to us now, its recurrent cycles out of step with the linear conception of time and progress that urges us forward. But I am glad to know that the oleaster in the courtyard might drive away evil spirits and that on the first day of 1983 my hearth is warmed by wood from the olive, the tree of the first month.

In the days that follow, Bosco buzzes with activity. It hasn't rained since the twenty-second, and the soil has dried out enough to be worked. Early the morning of the second, even though it is a Sunday, we are awakened by the sound of a truck. Mr. Amato has arrived, the *novararo* who has rented all our fallow land for the year in order to grow tomatoes and melons.

For all that it is very sketchily applied, crop rotation on unirrigated land in Sicily means alternating three main crops: durum wheat and fava beans, which grow in winter, and *novara*, tomatoes and watermelons that miraculously manage to survive summers without water and bear sweet and succulent fruit despite the dryness. For the last few years we have planted wheat, sown in October and harvested in June, and it is time for a change. Mr. Amato is new to us, presented by a *contadino* who worked for us in the past, and we are favorably impressed by the spit and polish on the tractor he unloads from the truck and, as the day wears on, by the precision of his plowing.

The deep plowing through the stubble of last year's wheat was done in September by the huge tractor belonging to the government extension agency. Mr. Amato makes a finer furrow, passing back and forth until the big clods of red clay soil are broken down to a fine grain. Our fields have never looked better. At the end of the week he makes the final furrows, a piece of metal piping tied across the front of the tractor, extending five feet on either side and dragging a length of chain from either extremity, so that he can plow perfectly parallel rows without wasting any land.

At the same time the vineyards spring to life, as Turiddu Vivona starts the annual pruning and plowing of the vines, untouched since September. Beneath the rows the thick carpet of sorrel and mustard is yellow with flowers and with the shriveled leaves that have fallen in the wind, leaving a brown haze of bare branches twining along the support wires. From the hilltop we can see Turiddu, a small gray figure against the yellow, working his way along the row, deciding how many buds to leave on each vine, choosing between a "fat" pruning and a "thin" pruning on the basis of last year's harvest and the health of the plant. Where he has passed, the empty wires glitter in the sun and the tangle of branches has fallen to the ground, waiting to be collected into a pyre and burned for charcoal.

Training the grapevines along wire fences or on overhead trellises is new to Sicily, where the production of low-proof table wine has only recently taken over from the traditional dark and strong Sicilian wine destined to make vermouth and to strengthen the thin wines of the north. The older vineyards are either pruned in the *alberello* style, low close-cut plants that do indeed resemble "little trees," or trained in the Alcamese fashion in which the branches of each vine are tied for support to a bunch of canes. The canes, replaced each year at pruning time, add new designs to the patchwork of the countryside: in some fields they are laid out in long gray stripes along the vine rows, ready to hand for the tying up, while other vineyards are tufted with stooks of canes leaning up against each other and awaiting distribution.

As each vineyard is completed, Turiddu gathers up the prunings and does the first plowing. The motors of the two tractors roar in counterpoint, first near, then far, echoing off the hillsides until it is difficult to tell who is where.

We move back to Palermo on Epiphany, the day in which the Befana fills the shoes and stockings of Italian children with candy and toys, or coals if they have been naughty. The Befana is an old woman; it is said that when the Three Kings stopped by her cottage to ask directions, they invited her to join them in bringing presents to the newborn King, but she said she was too busy with her housework. After they left she was seized by remorse and started off by herself with a bag full of presents. She is still searching, and she leaves presents as she passes at every hearth where there are children, just in case.

Never able to compete with the dead in Sicily anyway, the Befana has been further diminished by the government's efficiency campaign, a move that has been much criticized as unfair to children and disrespectful of all the most ancient Italian traditions. This year the Italian genius for compromise has triumphed: although the Befana has not been restored to the privileged ranks of the national holidays, the Minister of Public Education decreed that the schools would reopen on the seventh, thus saving both the goat and the cabbages, as the Italian proverb says.

According to another proverb, the Befana carries away all the holidays, and San Giuseppe brings them back again. Saint Joseph's Day on March 19 isn't a national holiday anymore either, but at least its arrival means that Easter is drawing near, bringing the incredible explosion of the Sicilian spring. For the moment, however, despite the swelling buds on the almond trees and the tips of the daffodils already fending the mulch in the garden, the

Befana carries us back to the city and to the two most wintry months, in which rain and mud and flu epidemics will keep us prisoners for two or three weekends in a row, until we all feel stir crazy and even the cat races around our small apartment in fits of demonic possession most becoming to his black fur and green eyes.

This time our return to the city is more reluctant than ever. The newspapers are full of what they have baptized as the *strage di Santo Stefano*, the "Saint Stephen's Day Massacre." On the day after Christmas five people were shot down by the Mafia, and more in the days that followed, bringing the total for 1982 to 150 murdered and again as many fallen to the *lupara bianca*, the "white shotgun" victims who disappear without leaving any trace, their bodies never to be found.

The twenty years that I have been in Sicily have witnessed two successive revolutions in the map of Mafia power. Originally a rural phenomenon, the influence of which was much curtailed though never extinguished under Mussolini, the Mafia entered new fields of endeavor in the wake of the Allied invasion in 1943. The American government released Lucky Luciano from prison to prepare the way for the landing, and the huge business of provisioning the American troops with its concomitant black market fell to the "friends of the friends."

The great expansion of Palermo in the postwar period, when it was designated the capital of the newly created Sicilian regional government, provided fertile ground for this new generation of mafiosi, who had replaced the old shotgun with the machine gun and adopted other innovations as well from their American cousins. Huge fortunes were made overnight as real estate speculation changed the face of Palermo, and at the end of the fifties a violent war broke out between the various *cosche*, or families, who were vying for control of the city. The last battle in this war backfired: a bomb in the luggage compartment of a car intended for a mafioso killed seven carabinieri instead, public indignation was ignited, and a parliamentary commission was instituted to investigate the Mafia.

The political influence of the Mafia outweighed the influence of the commission, and the special law passed to allow the police to place suspected mafiosi under house arrest far from their native territory only facilitated Sicilian organized crime in penetrating northern Italy, but the *cosche* thought it advisable to make peace among themselves and keep a low profile during the investigations, so the late sixties and seventies were years of relative peace.

The huge profits deriving from their increasing control of the drug market (Sicily is the channel through which a large part of the world's opium production is refined and distributed throughout Europe and the U.S.) created new problems, however. The need to recycle these profits, mainly through public works contracts, into respectability, made the Mafia more vulnerable to investigation and less hesitant about stepping into the limelight in order to remove obstacles to its progress. I can well remember how shocked Palermo was in 1971 when the top man in the local branch of the national prosecutor's office was shot down. It was the first time the Mafia had aimed so high, something that was to be repeated often during the next decade: top police officers, judges, even the president of the regional government were eliminated when they threatened the smooth functioning of this enormous machine. Yet still more blood has been shed in internecine quarrels among the families themselves. Entire clans have been wiped out during the last couple of years as a new power struggle has broken the precarious peace of the seventies and has seen skirmishes on both sides of the Atlantic: the body of one murdered mafioso came back in a coffin from New York decapitated, a macabre indication that his clan was now leaderless. The Saint Stephen's Day Massacre is only the most recent episode in all this.

The massacre took place in a pizza parlor and in a small glass factory, both belonging to the family of the boss Tommaso Buscetta. Neither site is far from our apartment, but it is less the fear of stray bullets that makes it difficult to return to Palermo than the sense of total impotence, the seeming impossibility of taking an effective stand, of braking the slow decay of this beautiful city.

Palermo is a splendid slavegirl, whom her masters—Muslim masters, Christians, emirs, Norman kings, and Spanish viceroys—have adorned, one after another. Weighted down by all her jewels, she sleeps in the sun.

Anatole France, "Lettera dalla Sicilia," in *Delle cose di Sicilia*

If he were writing this letter today instead of in 1896, Anatole France would perhaps concede that Palermo's sleep has become a comatose stupor, produced by infection and decay. I can bear to return only if I force myself to ignore this side of it and concentrate on the vestiges of former splendor. I have had in mind for a long time a children's book on the Norman period: now is the time to explore Palermo for this purpose, to trace the course of the Norman walls and search for the pleasure palaces that lay beyond them, surrounding the city "like golden coins hung about the neck of a full-breasted girl." Ibn Jubayr obviously had a one-track metaphor, but his is no doubt an apt description of the sensual beauty of Palermo in the twelfth century.

The Italian Middle Ages are so anomalous with respect to the feudalism versus growth of the nation-state pattern that evolved in northern Europe that most college history courses don't even attempt to cope with them. At the most a brief résumé of the evolution of the Italian city-state serves to explain the Renaissance. Southern Italy, which knew neither city-state nor any indigenous form of Renaissance, has a story that rarely gets told, and it is therefore startling to realize that Palermo at the beginning of the eleventh century had a population that is conservatively estimated at one hundred thousand inhabitants, second only to that of Constantinople among all the European cities, and that a century later, when the city had passed from Arab to Norman hands, King Roger II received an income from the city of Palermo alone that was greater than that which his Norman cousins to the north received from all of England.

When the Arabs arrived in Sicily in the course of the ninth century, they came to colonize; they brought with them highly sophisticated irrigation techniques and introduced many new crops:

lemons and oranges, date palms and melons, mulberry trees and silkworms, sugarcane and rice, all of which flourished in the fertile Sicilian soil. Small villages grew up throughout the island, and the languishing economy awoke to extraordinary vigor. Fifty years after the first landing, Syracuse, the western capital of the Byzantine Empire, fell into Arab hands. It required another hundred years to break down the last resistance, but by 965 the occupation of the island was complete, and in the last hundred years of Islamic domination, much of the local population, which had been almost entirely Greek speaking and belonged to the Greek church, converted to Islam and to the Arabic tongue.

In the meantime the capital of the Fatimite Empire had shifted from neighboring Tunisia to distant Egypt, and the Sicilian emirs, left to their own devices, fell to quarreling among themselves. Still fabulously wealthy but relatively unprotected, Sicily was a tempting morsel for any appetite. And there were plenty of takers in the neighborhood: Norman knights on their way home from the Crusades had discovered that southern Italy, torn between Lombard, papal, and Byzantine ambitions, offered good opportunities for those younger sons who sought to carve out by a bit of swordwork a piece of land for themselves. Among these, the sons of Tancred d'Hauteville had distinguished themselves as particularly ambitious and, led by the eldest, Robert Guiscard, had established control over much of southern Italy. In 1061 Robert Guiscard and his brother Roger embarked on a campaign to conquer Sicily, an endeavor that took them thirteen years: Palermo fell in 1078, and the last important Saracen stronghold, at Noto, was taken in 1091. Roger assumed the title of Great Count of Sicily, and in 1105 he was succeeded by his ten-year-old son, Roger, who in 1130 crowned himself king of Sicily.

The extraordinary tolerance and open-mindedness that the Normans demonstrated toward their Saracen and Greek Christian subjects were probably dictated in the case of Count Roger by considerations of strategy: a handful of Norman knights could not hope to rule the entire island unless they made use of the extant and highly developed Arab bureaucracy. With Roger II, however, preference was joined to pragmatism. Thanks to his mother, Adelaide of Savona, he was Mediterranean both in blood and in upbringing; his mother's choice of Palermo as the capital for her regency meant that Roger grew up in a city that was cosmopolitan, cultivated, and luxury loving, a striking contrast to the rough-and-tumble life his father must have led when growing up in the Hauteville castle in Normandy. The peaceful coexistence among Norman, Arab, and Byzantine created a most favorable environment in which science, learning, and art, encouraged by the curiosity and generosity of Roger and his successors, flourished beyond anything that Europe had seen since the Dark Ages began.

It was as short-lived as it was magnificent: Roger's grandson William II assured disaster when he married off his aunt Constance to the son of Barbarossa. When William died without a direct heir in 1189, Henry arrived to claim his wife's dowry. Swept into the struggle between pope and emperor, the Norman kingdom was doomed, despite the brief respite it was to know under Frederick II.

No doubt we must thank the piety of the French and Spanish conquerors who followed for the fact that the religious monuments built by the Norman kings, the Palatine Chapel and the cathedrals of Monreale and Cefalù, have survived relatively intact. No such respect has been shown to the pleasure palaces; we have inherited only bits and pieces that must be patched by contemporary descriptions and mortared with the imagination if one is to re-create any sense of the life they once knew.

I decide to begin with the earliest palace; on the first sunny day I ask my friend Maria Vica to accompany me to the eastern outskirts of Palermo to see Favara, much beloved of Roger II.

In order that none of the joys of land or water should be lacking to him, he caused a great sanctuary for birds and beasts to be built at a place called Favara, which was full of caves and dells; its waters he stocked with every kind of fish from divers regions; nearby he built a beautiful palace. And certain hills and forests around Palermo he likewise enclosed with walls, and there he made the Parco—a pleasant and delightful spot, shaded with various trees and abounding with deer and goats and wild boar. And here also he raised a palace, to which the water was led in underground pipes from springs whence it flowed ever sweet and clear. And thus the King, being a wise and prudent man, took his pleasure from these places according to the season. In the winter and in Lent he would reside at the Favara, by reason of the great quantity of fish that were to be had there; while in the heat of the summer he would find solace at the Parco where, with a little hunting, he would relieve his mind from the cares and worries of state.

> Chronicles of Archbishop Romuald of Salerno, quoted in John Julius Norwich, *The Kingdom in the Sun*

Actually, Romuald gives Roger a little more credit than is his due: the palace of Favara (which comes from the Arabic word *farawah*, meaning "fountain" or "spring") was built earlier, by Emir Jafar, and Roger only amplified it, adding a chapel and creating the artificial lake that surrounded it on three sides.

A great part of Favara's charm must have lain in its position on the narrow plain at the eastern rim of the Conca d'Oro; in sight of the sea, it is shadowed to the south by Monte Grifone, which rises rapidly and raggedly from the plain, its green hulk the first in the ring of mountains surrounding Palermo. The area, now called Brancaccio, has been designated as a zone for industrial development and is a squalid jumble of hovels and high-rises interspersed with small factories struggling to survive despite the fact that most of their profits go to paying protection money to the Mafia, which rules the neighborhood with such violence that the press sometimes refers to Brancaccio as the South Bronx of Palermo.

Without Maria Vica to guide me, I might easily have missed the narrow alley leading to the western facade of the castle. The blind arches, a constant decorative element in all the Arab-Norman buildings, are hardly recognizable for the bright green wooden shutters barring the windows cut into the ancient walls, while low sheds hide from view the small cupola marking the chapel, its round dome ringed by a cornice that gives it a curious, lidded effect. A young woman living in the alleyway opens the chapel for us so we can peer up inside the cupola, tall and narrow, the stones of its arches so weathered by the salt winds blowing off the sea that all sense of human artifice has been eroded.

Following the custodian through an iron gate we skirt the eastern wall of the castle and walk in what was once the lake, bordered on two sides by orange trees. The ancient stone banks have been brought to light, and to the north a row of small houses has borrowed the massive stones for its foundations. The lake itself is a vast and beautifully tended market garden, a variegated sea of green tossed by wave on wave of lettuces, radishes, and onions, and enviably free of weeds.

We retrace our steps, and the custodian shows us how to circle around behind the chapel to see the castle courtyard, which she warns us is inhabited. She has put it mildly: at least fifteen families have burrowed their way into the ruins, squeezing into niches and wrapping themselves about the columns, cutting a window, adding a balcony or a shed in an ingenious, almost fungal growth that has a certain sordid charm. In one corner the remaining half of a vault, quicklimed a brilliant blue, provides shade for a balcony, to the right one of the original arched windows sports pale green paint and a broom hung out to dry over flowerpots propped up on bricks to keep them from sliding down the tin roof of the shed below. A swarm of tiny children have interrupted their games to stare at us. A mother sweeps a little girl into her arms and kisses her in a series of loud smacks: *"Sangue mio*—my own blood!"

"You know," says Maria Vica as we walk out, "you don't hear that expression in Catania—it comes straight from the Arabic."

> Favara of the two lakes, you are the sum of all desires; pleasing sight, most marvelous spectacle.
> Your waters divide into nine rivulets; O most beautiful and branching currents!

Where your two lakes meet, there love had made its camp, and along
  your canal has passion pitched its tents.
O splendid lake of the two palms, O royal hostel which this embraces!
The limpid waters of your springs resemble lustrous pearls, and the
  surrounding meadows are the sea.

> From a poem by Abd ar-Rahmàn al Itrabanishi,
> Roger's secretary, in *Delle cose di Sicilia*

The good weather that accompanied us to Favara doesn't last
long: the temperature drops suddenly, and we have two days of
storms that leave the mountains around Palermo white with snow.
In the city, sleet and snow alternate in brief flurries, but nothing
sticks despite the ardent prayers of the young. Although nowadays it seems to snow much more frequently in the mountains
than it did when I first arrived in Sicily, the Palermitani still treat
a snowfall as something quite exceptional, and in January of 1981,
when we awoke one morning to find the streets buried under six
inches of snow, the city went mad.

In our part of the city the snow melted quickly, but farther
inland traffic was difficult, and the town of Monreale at the foot
of the nearest mountain was cut off except for the small elite of
ski enthusiasts who had chains for their tires. The storm had
knocked out much of Sicily's high-tension network, so we were
without light, and therefore heat and water, for several days, and
a couple of weeks of periodic blackouts followed in which we went
about with candles and flashlights in our pockets and trudged up
the stairs rather than risk getting caught in the elevator.

At the start, however, everyone was delighted: children skipped
school, drivers had big grins on their faces despite the hazards of
unfamiliar driving conditions, and the blackout was a joke as long
as outside there was a whiteout. On the Saturday we went out to
Bosco, arriving at sunset to find the roofs still white and a foot of

snow under the olive trees and between the rows of grapevines. It was melting fast, but the children managed a small snowman before it became too dark to see. The next morning we took a walk, sloshing down the hill behind the house into our neighbor's olive grove, where the little valley, protected by its steep slopes and ancient trees, still held snow deep enough for a furious snowball fight.

From the other side of the valley we could see the whole plain: the snow stopped just a little below Bosco, and from there to the sea it was green, but the ring of mountains was completely white and glistening in the sun, the peaks of Monte Iato and Rocca Busambra to the south looking more like some Alpine scene than our familiar Sicilian panorama, and illuminating for me the Greeks' enthusiasm for the snows of Mount Parnassus.

In a nearby vineyard the children found enough snow to make a proper snowman, but they needed a lesson in the basic techniques. The snow was thin and wet enough to roll up like a carpet, leaving its muddy underside outward, so our snowman had an olive complexion, and we gave him a purely Sicilian face: camomile flowers for eyes, an upside-down jack-in-the-pulpit for a nose, and a wild iris for a mouth.

In the early afternoon we headed back to Palermo along the mountain route, up over the pass behind Partinico and down into the Conca d'Oro and Monreale on the other side. The gas station attendant outside Partinico told us that the road had just been plowed open, and it felt very adventurous to be the first ones through. The thaw had barely begun up here, the snow was virgin on either side of the narrow lane created by the plows, and we stopped up at the top so that the children could have their first experience of plunging knee-deep into snow.

Once we were over the pass, the traffic became intense: all Palermo had come up to the snow, and well-equipped, down-padded families cavorted side by side with ladies in high heels and mink coats, fathers in business suits, and children in their Sunday best, all slipping and slopping about in the wet snow, slinging inexpert handfuls at each other and roaring with delight.

Custom dictates that those who go up into the mountains to see the snow must pile some up on the roof of their cars, preferably building it into a snowman, although even a mere heap will do. People who have baggage racks are lucky, as there is less danger that it will all slide off as one descends carefully into the city. For the point is this, the slow descent and triumphal entry, honking and laughing and showing off one's enterprise and bravura in conquering such a foreign element. At the traffic lights the cars are assaulted by gangs of street urchins who nip out and grab handfuls of snow off the cars to throw at each other, stealing snowballs just as they steal most of their other pleasures.

In the days that followed, Palermo's sports equipment dealers made a fortune. The Palermitani were quick to discover that they could consume the snow as conspicuously as they do everything else, and outfitted themselves with beautifully designed and hideously expensive padded jackets and pants and snowboots, just in case it should happen again.

❧ January 14: today is the fifteenth anniversary of the earthquake that devastated western Sicily in 1968. While most of the towns from Palermo west and south trembled, the fifteen that lie along the valley of the Belice River were severely damaged and several of them completely destroyed. The valley's population, already much reduced by emigration, which was still at that time the only viable alternative to the subsistence level farming of the Sicilian interior, lost what little they had to lose: their homes, their meager belongings, all the tangible expressions of a peasant culture that was already under siege. And many lost their lives.

The jackals were quick to scent an opportunity, and millions of lire have disappeared in the "reconstruction," first in the construction of temporary barracks to house the sixty thousand homeless (after fifteen years there are still twenty thousand people living in these uninsulated buildings, baking in the summer sun and freezing in the winter), and then in the mammoth *auto-strada*, the same superhighway that speeds our weekend trips to Bosco, which has embroidered the Belice Valley with cloverleaf exits worthy of Los Angeles, leading to deserted heaps of toppled houses or forlorn rows of barracks.

This morning the people of the Belice will gather once again to present their requests to the government, to ask that the permanent housing be completed and the work of economic reconstruction commence, but one wonders with what heart they march. They have won one Pyrrhic victory: they have entered the Italian language as a synonym for abandonment and desperation. After each new disaster, each earthquake or major flood, with the first relief a Minister comes, jumping down from his helicopter and declaring: "This will not become another Belice!"

The other evening at the movies I was telling some English friends who were with me an anecdote that ended, almost parenthetically, with "But of course it wasn't really an earthquake, it was just—"

"Oh, my God!" said Pam. "How is it possible that I have ended up in a place where someone can talk so calmly about earthquakes!" We have indeed had time to familiarize ourselves: in 1968 the tremors continued on and off for about four months and they have returned periodically ever since. An earthquake is interminable: I freeze, listening with my feet to this geological music, waiting to hear if it will fade out to stillness or build to a crescendo of falling masonry. It seems to go on for hours, although most tremors last only about twenty seconds. Fear comes over me afterward, as I see the hanging lamp, infallible seismograph, still swinging, and must decide whether to stay put, trusting in the reinforced concrete that is supposed to render our apartment building safe (although to judge by the rest of it, the pilasters are probably hollow), or to take the children out to join the crowd that is rapidly forming in the piazza. It is difficult to resist the pull of the running footsteps on the stairs; to succumb to it means to stand around for an hour in the piazza, everyone wedged between the school and the church, both low buildings that won't go far if they fall, awaiting some all-clear signal that will never sound. It is boredom that overcomes fear in the end; feet tire, the cold seeps in, and the crowd begins to dwindle as one by one the families return to their homes, children seeking once more the maternal bosom now that all anger is past.

It continues to be cold, but as always in Sicily the sun is hot, and turning the corner from shade to sunlight can mean a jump of ten degrees in temperature. We get three days of sun in a row, and I decide to take advantage of the warmth to go ahead with my quest for the pleasure palaces, this time those that lay in the Genoard, the huge park that stretched from the walls of the Royal Palace south into the Conca d'Oro. Started by Roger's son William I and continued by *his* son William II, this park covered many acres and was dotted with lakes and fountains and gardens, with summerhouses, pavilions, and palaces. Of all this splendor only traces remain, the Zisa, the Cuba, and the Cubula.

I don't know how much I shall be able to see. The palace of the Zisa has been subject alternately to restoration and to collapse since 1950, and although the basic work of consolidation has just recently been terminated, the restoration of the interior is still in progress. The Cuba and the Cubula are much smaller, little pavilions to provide shade and repose, but one is in a private garden and the other in a military barracks. So I take care to wear my most un-Italian clothes and to brush up my foreign accent, and with guidebooks in full sight, I start out to see what I can wangle my way into.

I leave the house in sunshine and park in front of the Zisa in pouring rain. It is immediately obvious that I shall not get to see the inside: since I last passed by here, the area around the palace has been fenced off with a very businesslike iron railing, cement mixers are churning, a workman is sandblasting an archway, a truck is being loaded with dismembered scaffolding, and more scaffolding is visible under the arches. But what I can see through the fence is glorious! The balconied windows of a later age have been removed, the big central arch leading into the interior has been reopened, and the warm rosy beige of the newly cleaned stone softens the austere geometry of the facade, three stories high, which is barely animated by two rows of blind arches and, on the ground floor, by three arched portals leading into the antechambers. Two lions rampant bearing a coat of arms are the only intricate note.

To the right of the palace lies a low line of buildings, once probably a cloistered walk leading to the chapel. Of this only the apse and the red Moorish cupola have survived, around which a baroque church has grown up and then fallen down, a marriage of opposites that have come to resemble each other through the centuries.

A carob tree and some twisted cedars are all that is left to remind one that the Zisa was once immersed in a park, but the outline of the reflecting pool that once lay in front of it is visible, together with the foundations of the little pavilion that stood on an island in the center. Although the city has grown up around it, there are still considerable open spaces both in front of and behind the Zisa, and the regional government intends to use the Zisa as a museum for temporary exhibits and to re-create the park and rebuild the pool, so that once more gardens will embrace the palace and still waters shimmer with the reflection of *al-Aziz*, "the Glorious."

For the moment, however, I shall have to be content with this view of the outside: for the interior I must turn to an account published in 1550 by a Dominican friar from Bologna, Leandro Alberti, in a book ambitiously titled *Descrittione di tutta Italia*, "A Description of All Italy." The most fascinating part is the description of the central hall, with its honeycomb vaults and mosaic friezes, and its fountain:

From an ingenious spigot a great abundance of water issues forth. And to the delight of the spectator, these limpid waters fall with great splashings onto stones of striped marble, and murmuring they descend the stones. . . . Above the spigot from which issues the water, one can see a most beautiful eagle in finest mosaic, and above this two delightful peacocks, one on each side, and between them two archers aiming their bows at birds perched on the branches of a tree. . . . The pavement is all of squares of white marble; in the middle the waters of the aforesaid fountain pass along a small canal and enter a beautiful and harmonious pool, four and a half feet square; this too is of the finest marble wrought with some curious mosaics. The bottom of the pool is divided into six sections, and beneath its limpid and transparent waters can be seen different kinds of fish, worked most ably in mosaic, the which, with the movements of the water, appear themselves to move. As they flow out, the waters are gathered once more into a canal similar to the first, and enter into another pool, . . . and then again into a third. . . . Near the center pool is a graceful table of candid marble, three feet on each side, raised not far off the ground upon four cleverly worked columns, where one can most enjoyably dine. And in this most pleasant spot and with no lesser delight one can sip of cooled wine, borne in jars upon the current along the aforesaid canals as far as this pool. Wherein, as they are borne along, the wine jars appear to seek battle among themselves, so agitated are they by the waters, more, or less, according to the impetus of the currents that carry them.

Leandro Alberti, *Descrittione di tutta Italia*, in *Delle cose di Sicilia*

Many of the little streets around the Zisa have been closed off because of the restoration work, and I have a hard time hunting out a route that will take me around to see the back. I finally find an excellent view across a wide stretch of fields and market gardens that have somehow resisted the low-cost public housing that has flooded the area. From this distance I can see three pavilions that were built onto the roof in the seventeenth century, their pink and yellow stucco and their curlicued outlines peeping over the crenellations in playful contrast to the severity of the palace below. It is exciting to witness the rebirth of this monument, proof that not all of Palermo's decay is irreversible, and to think that we owe the accuracy of the reconstruction in great measure to Fra

Leandro, who justified the detail of his account with remarkable foresight:

> I have dwelt at length on the description of these buildings, going beyond our original intention; yet it has seemed fit to me to describe this building for the satisfaction of all curious minds in order that, when much of the building is no longer, which impends in as much as there is no generous soul who will preserve it, and when it can no longer be seen in stone, its memory may at least remain in writing.

From the Zisa it is not far to Corso Calatafimi, the main road leading from Palermo to Monreale, flanked with seventeenth-century villas, nineteenth-century townhouses, and twentieth-century high-rise condominiums, tossed together in the grab bag of the city's chaotic growth. I have little difficulty in locating the barracks that hide the Cuba from view, but the soldier on duty outside the gate has no intention of letting me in.

"You need permission. You have to go to get permission somewhere and it really isn't worth it. I mean, you can't go inside or anything, only look at it from outside, and it's just a few old walls."

I am provoked but not really surprised: last summer the Red Brigades attacked a couple of munitions depots near Naples, and the military has tightened surveillance.

"Where do I get permission?"

"Well . . . maybe from the Comiliter."

"Where's that?"

"Well . . . maybe at the Caserma Garibaldi."

"Where's that?"

"Well . . . you go down this street and then there's a church, and next to that there's the Caserma Garibaldi."

From the Caserma Garibaldi I go to Piazza Bonanno, where the sentinel at the carabinieri barracks directs me to the Comiliter, which in turn sends me to the Ufficio Presidio, which is in a handsome eighteenth-century building across from the Royal Palace. The huge old wooden doors have a smaller door cut into them for foot traffic: when I ring the bell, this door opens on a chain and a soldier peers out like a suspicious housewife. Inside, behind bulletproof glass, two soldiers, their waists thick with daggers, hand grenades, and other sinister-looking gear, are watching Betty Boop cartoons on television, while a third takes possession of my driving license, issues me a visitor's pass, and then accompanies me to the offices, where he knocks on doors saying, "This lady here wants to see some cupola," until we find a major to whom I am allowed to make a written request for permission to visit the Cuba for "*motivi di studio*." The next morning I go to pick up my letter of permission and present it to the soldier who is on duty today.

"Why, you didn't need permission, not unless you wanted to take photographs or something; we *always* let people in."

It's not worth the energy to get upset, and in any case I am grateful that my visit to the Cuba has been postponed for twenty-four hours, enabling me to see it in today's brilliant sunlight. It is much bigger than I expected, only slightly smaller in dimension than the Zisa and very similar in its facade. The arched windows give onto blue sky: the cupola from which it probably derived its name has long since collapsed. Through the doorway, six feet off the ground at the water level of the lake that once completely surrounded the palace, I can see the bare branches of a tree growing in the courtyard, and some last remnants of arabesqued stuccowork clinging to a vault. Like the Zisa, the color of the stone, warm in the sun, softens the harsh lines, and the play of light and reflection between stone and water must have been delightful, the shadowy interior an invitation to cross the little bridge, long gone, and escape from the hot Sicilian sun. It is still inviting despite its dismal surroundings, and I would like to linger, but the bored soldier is breathing down my neck.

Reluctantly I take my leave and continue on up Corso Calatafimi in search of the small lane that leads between apartment buildings to the gate of a lovely but very decayed villa, typically Sicilian in its baroque facade and double staircase curving up to the front door. Three tall palms and an enormous magnolia rise up behind the villa while orchards stretch out on either side, a sunken pool of green amidst the high-rises. A custodian opens the padlock on an iron gate and tells me to follow the path.

This leads me between two ancient stone walls bordered by orange and lemon trees, heavy with fruit that gleams in the bright sunlight. After a bit the path curves and opens into an orchard where citrus trees are interspersed and shaded by medlars, taller and duller in color, their fruit still tiny and dark green. The trees are close together, barely allowing the sunlight through to dapple the dense undergrowth of ivy, angelica, and acanthus. The path narrows—I have walked some two hundred yards—and I can see at the end some palm branches. As I draw closer I realize that I am looking at them through the Cubula itself, a small stone cube topped by a cheerful red dome, each of its four walls pierced by a tall pointed archway opening onto the single vaulted room. It is thought that there was once a whole series of these pavilions forming an intermittent portico of shady spots wherein to stop and rest while strolling through the park. The Cubula is the only one left, and this of itself seems quite miraculous: one emerges from the shady orchard to see it silhouetted against the beige stucco of an unfinished apartment building less than fifty yards away, and only three yards to the right a barbed-wire fence skirts a huge pile of metal scaffolding. A crane turns overhead, and the whine of an electric saw drowns out the singing of the birds in the orchard.

I hasten to retreat along the path so that I can look back again through the branches of the medlar trees that blot out the construction work, wreathing the Cubula in its original frame of foliage. The slightest of breezes shifts the leaves and their shadows, a birdsong is interrupted abruptly, and only my presence impedes the arrival of king and concubine to restore themselves in the shade of the Cubula with wine that has been cooling in the fountains of the Genoard.

❧ It is too easy for me to consider Bosco the repository of all that I love in Sicily, and Palermo the incarnation of all that is worst. I stand rebuked by this morning's newspaper, which bears a reminder that pastoral settings are not reserved for idylls. Two sons of our local shepherd have been arrested, together with some twenty-five other people of the area, on charges of belonging to a criminal organization and of attempted extortion. During the night the carabinieri cordoned off the area between Partinico, Balestrate, and Alcamo and arrested the whole gang, mostly shepherds, who they claim have been exerting pressure on local landowners to rent or even sell land for pasturage at very low prices.

Tonino had heard no rumors of anything like this, and we speculate as to whether it is generational turnover or indicative of the power void at the top. All the local *"pezzi di novanta,"* the big shots, are in hiding because of the drug war, and a lot of petty criminals are making amateurish attempts to carve out a space for themselves in the absence of the bosses.

I have long been a champion of shepherds, albeit for ridiculous reasons: just about the best thing one can eat in Sicily is a bowl of hot curds and whey ladled from the cauldron in which the shepherds are making ricotta, and I bitterly resent the fact that we are seldom on visiting terms with the shepherds who live nearby. Perhaps it was basically greed that prompted me to consider Tonino's profound distrust of shepherds as an inherited and unreasonable prejudice, something out of *Oklahoma*. "Oh, the cowboys and the farmers should be friends" would run through my head whenever he embarked on the subject.

When we first began to spend time at Bosco, the shepherd whose house and sheep pens are just up the road sent his son to ask permission to pasture the sheep in the stubble after our wheat had been harvested. It seemed that this might mark the onset of a thaw in our relations with shepherds, and the following Easter

I took Natalia and her cousin Martina to get some ricotta, as we had been invited to do. Following Tonino's instructions we walked up the road, forked left and left again onto a track that led up over a little rise and into a muddy yard blackened with sheep droppings and pockmarked by the passage of tiny hooves. In front of us was the traditional whitewashed one-room farmhouse with a sloping tile roof, to the left a shed and a modern, flat-roofed house stuccoed in a pattern of brown and green, to the right the railings of the sheep pens and a small vegetable garden.

Smoke was coming out of the shed, and it was there that we found the shepherd's wife, a gray-haired woman perhaps in her early fifties, and her teen-aged daughters, hard at work on the ricotta from the morning's milking. In the summer they have to make the cheese twice a day, but in April the nights were still cold enough to keep the evening's milk from spoiling so that the two batches could be processed together. The first lot of milk had already been boiled and separated, and the curds, destined to become pecorino, had been packed into rush baskets and were draining on wooden trays in one room of the shed. In the other room the women were taking turns at stirring the whey that was heating together with more milk in an enormous copper cauldron, big enough to take a bath in, propped up on stones in one corner of the shed over a blazing fire fed by four- or five-foot-long logs that were shoved farther and farther into the flames rapidly consuming them. The smoke circled the rafters and went out the door; the women seemed accustomed to it, but the little girls and I couldn't manage to stay in the room for more than a few minutes at a time.

As she pushed the long-handled twig brush round and round to keep the milk from scorching and sticking to the bottom of the cauldron, the wife talked to me about her life: the hard work involved in making cheese twice a day (as welcome as the open fire was in the damp chill of an April morning, it wasn't difficult to imagine what it would mean in the Sicilian summer), the difficulties and the loneliness of bringing up seven children out in the Sicilian countryside, without electric light or running water until eight years ago, her worry that her sons would be unable to find wives willing to put up with the hardships of a shepherd's life. They managed to get a good price for their cheese, she said, because instead of selling it to a middleman she herself took it in the car to Partinico every day and delivered it direct to her customers. I remarked on how unusual it was to find people living full time on the land. Her husband had always needed her help, and although they had had a house in Alcamo "with all the proper furniture," somehow she had never managed to live there, and finally they had saved up enough money to build a house with all the modern comforts here in the country.

"Come, let me show you." Turning the brush over to one of her daughters, she led us to the brown and green house we had seen as we came in. "There wasn't any point in letting my furniture just rot there in Alcamo where nobody could see it."

With great pride she showed us through a shiny, tiled and marble-floored house full of brand-new furniture that looked as if it had never been sat on. It was all what the Italians call "*in stile*," modern replicas approximating styles from the past, as opposed to *moderna*. (But then there is also what an architect I know calls "*stile moderna*"—built by someone who has heard of modern furniture but never seen any.) A sofa and armchairs upholstered in velvet and fringed in silk sat about a dining room suite that was vaguely French in inspiration, heavy with gilt and pink marble. The kitchen had the matching cabinets known as "*all'americana*"; the master bedroom was, she proudly announced, "*stile veneziana*" and was very handy when her married daughters came to spend the night. Of the other two bedrooms, only the one where her son slept showed any sign of human passage, and I couldn't figure out if the gleaming ceramic tiles of the bathroom got polished up every morning after the men had washed or whether that too was off limits for daily use.

When I asked her if she had learned the art of cheese making from her mother, she seemed almost offended. "Oh, no, signora, I wasn't born to this. I grew up in Balestrate, my father was a *bottaio*, a cooper." The craft of making and maintaining wine casks is many rungs above shepherding, so she saw her life as one of disappointment and decline.

When we returned to the cheese shed, the milk had boiled and curdled and she pronounced it ready. Her daughter lifted up the brush, shook off the drops of whey clinging to the twigs, and passed it over the cauldron in the sign of the cross before carrying what was left of the logs outside to plunge in a bucket of water.

The shepherd's wife filled up my plastic container with ricotta from the cauldron and then insisted that we eat some while it was still hot. Natalia and Martina could not manage the soup plates full of steaming whey while standing up, so one of the daughters ushered us into the old farmhouse and sat us down at a table. One look showed me that this was where the real business of living was conducted. The room that occupied the front half of the house was at once kitchen and living and dining room; to the back were two alcoves, closed off by curtains, where presumably the parents and the two daughters still living at home slept. The flaking whitewashed walls were dotted with pots, coat hooks, and pictures of saints, and the furniture was old and lopsided, whatever *stile* it once had had blurred by many coats of paint.

As we sat at the table mopping up the ricotta with fat slices of fresh bread, a voice, high and wavering with age, suddenly spoke up from behind one of the curtains. I couldn't make out anything it was saying, until I realized to my astonishment that it was declining a Latin noun.

"*Buon giorno*," I answered, at a loss for any more adequate response.

The answer came in Italian, quite correct and without a trace of dialect: "You aren't Sicilian, are you, signora? By your accent I would say you were either English or American."

"You're quite right, I'm an American," I replied, still having no idea to whom I was talking, or even if it was a he or a she.

"English is a *very* beautiful language." This time the voice was speaking in English. The daughter who was attending to us must have noticed my growing perplexity, for she intervened.

"My father has very bad legs, and ever since his gallstone operation last fall he hasn't been able to get out of bed." She drew back the curtain just enough so we could see an elderly man in a woolen nightcap propped up in a large double bed under many layers of blankets. I bowed, he nodded, and we continued our conversation, this time in Italian.

The old shepherd was greatly saddened that age, sickness, and the harsh adversities of the pastoral life to which fate had so unjustly delivered him were such that they prevented him from rising from his bed of pain to greet me properly, honored as he was to welcome to his humble dwelling someone who not only belonged to a family with which he had long had the honor to be acquainted and of which he held particularly sacred the memory of the *buon'anima* ("the good soul," the Sicilian way of saying "the late") of Don Turiddu, in whose footsteps his grandson (Tonino) was following, a man of honor the Cavaliere Simeti, respected throughout the neighborhood for his honesty and beloved for his generosity, of which he, the shepherd, was not the only beneficiary, for Don Turiddu had ever been ready to lend money to some poor unfortunate without ever asking as much as a *soldo* of interest, but also he was honored to welcome someone who spoke English, which was music to his ears, bringing back to him as it did the time when he had been in the service of the British crown, for he had studied English in school, since he had not been intended for the miserable life of a shepherd but would have been an accountant had not the war intervened, sending him to fight in Africa, where he was taken prisoner by the British and sent to Ceylon, where he was interned in a prison camp in which he was able, by virtue of his knowledge of the English language, to serve as an interpreter, but this was the last stroke of fortune in a long and luckless life, for upon his return to Alcamo at the end of the war he was to discover that his widowed father had first remarried and then expired, and that all that was to have been his had finished in the pockets of a son by a previous marriage of his wily stepmother, save for the small piece of land on which this house where we were was built and some few sheep, and if it hadn't been for the *buon'anima* of Don Turiddu, who had lent him the money to enlarge his flock, he didn't know where he would be, but as it was, thanks be to God and ever struggling against the bestiality and the suffering of a shepherd's life, which is certainly the most desperate and *disgraziata* occupation that God ever created for man, he and his family had managed well enough, although after all he had endured he was now still further tried by the pains in his legs, but he and his family did their best to maintain their dignity and furthermore he was in frequent correspondence with Queen Elizabeth II!

That visit marked the high point in our relations with this family. The warm weather allowed the old shepherd to hobble about with the help of canes, and he and his wife returned the visit, but it soon became clear that we would have to look sharp. Things borrowed took a very long time to come back, the sheep wandered too often out of the stubble to nibble on the grapevines, the flock took shortcuts over freshly plowed fields (even though their hooves are tiny, when a flock of sheep passes through a vineyard, it packs the earth down solidly, suffocating the vine roots), and then the youngest son took a fancy to Christmas trees.

One day some carabinieri in a patrol car jolted down the road and stopped to ask me directions to the shepherd's house. With my usual naïveté I thought they probably wanted to buy some ricotta. That evening we heard that the elder son was being held for questioning in connection with a murder. (The case was never solved, and the boy was released after a few months.) When he came over once with his father to protest the fact that another shepherd (quite uninvited) had brought his flock to graze in our stubble, which they considered to be their own monopoly, he said, by way of recommending himself to me: "We treat your things as if they were our own!"

Tonino, not in the least surprised by the news in this morning's paper, explains to me that violence is almost inevitable where shepherds are concerned: very few of them own their pasturage, their margin of profit is too low to allow them to pay much rent—

especially in an area like ours, where land values are high—and they are therefore hard put to keep their flocks alive without resorting to prevarication, poaching, and deceit.

We are so vulnerable at Bosco. The house is empty so much of the time, the comings and going of Turiddu Vivona are easily predictable. I am alone there very often, with only the company of a dog who is all bark (when she can be bothered) and no bite whatsoever. There are no guns of any sort in the house, my private and perhaps irrational statement in a land where violence is too often the first resort, and I feel myself totally unequipped to deal with the devious, read-between-the-lines negotiations that are necessary with people like the shepherd and his sons. Yet I feel much less threatened by them than I do by the impersonal, random violence of the city, the purse snatchings, the holdups, and the Mafia massacres that have proliferated in the last ten years, as if I think that some principle of order and civil coexistence, long since vanished from the urban setting, still survives in the countryside, making Bosco a safe haven from all that I cannot accept in Palermo.

II SPRING

The symbol of Spring is the flower,
the protagonist of the feast day, which
it resembles in that it augurs a long
and fruitful life. Like the feast day the
flower is ephemeral, and finds its only
strength in the possibility of perpetual
rebirth. And yet, if it is a cut flower
that is being offered—a flower gathered,
that is, before it has had time to
transform itself into fruit—it recalls
the idea of sacrifice, the very sacrifice
most dear to the gods, that of the
young and virgin victims who have yet
to reach maturity.

   And it is just this fate—either
to ripen into fruit or to be gathered
before its time—that explains why . . .
the flower has often been taken as the
symbol of human destiny.

Franco Cardini,
I giorni del sacro: il libro delle feste

VILLA DE CORDOVA, PALERMO

Chapter Four

The winter has been as punctual as I had feared in delivering influenza and bad weather, so ever since the end of the vacation our visits to Bosco have been limited to wine pickups, lasting the time necessary for rinsing out twenty or thirty ten-liter demijohns, round glass bottles in plastic baskets, and filling them up again with red or white wine to be delivered to our customers in Palermo. This service, started for the benefit of friends and neighbors, has expanded to absorb almost a third of our production, and although Francesco and Natalia, who often manage the whole bottling operation by themselves, grumble frequently about what a pain in the neck it is, we can get more than twice the wholesale bulk price this way, and, equally important, the satisfaction of knowing that all the effort we put into making the wine is appreciated.

It has been tantalizing for me to come and go so rapidly, and I am delighted when the presence of the *bottaio* obliges us to spend the whole of February's first weekend at Bosco. Tonino goes out on Friday, Francesco is staying behind in Palermo, so Natalia and the animals and I are the only ones who drive out on Saturday as soon as school is dismissed. The rain has gone but the cold lingers, and the snow on the mountains has not yet melted despite the bright sunlight. The almond trees are in bloom, puffs of palest pink blossom that echo the dance of the cloud shadows across the snow-covered mountaintops. First of all the trees to flower, the almond was a symbol of hope to the Greeks; Virgil was even more specific:

> Observe, too,
> When the almond tree that grows so thick in the forests

Puts on her blossoms, curves her fragrant boughs:
If the fruit abounds, abundant crops ensue,
And heavy threshing comes, intense with heat;
If shade predominates, with wealth of leaf,
Your floor will thresh stalks only rich in chaff.

Virgil, *The Georgics*

Today the almond's fragrant branches curving out to the blue sky do at least seem a promise that Persephone's return is not far off.

On closer inspection the countryside bears many harbingers of spring. The roadsides are thick with tiny flowers, much smaller and less ostentatious than those of April and May. The wild calendula speckle with orange the snowfall of camomile that spreads its miniature daisies throughout the vineyards, while great swathes of brilliant lemon yellow mark the advance of the wood sorrel. I would like to have a word or two with whoever it was who brought wood sorrel from South Africa to Europe. The delight of my eye yet the bane of my gardening, it grows everywhere; the single stems, each bearing a round bouquet of trefoil leaves and yellow flowers, pop up in any terrain, hugging close to arid soil but stretching out where it is damp as much as thirty centimeters to poke their heads through mulch, underbrush, woodpiles, and any other discouragement. At least 70 percent of the weeds that I pull out each winter are wood sorrel, and each root leaves behind a tiny bulb, ready to proliferate again the next year.

Yet the cushiony green leaves and the acid-yellow flowers are so beautiful and so much a part of the Sicilian winter scene that it is difficult to remember that wood sorrel is a relative newcomer. In fact, many of what one would consider the most characteristic elements of the Sicilian landscape were missing from Magna Graecia: the palms and the citrus trees that arrived with the Arabs, the agave and the prickly pear that the Spanish brought back with them from the New World. Almonds were already there and thick oak forests covering the now barren mountains; the olives were young and slender trunked, brought by the Greeks themselves.

We arrive at Bosco to find the road blocked by the *bottaio*'s huge filter, which is parked in front of the wine cellar. Tonino, Turiddu, and the *bottaio* himself are all at work, and cane markers stuck into the furrows at regular intervals testify that Mr. Amato has been getting ready to sow his tomatoes and melons.

The *bottaio*'s contribution to the process of wine making is twofold: he builds and maintains the great casks for fermenting and aging the wine, first cutting and bending the long strips of hickory or chestnut wood and binding them together with bands of wrought iron, and then scraping and cleaning the casks each summer to prepare them for the new must, checking to make sure that the wood has neither mildewed nor absorbed acid residues that would cause the wine to turn to vinegar. Then he returns in the winter to open the casks at the moment of the *travaso*, the decanting, when the fermentation is over and all the sediments have settled to the bottom of the casks, leaving the wine clear and sparkling. One cask, left empty at harvest time, receives the wine of its neighbor, which is then emptied of sediment and cleaned to receive in turn the wine of the next cask, and so on all the way around the wine cellar until all the wine has been decanted and all the sediment scraped out and run through the *bottaio*'s filter, once a hand press, now a complicated electrical machine. The wine that is filtered out is pumped back into the casks, the solid residue packed into sacks. This the *bottaio* takes in partial payment for his labor and sells to a distillery for the production of rubbing alcohol. He also gets to take away the tartar that has accumulated on the walls of the casks, which will go to making cream of tartar, for medicine and meringues.

The number of *bottai* still practicing their craft is dwindling rapidly: by far the majority of grape producers now take their grapes to the big cooperative wineries that store the must in gigantic steel tanks and have their own equipment for filtering the dregs. Even people like us who still make the wine at home have mostly converted to reinforced concrete or stainless-steel cisterns, which can neither mold nor absorb vinegar. We keep a few wooden casks in operation for seasoning the red wine, since wine matured in wood has a different, fuller taste, but the greater part of our production is stored in steel cylinders about twelve feet high and eight feet in diameter, which also have the great advantage of being easily cleaned, since each one has an oval door in the side through which a thin person can squeeze. Tonino and Francesco spend many wet and noisy hours with bathing suits and hoses inside the cisterns, scraping and singing. A steel wine cistern far outdoes a bathtub in resonance, and even tone-deaf Tonino sounds like Luciano Pavarotti as he scrubs away. I have always been tempted to try, but the door is small and I see myself stuck halfway like Winnie-the-Pooh, and desist.

Natalia helps me unload the car, eager to begin our ritual round of inspection in the garden. Not quite twelve yet, she still enjoys our weekends at Bosco, happiest when we bring one of her school friends with us, but perfectly content to be here by herself, to go for walks with just the dog and her imagination for company, or to curl up and tell herself stories in the crook of the mulberry tree.

Natalia gets her looks from her father, but her character is her own, powers of self-discipline and concentration that leave us all agape, dissolving into thunderstorms of emotional release. Timid and reserved until she feels at ease with people, she has had ever since she was tiny a very clear sense of what she did not feel ready to face, together with the courage and determination to go after what she really wanted.

This is a year of passage for Natalia as well, although she has not quite decided yet whether or not she feels ready for adolescence, and finds little help in the lurid stories about his contemporaries with which her fourteen-year-old brother hopes to shock us. Square and stocky as a little girl's, Natalia's body is rapidly catching up with her hands, which have always been remarkably long-fingered and graceful, and sometimes I can detect a seed of self-confidence in her shy smile. I too am changing in her regard: her "otherness" no longer disconcerts me, nor do I mistake strength for stubbornness, or feel anything but proud delight to note the difference between my own adolescent self, overweight and awkward, and the willowy nymph that Natalia now seems destined to become.

She is like me, however, in her love of flowers, and she rushes about the garden with the eagerness of Persephone, crooning over the cautious flowering of the crocus and reveling in the heavy, honeyed perfume of the blossoms on the almond trees. The daffodils are showing their buds as well, and it is only a question of days before their yellow competes with that of the wood sorrel. We find some newcomers to the garden: Tonino has asked Turiddu to dig up some suckers from the sorb apple tree down the road and plant them in front of the house. Sorb apple trees are very pretty with their tiny bouquets of white flowers in spring followed by bunches of little yellow fruit that grow rosy patches by October. The fruit is very astringent and puckery—it ties up the mouth, as the Italians say—unless you wait until it is overripe and looks almost rotten. People here string bunches of ripe sorb apples, surrounded by their leaves, onto wires to mature; hanging against the whitewashed walls they look like little Della Robbia plaques.

I often regret that I know nothing at all about the principles of landscape gardening and that I have never succeeded in imposing a scheme of development on that part of the land around the house that I call "the garden," which lives in uneasy coexistence and occasional rivalry with "the farm," its boundary line ebbing and flowing according to my supply of energy and the demands of the agricultural calendar. I hoe and plant on impulse, my point of departure the vestiges of the old garden—the clumps of oleanders and the hedges of asparagus that were planted by Tonino's grandfather—and my only guideline the pleasure that a plant gives me both in its aspect and its associations. So the sorb apples, even if they have been plunked down wherever Turiddu's fancy dictated, are welcome on both accounts: they will be lovely to look at, and it is fitting that they come now, to celebrate the second month of the tree calendar, a month consecrated to the rowan tree, or mountain ash, a most magic-laden tree that does not grow in Sicily, except perhaps in the high mountains. If I cannot have the rowan, the *sorbus aucuparia*, at least I now have its domestic cousin in the garden.

Despite the sharp wind it is warmer outside in the sun than it is in the house, which is damp and cold after a month's abandonment. Tonino has already lit the fireplace, but as soon as dark falls we turn on the central heating for the upstairs and start to fill the big brass braziers with coals from the fire. The brazier has always been the principal method of heating in Sicily, and what it lacks in effectiveness is compensated for by its beauty. The brazier itself is a round brass tray, about two feet across, with a wide, double-handled rim that curves down and out to accommodate toes in need of warming. It sits in a tripod whose brass feet end in leonine paws, and in a proper Sicilian household, which mine unfortunately isn't, it has an enormous and highly polished lid of pierced brass that rises in sinuous curves for about three feet and ends in a spire on which a cupid balances on tiptoe. A brazier doesn't give very much heat, and the coals tend to smell (that can be counteracted by adding a little tangerine peel), but it does have one singular and marvelous advantage over almost any other form of heat—you can take it to bed with you. The tray, well stoked with coals glowing red in their nest of ashes, is carried upstairs and tucked into bed, under a dome of woven willow branches (still known in the mountain towns by its Arabic name, *cuba*) to keep the covers from catching fire. Of course you can't sleep safely with the brazier, and the question of who is to get up out of the warm bed at the very threshold of sleep and scamper across the cold floor to close the brazier in the bathroom may cause some slight marital friction, but that is a small price to pay for the incomparable luxury of nestling into such well-toasted sheets.

On my return to Palermo Sunday evening I receive a telephone call inviting me to a screening and discussion of the movie *Il giorno della civetta* at Natalia's old elementary school, as part of a seminar preparing the teachers for anti-Mafia education. The very existence of such a program is an indication of how much Sicily has changed in the twenty years since Leonardo Sciascia wrote the novel on which the film was based. In those days a good portion of the Sicilian population would never have admitted the existence of the Mafia, and Palermo's morning newspaper never printed the word. A pastoral letter from the late Cardinal Ruffini, then the archbishop of Palermo, which was read in all the churches one Easter just after I came here, claimed that the Mafia was a calumnious invention and that the three great impediments to Sicily's peace and prosperity were Danilo Dolci, Tomaso di Lampedusa, and the foreign press, all of whom had slandered Sicily in their publications.

The change in the Mafia itself, a change that Sciascia recently defined as a "transformation into a 'multinational of crime,' . . . which no longer observes the rules for coexisting and conniving with the power of the state and with the morals, the traditions, and the way of life of the Sicilian people," a change that has ruptured the equilibrium between bosses and politicians and left a long list of "excellent cadavers" in its wake, is in turn slowly altering both the official commitment to combating the Mafia and the approval, acquiescence, or at best indifference with which a great many Sicilians have traditionally considered the phenomenon.

This slow metamorphosis was abruptly accelerated last September with the murder of Carlo Alberto dalla Chiesa, a general of the carabinieri, who had begun his campaign against the Mafia early in the sixties, when he commanded the carabiniere forces in Sicily, and who was later one of the leaders of a successful campaign against the Red Brigades and the other terrorist groups operating in the north of Italy. In March of last year he was appointed prefect of Palermo and was promised legislative support and special powers in what was announced as a full-scale offensive against the Mafia. Having made the gesture, the government began, in the opinion of many, to drag its feet. Dalla Chiesa's official installation took place only and precipitately the day after

Pio La Torre, the regional secretary of the Communist party, was murdered by the Mafia, and the promised powers never came, while the law that would allow the police to investigate the bank accounts of presumed mafiosi languished in Parliament.

During the four months he was in office, however, dalla Chiesa did much to correct the traditional Sicilian view of the policeman as *sbirro*, or spy. He visited schools, factories, civic groups, and drug-rehabilitation centers in an attempt to drum up popular support for his battle and to convince the people of Palermo to abandon the *omertà*, the code of fear-inspired honor that imposes silence and prevents the police from ever finding a witness to any Mafia crime.

On the evening of September 2, 1982, as he was being driven home from the office by the young woman he had only recently married after years of being a widower, his car was ambushed in a narrow Palermo street, and a spray of machine-gun bullets killed dalla Chiesa, his wife, and the two men in the escort car behind them. The next morning the sidewalk where they had died was heaped with flowers, and a crudely lettered sign stuck to the wall read, "Here died the hope of all honest Palermitani."

The funeral was impressive and deeply moving: an enormous crowd followed the coffins from the prefecture to the church of San Domenico, where the archbishop of Palermo, Cardinal Pappalardo, officiated at the requiem mass. It was an unprecedented assemblage, come from the new middle-class neighborhoods and from the slums of the old city, all outraged that the Mafia should have broken with tradition in having killed the wife as well, all cheering the coffins and hooting at the arrival of political dignitaries. The cardinal's sermon, an outspoken denunciation of the local connivance and the national neglect that had allowed the Mafia's power to proliferate, was delivered to absolute silence and followed by an ovation of spine-tingling dimensions. For the first time in Sicilian history a policeman had been admitted to the ranks of the popular heroes that had heretofore been reserved for rebels and outlaws such as the bandit Salvatore Giuliano.

Amidst the conventions, publications, exhibitions, and commemorations that have expressed honest commitment or paid mere lip service to the crusade against the Mafia, the Sicilian regional government has financed seminars on the Mafia for both teachers and students at every level of the school system, thus allowing the schools to buy books and to rent films and exhibits on the subject. It is in this context that I have been invited back to Natalia's old elementary school, where I served several years as president of the local elementary school board. I decide, somewhat reluctantly, to go, if only to show what support I can for the program and for the woman who has organized it as part of her almost single-handed battle to shake her fellow teachers from their complacency.

The film itself is the story of a carabiniere captain from the north who, in the course of unraveling a murder case in the small Sicilian town where he is stationed, finds himself on the track of high-level corruption and graft and dares to arrest the local boss. False testimony destroys his case, and he is transferred away from Sicily, somewhat to the regret of the boss, Don Mariano, who, in a world that he himself describes as populated mostly by "half-men," "manlets," and "quackers," has almost enjoyed engaging arms with a true man.

The original novel, commonly believed to have been inspired by the figure of dalla Chiesa although Sciascia has denied this, is a beautifully drawn portrait of the Mafia twenty years ago, and phrases from it have become part of the standard lexicon used in handling the subject. The movie makes some sacrifice to the spectacular, but it is nonetheless a good piece of work, and I am not sorry to be seeing it again.

The screening was to begin at five o'clock, to be followed by a debate. Unable to shed my American training, I arrive punctually to find only about five others; a gradual trickle fills the room with about twenty-five teachers (out of the fifty plus invited) and three of the nine parents now serving on the board. At a quarter to six the projection finally starts, but no one has bothered to find out how long the film lasts, and by the time the last reel flaps out of the projector it is seven-thirty, and the audience, with supper to prepare, is perched on the edge of its seats ready for flight. It takes twenty minutes of animated if shapeless discussion to decide upon postponing the debate until the following week.

When the debate finally does take place, in the presence of little more than a dozen teachers, the headmistress, and myself, it is a compendium of all that has made me flee from civic commitments in Sicily: it starts at least half an hour late; there is neither agenda nor chair to impress form or order on the discussion; all talk at once, heedless of relevancy, narrating at length and at the top of their voices their own personal experiences and problems.

It is, however, a golden opportunity for rhetoric: about the person of dalla Chiesa, about the need for commitment to human values, about the courage required to do one's duty. I try to bring the discussion down to earth and into the classroom with a criticism: to my mind the film has turned Sciascia's subtle portraits of the Mafia into grotesque caricatures, and this may tempt us into considering the Mafia as something foreign to our everyday experience, whereas I believe it important for students to discover just how much their lives are affected by the Mafia, in the cost of living, in the form that the city's growth has taken, etc., etc. But no, I am a foreigner, I don't know what the mafiosi in the small towns were like twenty years ago. I can't be bothered to explain that twenty years ago I was living in the very town where the movie was filmed and that when mafiosi were pointed out to me I was always surprised at how ordinary they looked. As usual, as soon as I ask people to look at things in a different light, I am reminded that I am not a Sicilian and therefore do not understand.

This is the first winter in almost ten years in which I have no civic commitment other than a very minor and undemanding role as class representative at Natalia's junior high school. As I have tested the waters or swum with militant stroke through the most disparate seas, from neighborhood improvement campaigns to feminist encounter groups, from a radical cooperative bookstore and documentation center to the middle-class and middle-of-the-road parent-teacher associations of the local schools, I have encountered more similarities than differences: endless and unproductive debating abounds everywhere, together with all-invasive ideology and an initial and unrealistic enthusiasm that is unaccompanied by the dogged plodding necessary to effect change in a bureaucratic world. And nowhere has the impact been more frustrating to me than in the schools.

Parent-teacher associations are a very new phenomenon in Italy, where the schools have always been controlled directly by the central government. Teachers are assigned to their posts according to their scores on a provincial point scale, and only the most self-confident and dedicated overstep or alter the nationwide programs of the Ministry of Public Education that dictate what material must be covered each year. It was only ten years ago that the Italian government passed a law instituting the election of school boards representing both parents and teachers within the school administration. Francesco was just starting school at the time, and I was eager to participate, my share in the general enthusiasm fanned by my desire to find a niche for myself in Sicilian society and by my conviction that, coming from America, I had much to contribute.

It rapidly became apparent that these newly instituted boards, with no tradition behind them, very little experience in direct democracy at the local level, and very limited powers, were for the most part quite unable to cope with the resentment of a fair share of the administrators and the teachers, who identified interest with interference. They were crippled by often irrelevant ideological divisions bequeathed them by the political parties whose initial interest waned as soon as they saw that there was no real power up for grabs, and they were stymied by the immobility of the bureaucracy.

If my own particular condition inflated my enthusiasm, it also aggravated my frustration. My children's schooling seemed in so many ways inferior to that which I had received in America (admittedly as part of a privileged elite) and to that which the children of my sister and my college classmates are receiving today. I regard this as the single irreparable ill consequence of my choice to expatriate, a source of anguish and guilt that no amount of parent participation has been able to assuage.

This ambivalence of mine may also be tinged with unconscious rivalry. The mother is said to be responsible for transmitting cultural values, a dilemma for the expatriate, who often behaves as if she were besieged, patrolling the perimeters of her offspring's consciousness, ready to repel the onslaughts of an alien culture in favor of her own. Mistakenly believing that I could command the spaces of my children's minds, I have perhaps looked on the schools here as the enemy.

Natalia, who has always been in love with the process of learning, seems to have emerged miraculously unscathed from all this conflict, which may even have given a salutary sharpening to her critical sense. Not so my firstborn, who closely resembles me in looks and in temperament: Francesco absorbs my ambivalence and uses it, together with his own desire to know everything without effort and his objective bad luck with teachers, as an excuse to limp his way through school, trusting to fortune and to native intelligence to save him from disaster each June.

But all this is hindsight. I come home depressed by the debate at school and wearied by my own internal debate, the endlessly regurgitating struggle between an acquired Sicilian fatalism and an inherited American belief in civic commitment. The guilt generated by this year's withdrawal from any form of involvement has been reawakened by the one small seed of optimism I carry away from this evening's meeting, an anecdote told by a woman who teaches at Cruillas, a rural village that has been swallowed up in Palermo's expansion and is permeated by the Mafia value system. When she assigned her class a composition on "What I would *like* to read in the newspapers," one child wrote that he would like to read that Sicilians no longer called policemen *sbirri*.

🌿 Returning from our next weekend at Bosco, we decorate our usual load of lemons, wild greens, and demijohns with some seasonal additions, a few flowering almond branches and a bag stuffed with costume jewelry, a dress from Tunisia, a Spanish mantilla, and an old felt hat. February is Carnival time, and Francesco and Natalia are planning their costumes. For weeks now the stores have been doing a steady business in streamers and confetti, in practical jokes, false noses, and plastic horns, and their windows glitter with elegant costumes—Arlecchino and Pulcinello next to Zorro and Chief Sitting Bull, ladies with hoop skirts and powdered wigs mingled with dairy maids and odalisques. Each year a few newcomers reflect the latest successes of television and cinema: Marco Polo and E.T. are said to be this season's hits. Italians are willing to spend conspicuous sums on their children's costumes, and by the last week in January the streets are full of proud parents strolling along with their children on display, while the parks buzz with tiny musketeers dueling miniature cowboys and with fairy princesses hiking up their skirts to run after pygmy Primaveras in a cloud of hoops, ruffles, flounces, and artificial flowers.

For years Carnival in Italy was reduced to a children's holiday, and while one heard of the occasional costume party or masked ball for adults, the old sense of liberation from the restrictions and oppressions of every day, of overturning the social order for a week or so and admitting any sort of licentious behavior, lived on only in the fervid attachment of small children to this one occasion in which their wildest dreams could be acted out. Recently, however, Carnival has come back into fashion, washed in on the wave of the *riflusso*, of reaction to the puritanical, revolutionary fervor of the years following 1968, when all that was personal became political and all that was frivolous or extraneous to the ideals of the student movement was ignored. The disappointments of that era and of the revolution that never materialized have swept the survivors into one of two directions, either into the Red Brigades or into the "reflux," the ashrams of India, the dreamworld of drugs, the rediscovery of the personal, the physical, the emotional, etc.—and into costume for Carnival.

In the week before Ash Wednesday the evening streets are busy with cars shuttling masked students from one stereo-rocked apartment to another, and firecrackers punctuate the night with their sinister explosions. At noon Natalia comes home from school with stories of stink bombs and peppery chewing gum, while Francesco arrives aged fifty years, his hair and clothes white from the flour with which he and his classmates have battled, two to a motor scooter, one driving and one throwing. The newspapers announce that ancient traditions are being revived in many of the smaller towns, to delight the inhabitants and attract the tourists, the quadrille danced in the main square at Regalbuto and San Marco d'Alunzio, sausage festivals at Sciacca and Chiaramonte Gulfi, while the list of towns that are planning a parade of allegorical floats has doubled.

Most scholars tend to see the origins of Carnival as a compendium of various classical festivals: the Saturnalia, in which great license and revelry were permitted to the slaves and a young slave was crowned king of the festival, only to be put to death at the end; the rites in honor of the goddess Isis, in which a boat-shaped cart (the *currum navalis*, from which the word Carnival is thought to come) was drawn through the streets in procession; the Lupercalia, when youths dressed in animal pelts would run about the Palatine slapping the women they met with leather straps to make them fertile (the throwing of streamers and confetti supposedly started here); and the Bacchanalia or Anthesteria, rites of Greek origin that were very popular in southern Italy. In their later, Olympian form, these three days were dedicated to Dionysus: the casks of new wine were opened on the Day of the Casks, the Day of the Cups was devoted to drunken revelry, and the festival ended with dramatic contests held on the Day of the Pots. In the archaic period, however, this may have been a festival of all souls, in which the casks were grave jars and the cups signified the pouring out of libations to the souls of the dead, who, once feasted, were bidden to depart on the third day through the natural, chthonic potholes of the earth. Seen in this light the Anthesteria becomes a feast of revocation, a closing of the *tempus terribile*, a purification of the gates of Hell before the last resurrected One passes through.

In its heyday Carnival went on for over a month, starting in mid-January and continuing until Ash Wednesday in the second half of February, although the fervor and extravagance of its celebration varied, curtailed by famine and plague or encouraged by authorities eager to distract the masses from their discontent, an essential ingredient in the recipe for government by the three Fs, *Feste, Farina, e Forche*—Festivals, Flour, and the Gallows. The streets were filled with people in costume, with masques, tableaux, processions, and pageants, while violent battles were waged with bran (the use of flour is a sign of our modern affluence) or with bitter oranges.

> In the old days the gardens and the parks belonging to the nobility and the peasantry were filled with groves of common oranges, those good only for making juice or polishing copper. During the Carnival period the populace would battle with these oranges, grouping themselves into companies that had no real military rank. The size of the companies was such that the battle would swell and become heated, and would attract a prodigious number of spectators. The many carriages which arrived would draw up in a circle, thus delineating unwittingly the battlefield. This sort of game was most satisfying, the amusement which more than any other gave pleasure to the populace.
>
> Diary of the Marchese di Villabianca, quoted in Giuseppe Pitrè, *Usi e costumi, credenze e pregiudizi del popolo siciliano*

In the descriptions the Marchese di Villabianca and other Palermo diarists have left us of Carnival behavior, and in the laws and decrees with which the governments attempted its regulation—for instance a proclamation of 1499 prohibiting "any person, either citizen, or foreigner, from presuming to play at Carnival with oranges or water or in any like manner"—three traditions are particularly recurrent.

Two of these have very ancient roots, the first being a transformation of Isis's *currum navalis* into a boat made of cardboard and slats that was propelled about town by fishermen pretending to row, while in fact walking with their feet stuck through holes in the hull. As the boat stopped in front of stalls and shops, one of the crew would reach out with a boathook and pull in a length of sausage, a bunch of onions, or some other delicacy.

The Nannu, or "Grandfather," modern descendant of the King of the Saturnalia, was the most important figure of the traditional Palermo Carnival. Impersonated by a straw-stuffed effigy or by a live person, the old man was carried about the streets seated on a chair, before a great throng of servants and merrymakers who alternated shouts of joy with laments bewailing the Nannu's imminent demise. At the end the public notary was called to draw up and read out the Nannu's last will and testament, a long poem in Sicilian dialect in which each profession and social category got its due, to the general satisfaction and hilarity of the crowd.

The last of these traditions, known as the "Castle" or as the "Master of the Field," is relatively modern in comparison, since it was inspired by an incident that took place at the beginning of the fifteenth century, in the early years of the Spanish domination, when the Kingdom of Sicily was still separate from the Kingdom of Aragon and was ruled by a regent, the young Queen Bianca of Navarre. The king of Aragon's principal spokesman on the island, Bernardo Cabrera, Count of Modica, decided to force the queen to marry him, thus satisfying in one move both his elderly lust and his desire to control the whole island. Escorted by an armed band, he left his castle in Alcamo in the dead of night and stormed the Palace of the Steri in Palermo, where the beautiful young queen lay sleeping. In the confusion she and her ladies-in-waiting managed to escape by boat and take refuge in the Castle of Solanto, thus defeating Cabrera's plans. Legend has it that when Cabrera burst into the queen's bedroom and found it empty, he shouted out, "If I have lost the partridge, I have gained the nest!" and threw himself into the still-warm bedclothes, "snuffling like a bloodhound."

Cabrera's assault on the Steri was reenacted every year at Carnival, first in elaborate pageants with wooden castles built for the occasion, where a king and queen held court with dances and games until the arrival of the Mastro di Campo, the "Master of the Field," with his army. The assault would last as long as possible, with the Mastro di Campo attempting to climb up a siege ladder and falling off repeatedly in a great display of frustrated rage and acrobatic ability. This was the high point of the show, so much so that by the middle of the nineteenth century the elaborate setting had disappeared and what remained was:

A man dressed in the Spanish fashion with an orange mask and an enormous moustache climbs up on a ladder which is supported by other men in costume, while on the ladder a *schiavottino*, a young boy in Moorish costume, brandishes a sword and prevents him from reaching the top. The Pappiribella, as the Mastro di Campo is also called, attempts in all manners to reach the top, but when the threatening gestures of the little Moor at the top of the ladder defeat him, he bites his hands and twists himself about in a monstrous fashion, to the indescribable delight of the people watching.

Carnival ends on Shrove Tuesday, traditionally celebrated with a big family feast in which everyone stuffs himself with pasta and tomato-and-pork sauce, with sausages, and with cannoli. "Every pig meets his Carnival," the saying goes, and in fact for the very poor this would have been the one day in the whole year when meat would grace their table. The feasting was naturally accompanied by laughter, music, and practical jokes, a last ribaldry before the rigors of Lent. *"Divertèmmuni, cà dumani acchiana lu furfanti ò pùrpitu!—*Let's enjoy ourselves, for tomorrow the old knave climbs into the pulpit!"

In pursuit of calendars I have discovered that according to the official calendar in use in Athens, as opposed to the sacred and secret tree calendar, we are now in the month of Gamelione, in which the Gamelie was held, a festival celebrating the marriage of Hera. This was therefore considered the most propitious month for weddings, which, come to think of it, means that we have merely switched our allegiance from the Greek to the Roman tradition: all our June brides must be the handmaidens of Juno. But how tenuous our connections with our calendar are, in comparison with the Greeks, for whom the name of each month was a direct reminder of the festivities that would be celebrated. Even where such connections still exist, few of us are aware of them. It is only the writing of this that prods me to look up February in the dictionary to discover that it comes from *februa*, "purification," a vestige of the classical rites that gave birth to Christian Carnival and Lent.

Either ancestral forces or coincidence is at work. We must find time between one Carnival party and another to go to Alcamo and deliver a house plant, a present for Turiddu Vivona and his wife, who are celebrating their twenty-fifth wedding anniversary. We arrive just before noon, an awkward hour since they are getting ready for church, where during the service they will reconfirm their marriage vows. But there is time for them to offer us vermouth and chocolate candies, to show us the presents they have received, displayed on the dining room table in readiness for this afternoon's party, and to give us our *bonboniera*, the beautifully wrapped souvenir packet containing a silver-plated ashtray and a little tulle bag tied with ribbons and flowers in which there is a card printed with their names and some sugar-coated Jordan almonds, four white ones and one silver.

Try as I may, it is impossible for me to have any idea of what might be going on in Turiddu's mind today as he contemplates the last twenty-five years. If I were to ask him whether he had dreamed as a bridegroom of obtaining so much, he would no doubt answer, *"Eh, no, signora, purtroppo!"*—*purtroppo* being an Italian word for "unfortunately" that Turiddu has adapted into a generic but by no means adverse comment on life. In 1958 Sicily was just beginning to pull itself out of the extreme poverty of the postwar period, thanks to the great flow of emigrants leaving to work in the factories of the north. Turiddu was one of many children in a family of agricultural day laborers and sharecroppers; four years of schooling—after three years in first grade he was promoted "for reasons of age" into second grade, which he abandoned after one try—and he was sent to work in the fields, where he was treated by his padrone in ways he once told me he does not like to remember. But he is in turn the "old-stone savage armed" of the Frost poem about mending walls, or worse: suspicious, quarrelsome, and violent in his reactions, he nurses a running dispute with every single one of our neighbors, which we always fear may flare up into outright battle. At work he is honest and loyal but easily offended, and some sort of record has been achieved in his remaining with us for almost ten years now; at home he appears to oscillate between childish good humor and tyrannizing.

Yet here they are in the house they have just built on the edge of town: the ground floor is a garage for farm supplies, their tractor, and Turiddu's car, while for lack of space the secondhand cars belonging to the two sons are parked in the street outside. The second floor is their apartment: three bedrooms, a dining room with a very fancy stereo, a living room with suite in imitation leather, the phone that was installed when the eldest son went north to do his military service, a modern kitchen with the *"all'americana"* cabinets in lacquered wood and a large color TV. Above us there are two more floors, unfinished apartments so that each one of the three children will have one, and a roof terrace complete with rabbits and chickens. And as far as I know, it is all paid for.

This is a collective conquest, of course: the boys have both worked since they finished eighth grade, and on weekends and vacations before that; Teresa has done hand embroidery on commission and the daughter embroiders by machine. But it is Teresa's intelligence and character that have acted as a counterweight to Turiddu's erratic personality. She is unfailingly calm and good-natured, measuring out indulgence and sympathy in doses sufficient to cushion but not to undermine her husband's heavy-handed authority, guiding the family investments with good sense and practicality. She actually cooks in her fancy kitchen, unlike many peasant households where the shiny stove and matching cabinets are considered too good for everyday, and the cabinet doors are kept open to display carefully arranged wedding presents, while the cooking is done on the old two-ring burner hidden in a closet under the stairs. Thanks to Teresa the children are cheerful, intelligent, and hardworking, despite the paternal turbulence that does come through in the slight stutter that afflicts both boys.

The younger son is an expert hand with plow and tractor and did a lot of work for us before he finally refused to work any longer at his father's side. The elder, an electrician, is much shyer, has a more severe stutter, and at first gave the impression of taking after his father. Then one evening when the whole family was staying at Bosco for the grape harvest, he asked me if he could look at some of my books while he was waiting for supper to be served. I expected him to put back immediately the book on Sicilian baroque architecture that I presumed he had picked up by mistake and was very startled when he began to point things out to his mother and make comparisons between the churches in the photographs and the ones in Alcamo. He apparently reads everything he can get his hands on and loves the educational programs on television, much to the disgust of his father, who thinks that too much reading is harmful and who hurries home at the end of the day to watch "Fury, the Fastest Horse in the West" on the children's hour.

But if my mind boggles in an attempt to encompass the jump that they have made, Turiddu seems unperturbed by it. Teresa is flustered by the extent of the celebrations that children and relatives have talked her into, but Turiddu is wreathed in smiles.

"Eh, *purtroppo*, signora, twenty-five years!"

We stop off at Bosco on our way home to pick up some wine. The very first of my beloved daffodils are out, their deep yellow petticoats tossing in the wind that blows hard and cold from the south, whipping the dark clouds across the sky and shredding the earlier promises of spring, the almond blossoms, into a shower of white petals, confetti for Carnival and for weddings, a symbolic sowing that links field and family in a prayer for fertility, for new crops and new generations. The link persists even in the etymology: we have borrowed the word "confetti" from the Italians, who use it to denote the sugared Jordan almonds that are distributed at weddings, like the ones Turiddu and Teresa have given us, while the small disks of paper the children throw at Carnival are called *coriandoli*, "coriander seeds." At Greek weddings the bride entered her husband's home "to the cheers of the inmates, who by way of a lucky omen rained upon them a shower of all kinds of fruits and sweetmeats." They must have been a bit sticky— today's brides are probably better off with rice.

The next Saturday we have again to come to grips with Gamelione, this time as guests at a very elegant wedding in the city. Palermo brides must have a very difficult time deciding where to get married: civil ceremonies are performed amidst the Bourbon frivolity and chinoiserie décor of Queen Maria Carolina's pleasure pavilion in the Favorita Park, while the choice of religious setting runs from the stark stone beauty of the Norman church of the Magione to the glittering gold mosaics of the Palatine Chapel, the almost overpowering splendor of the baroque marble inlays at Casa Professa, or the mysterious Byzantine intimacy and the Greek rite at the Martorana. The bride in question gets high marks for good taste: she has chosen to be married at the Oratory of the Rosary at Santa Zita, a setting as appropriate as it is beautiful, for the frothy white stuccowork of this chapel bears a close resemblance to the frosting on a wedding cake.

There are three such oratories in Palermo, each one the work of Giacomo Serpotta, one of the most famous of Sicilian sculptors, who lived and worked in Palermo at the turn of the seventeenth century. Each is the private chapel of a confraternity, presumably of nobles but whether clerical or lay I have yet to discover. In any case, the confraternities had both the taste and the means to commission what are justifiably the most famous monuments of Baroque Palermo.

One enters the oratory at Santa Zita from a narrow street running to the left of the church. An unassuming door gives onto a broad marble staircase open on one side to a small courtyard; at the head of the stairs is an antechamber hung with portraits of the various leaders of the confraternity, starting with quite recent paintings and going back through a succession of fashions and beards to the epoch of the oratory's construction and beyond, the ruffs and the pointed beards of the Spanish domination dark with age, the paint of the twentieth-century spectacles and smooth-shaven cheeks still glistening.

The oratory itself is a triumph of white and gold, the simplicity of its rectangular floor plan and unadorned vaulted ceiling a perfect frame for the riot of white plaster putti who cling and tumble about the windows that occupy much of the side walls. Life-size allegorical figures of the Virtues perch on the window-sills, guarding small plaques of tiny freestanding figures that represent the mysteries of the Rosary. On the rear wall five more such plaques surround a larger central scene showing the defeat of the Turks at the Battle of Lepanto in 1571, with the aid of the Madonna of the Rosary. On high the Madonna, supported by clouds and angels, hovers ready to intervene in the battle waged below between rows of galleys, each miniature ship completely rigged with spars and oars no bigger than toothpicks. These plaques are set in a tumultuous sea of scrolls and swags, of putti and birds, shells and flowers, all done in white stucco of the most amazing intricacy and detail.

For the occasion the chapel is filled with large bunches of white and pink carnations and gladiolas, and the white frills and flounces of the bride's dress, the gold and white brocade of the prie-dieu where she and the groom are kneeling, blend into the perfect harmony of the setting. Never have I been so glad of the length of an Italian wedding, but as I feast my eyes on the joyful surroundings, it is difficult not to wonder at how my own marriage has so conditioned me, it seems, that I cannot come to this oratory without experiencing acute discomfort. When I look at the accumulation of gray on the curls of the putti, I am both appalled and compelled by the thought of dusting it all.

❧ Carnival supposedly brought the *tempus terribile* to an end, but suddenly the gates of Hell yawn before us. A man in Alcamo with whom Tonino has worked closely as an agricultural consultant receives an anonymous phone call asking for 100 million lire. This request is, among other things, totally unrealistic: the man's consultancy business is only moderately profitable, and he is loaded with debts from building a new house.

Tonino seems to think it perfectly possible that similar miscalculations might be made about us. We try to find reassurance in the fact that we live in Palermo and have a very low profile in Alcamo, since we dress shabbily by Sicilian standards and drive inexpensive cars that age prematurely on the dirt roads around Bosco.

A week later the farmhouse that our friend's father has just finished rebuilding is blown up. It is done with canisters of bottled gas, to make it look like an accident: the roof lands some hundred yards away, and the damage amounts to about 50 million lire, a very neat and professional piece of work.

The phone calls continue: if you don't want to end up like your house, pay up. The man talks unofficially to a friend of his in the carabinieri, who advises him to "settle it outside." When he asks if the police could tap his phone, he is told that it is very complicated. But the calls come every day.

Tonino is very nervous. Sunday afternoon while we are at Bosco a car comes up the hill on the lower road and stops suddenly when it is near enough for the occupants to realize that we are there. They make a show of getting out to look at something across the valley, then leave. Tonino keeps finding excuses to go to Bosco during the week: he says nothing but I am sure that he holds his breath each time he drives up the hill, until he is close enough to see that the house is still intact.

❦ Palermo is papered with posters announcing a march against the Mafia and against drugs, to be held on the last Saturday of the month. It is being organized by the coordinating committee of high school students for Palermo and Bagheria, with the participation of the People's Committee of Casteldaccia.

Bagheria and Casteldaccia, together with Villabate, are small towns on the eastern outskirts of Palermo, the three corners of the area baptized last summer by the press as the *triangolo della morte*, the "triangle of death," after a particularly bloody Mafia feud produced a corpse a day for several weeks running, despite heavy police surveillance. The succession of murders was apparently intended as a challenge to dalla Chiesa, and in fact the prefecture received an anonymous telephone call, just a few days before the general himself was murdered, announcing that "the Operation Carlo Alberto is almost finished."

The high school students in Palermo have been very active in organizing marches and conferences about the Mafia this winter, a commitment that goes beyond mere youthful enthusiasm to an acute sense that their generation is both target and victim of the Mafia-controlled drug traffic, but this is the first time the marchers will desert the center of Palermo to invade the very heart of Mafia territory, the Vallone, the wide valley of rich lemon groves that lies between Bagheria and Casteldaccia.

The students have chosen for their poster a poem that they attribute to Brecht:

> The great oak,
> the glory of the emperor,
> is falling:
> and who would ever have said so?
> It was not the river, not the storm
> that split the great trunk to the roots, but

the ants, thousands of ants,
working every day together,
organized, for years and years.
Soon you will listen to its fall
and the tremendous crash, and an immense
cloud of dust
will rise after the fall.
And the little plants of the world
will finally see the sun.

I worry that the ants will not be counted by the thousands but by the tens or the hundreds, and right now it seems especially important to me that this peaceful invasion of the battlefield be multitudinous, so I decide to go together with some other unaffiliated adults to swell the ranks.

Unable to be at Bagheria for the 9:30 departure, a group of us drive ahead to Casteldaccia and walk out to meet the marchers. The day is unexpectedly warm despite the misty clouds that hide the sun. The march is following a small country road that weaves up and down through terraced valleys of lemon trees laden with fruit, a bumper crop, most of which will not even be picked because prices are so low. The branches bend down to the ground under the weight of their golden burden, the bright yellow of the lemons merging with that of the wood sorrel growing underneath. There is no traffic on the road; an occasional motorcycle cop putts purposefully by, but otherwise the silence is broken only by the birds and the barking of a dog. We pass a stand of nasturtiums run riot, the leaves as big as plates, that slither down the bank to the road in a splash of orange, the only exception to a limited palette, lemon yellow, emerald green, both muted by sky gray.

We walk on for almost two miles before the quiet is invaded by a distant hubbub of voices that soon resolves itself into a rhythmic chant: "*Pace sì, Mafia no! Pace sì, Mafia no! Pace sì, Mafia no!*" In a burst of color the march rounds a curve and comes into sight. Behind the police on motorcycles come the official banners of Palermo and Bagheria, the red banners of the trade unions, the delegations from the political parties. Then a tractor and cart belonging to a farmers' cooperative, filled with gray-haired peasants, their faces baked to a rich brown crust by years of Sicilian sun and wind, their red flags streaming behind them. And then the flood of students, some behind the flags of the youth federations of the various political parties, others behind banners bearing the names of their schools, still others carrying the rainbow flags of the peace movement. The students themselves are a multicolored tide of down jackets and patterned sweaters, laughing, joking, taking up a slogan or a song and letting it wash down the line, then resuming their conversations.

Here and there are other small groups of adults like ourselves, but we are very few in this sea of youth. We fall in behind one banner, are overtaken by another, uncertain where our place in all this is. Toward the end, a group of white banners with a cross on them, the flag of the ACLI, the Catholic Workers' Association, seem strangely tattered. Looking back as we go over the crest of a hill, I can see that we have left a wake of lemon peels behind us.

As the march passes through the outskirts of Casteldaccia and into the main square, small knots of men watch us, their black caps low on their impassive faces: it is impossible to catch any inkling of reaction. The mayors of Casteldaccia and Bagheria are waiting for us on a wooden grandstand, together with dalla Chiesa's daughter, the parish priest from Villabate, and a couple of students from the organizing committee. The crowd cheers when a telegram of solidarity from President Pertini is read aloud and again when Rita dalla Chiesa steps up to the microphone with a brief message of greeting, but the other speakers receive at best a very perfunctory attention. We ourselves decide to skip the speeches and head for home.

When Francesco comes home in the evening I ask him what the beginning of the march was like.

"Pretty good. At Bagheria even some little kids from the elementary school came out and sang a song for us. But Palermo is really disgusting—if the Catholics organize something, then the Communists and the extreme left won't participate; if the left starts something, then the Catholics don't want any part of it. It's a miracle anything *ever* gets going! As soon as we got out in the country some guys started throwing lemons—did you see the state that the ACLI banners were in? They got the worst of it. . . . But, actually, it was kind of fun. We got a real battle going, just like those ones with oranges at Carnival that you were talking about the other day."

Chapter Five

There are no lions or lambs in Sicilian iconography: March is quite simply considered mad. Dark clouds scud back and forth across the sky, caught in a cosmic tennis match played out between the *scirocco*, the hot wind blowing up from the Sahara, and the *tramontana*, whose gusts have been chilled by Alpine glaciers. The temperature changes abruptly at every swing, and the pace is furious, allowing the clouds no pause to unload their precious burden of water. Despite the many gray days this winter, little rain has actually fallen into the reservoirs, already depleted by two years of drought, and the prospects for the summer are very grim. Water in Palermo has been rationed for more than a year now, in theory at least, but the supply system is such a tangled maze of modern tie-ins to Bourbon conduits that the aqueduct office is hard put to know how the water gets from one point to another, much less to insure an equitable distribution. At least a third of the input leaks out through the rotting pipes before it reaches its destination.

The situation is much worse in the towns in the interior, where water often arrives only every five or ten days. Here too it is man who is at fault, not nature, for Sicily is rich in water that flows to the sea unexploited. The government's neglect is part ingrained, part instigated: the Mafia controls the major wells and springs that tap the subterranean water layers, and it sells its water at high prices. One must admire, however, the Mafia's adaptability; when a popular movement led by Danilo Dolci forced the government to approve the construction of a huge dam on the Belice River, local mafiosi bought, for next to nothing, some of the wheat fields that were to be flooded and applied for government subsidies to transform them into first-class vineyards (the government foots 60 percent of the bill for this kind of land improvement). When the land was expropriated for the dam, the government reimbursed these new owners at vineyard prices, which were much much higher than what it would have paid for the original wheat fields.

On the few days that rain does fall, the clouds, exhausted by so much activity, drop everything at once. The water descends in a solid wall, choking Palermo's inadequate sewers and bringing traffic to a standstill. The countryside is overcome, unable to drink in such an exuberant serving, the water drains off to the sea, carving deep furrows in the plowed fields and carrying away the seeds and seedlings of the farmers who had hoped to get an early start on their *novara*.

Beneath the gray skies the fava beans are in bloom. These flowers alarmed the Greeks, who read in the black markings on the petals a *theta*, the first letter of *thanatòs*, of death. In fact, the Greeks used fava beans for funerary rites rather than as food; the Pythagoreans even considered eating a fava bean to be cannibalism, since the stalk, one of the few in nature to be absolutely hollow, was the passageway for the exchange of souls between the living and the dead. Fortunately for us, the Romans recuperated the fava bean to the table of the living: picked while they are still small, very green and tender, and cooked with bacon, or in *fritedda*, sautéed in olive oil and a little broth together with new peas and finely sliced artichokes, fava beans deserve their place in spring's cornucopia.

Another Lenten flower stands sentinel along the roadsides: the asphodel, gray-green stalks supporting a spear of pallid flowers, white barely tinged with pink, pale flesh, the flowers that covered the meadows of Hades. I remember—and am touched by how telling a memory it is—that my mother was bitterly disappointed by her first sight of the asphodel, for the poets had led her to expect something far more magnificent.

Except in Arcadia, where acorns were plentiful, the roots and seeds of the asphodel were probably the basis of the Greek diet before the introduction of grain, and Pythagoras thought this, the spontaneous production of nature, to be the perfect food. Chased to the Netherworld by the introduction of agriculture, the asphodel has now returned, together with the poppy, to invade the fields abandoned in the exodus from the countryside, a white flag marking capitulation to poor soil and inadequate cultivation.

But Lent is also a time of preparation, to which nature contributes by adding new colors to her palette. The hedgerows, still yellow and orange from February's flowering, are now awash with the watery blue of the borage flowers and streaked bright pink by the campion. In the garden the daffodils herald the change in season, the big gold trumpets that multiply each year towering over the miniatures I put in last December, while round them the grape hyacinths run a ribbon of purple-blue. Each day brings some new flower, some new sign that spring is coming, though not in the sense of a New England spring, as tenuous promise, veiled allusions of green over gray, pastel colors and faint perfumes. The Sicilian spring is building up to a vivid and violent explosion of bloom and heat and color and smell, of pagan rite and Christian procession, in which nature, agriculture, and cultural tradition meet in perfect synchronization.

In the city March begins with another sort of explosion, literal and tragic. On the afternoon of the first, a bomb goes off in the courtyard of the new police commissariat in Brancaccio, the "South Bronx" neighborhood where the Favara Palace lies. Nine people are injured; one of them, a young policeman, is on the critical list.

This storm has been brewing for some time, ever since the Minister of the Interior and the prefect of Palermo announced their intention to introduce a commissariat into this neighborhood as a response to the Mafia violence that has been steadily increasing there over the past two years. The only available site was a pair of adjoining apartments, the property of the municipal government, in a new building in the heart of Brancaccio, just down the road from the Favara. The building's residents rebelled, protesting that the commissariat would constitute a danger for them and their families and that the coming and going of patrol cars would prevent the children of the building from using the courtyard as a playground. But after several meetings with police representatives they seemed to have accepted the government's decision.

And then this afternoon a car drove into the courtyard, and a young man leapt out and threw a bomb under the patrol car parked there. Attracted by the cries of a man who was sitting at a window, one of the policemen doing guard duty at the still-unopened office ran out to see what was happening. As he neared the car the bomb went off, tearing the patrol car in two and smashing the car next to it against the wall. The policeman lost both legs, and flying glass slightly injured other people. Fortunately the weather was not good; otherwise the courtyard would have been filled with children.

After a moment of shocked silence a crowd formed rapidly in the courtyard, on one side the building's residents, some wounded, some in shock, all terrified and angry; on the other, the police, distressed by the fate of their colleague, dismayed and embittered to find themselves under attack from the people they believe themselves to be defending.

In Alcamo, our friend has made a formal complaint to the police, and as of yesterday morning his phone has been tapped. In the afternoon a phone call comes, but to his father's house:

"Tell your son we are waiting for an answer."

Apparently it is not uncommon in Alcamo for professionals to pay protection; one of Tonino's friends says that several people have come to the bank where he works, desperate to raise the money.

"You're lucky," this man has told Tonino, "to live in the anonymity of a big city."

I have seldom felt such a stranger to Sicily as in the past month. I keep remembering the occasion, shortly after Tonino and I first met, when we were chatting, apropos of traffic or some other noise, about how soundly we had slept as children, and in reply to some banal anecdote on my part, Tonino said, "Yes, me too: when the Mafia threw a bomb in the window I didn't even hear it go off." His grandfather had been threatened for refusing to sell a piece of land, and the family had taken the precaution of moving their beds to a room without windows onto the street. The crack in the marble balcony is still visible.

I laughed and laughed: it was such exotic one-upmanship. But it was a tale of childhood, as remote and unreal to him as dancing classes in the Colony Club ballroom are to me. I can't believe that this is real either, or that it is possible to be so defenseless. And I am surprised and frightened, yet somehow relieved, to see that Tonino doesn't feel any more equipped than I do. We debate endlessly.

"If you pay once, then you've subscribed," Tonino says. I think I believe that the only thing to do would be to go to the police and make as much noise about it as possible, write to the press, capitalize on all that has been said recently about the Mafia, about *omertà* and having the courage to cooperate with the police. It wouldn't have worked in the past, but right now it just might. But I do not want my courage and my conscience put to such a test.

I have always tried, in my conscious attitudes at least, to be equitable, so that my children might take pride in each side of their double heritage and might choose freely and serenely, when the time came, whether to make their future here, or elsewhere in Italy, or in the United States. This has not been mere devotion to an abstract ideal of justice, since I have found much to criticize in the United States and much to care deeply for in Sicily, but it has been posited on the belief that one could draw one's own boundaries. For all that Sicily does indeed have what Sciascia once called a "low moral latitude," where moral absolutes tend to wilt, and for all that I, like every other person living here, have had to make my own accommodation to the climate, choosing when to stand upon my principles and when to nudge them to the side a bit, I have always thought the choice was mine. I believed that barring the unlucky but unlikely event of witnessing a Mafia execution, it was possible to live a normal and honest life in Sicily, without fear. But if our phone rings and our turn comes, if this is what living here involves, then perhaps I should begin to encourage the children to make their future elsewhere. Perhaps I should weed out those most un-American sentiments of tradition and stability that have germinated in twenty years here and accept that whatever we make of Bosco, whatever tree we plant or wall we build, is for us, but not for them or for their children.

At the wedding last month the father of the groom asked another guest, a Polish woman who had also married here, and me what we thought of Sicilians. This is typical Sicilian masochism, which can be satisfied only by a negative opinion couched in such terms as to become a compliment. I made my standard reply about liking them very much except when they are behind the wheel or disposing of their garbage, which I always cap with the story about the doctor living downstairs from us, who drives off to the hospital each morning with his plastic bag of garbage on the hood of his car. At the corner he brakes suddenly in front of the collection bin, and momentum carries the bag onto the heap. Of course the bag doesn't always go *into* the bin, and sometimes it breaks on impact and the orange peels and empty bottles roll about the street, but what is a little litter in the face of such style! As I bantered on, this time I thought to myself that it was becoming difficult to cope with the idea that "Sicilians" include both the elegant and distinguished people around me and those who are telephoning to our friend, and I wondered whether, if a bomb were to blow up Bosco, I would have the strength and the objectivity to maintain my distinctions.

The clouds disperse as Saint Joseph ushers in the spring and brings the feast days back again as promised, just two days before the equinox. San Giuseppuzzu, as he is familiarly known on the island, is much beloved by the Sicilians, for whom he is the advocate of lost causes, taking the side of mercy in the debate with divine justice; the patron of the poor, the orphaned, and the needy. And in honoring Saint Joseph, the Sicilians celebrate the change of season and invoke celestial protection for the new crops that are sprouting in the fields. The forms of the celebration vary from town to town but always include the preparation of special bread, and the menu always centers about dried beans or lentils, so all the last remnants of the previous harvest are consumed in a collective banquet of such vast proportions as to call forth a similar generosity on the part of the saint and of the new harvest.

In the past I have always gone to Alcamo for San Giuseppe, where the celebrations are private votive offerings. The family that has made a vow to Saint Joseph prepares an altar in their living room, decorated with flowers, candles, and elaborate forms of bread and swagged with the best tablecloths or, if family finances will allow it, staged in a rented setting of spiraling baroque columns and garlanded putti. In front of the altar a dinner is laid out, dish after dish of pasta, meat, fish, vegetables, fruit, and pastries, running to as many as thirty different courses at the very fancy altars.

A small table holds three places set with the best china and silver. This is where the *virgineddi* will eat, the "little virgins," an old man, a young girl, and a little boy recruited from the town poor and dressed up to represent the Holy Family. The head of the household waits on them, setting plate after plate in front of them until they can't eat any more (they get to take the leftovers home).

Here as elsewhere in Sicily on Saint Joseph's Day the central

element is the bread. Mainstay of the peasant diet and fruit of the
island's principal crop, bread is always sacred, so much so that
according to an old superstition he who allows a crumb to fall on
the floor will be condemned in the afterworld to gathering it up
with his eyelashes. In its simpler manifestations the bread baked
for San Giuseppe is either a long loaf that is supposed to represent the saint's beard, or a ring-shaped loaf, of which Pitré describes a particular version:

> Now, since it is an offering to the "Father of Providence," as Saint
> Joseph is called, everything must be big and spectacular. The bread
> gives the measure of the providence of the day: and a ritual bread
> which, if it were lacking, would mean some sort of sacred duty be-
> trayed, is the *cucciddatu*, bread baked of semola flour in the shape of
> a doughnut, but so big that in order to put it in the brick oven it is
> necessary to enlarge the door. The *cucciddatu* at Chiusa Sclafani weighs
> twelve kilos and measures a meter and a half in diameter.
>
> Giuseppe Pitrè, *La famiglia, la casa, la vita del popolo siciliano*

This was at the turn of the century; I don't know if time has
diminished such munificence at Chiusa Sclafani. In Alcamo the
art of ritual bread making lives on, although it is questionable for
how much longer, in the hands of a few elderly ladies who direct
the female members of the household in preparing the bread for
their altar. The forms here are considerably smaller but much more
elaborate, and their symbolism and how they are placed on the
altar follow the rigid dictates of tradition. Vases of flowers, baskets of fruit, and angels bearing seven-branched candlesticks garlanded with roses flank the central forms: the monstrance bearing the Host; the initials of the Virgin Mary intertwined with
fruit and flowers; and Saint Joseph himself, complete with cowl,
crook, and black currant eyes, leading the Christ Child through
an intricate baroque bower of flowers and angels. A myriad of
smaller pieces, the *pani di cena*, in the shape of fruit, flowers, fish,
and birds, are tucked into the empty spaces and will be distrib-

uted to the people who come to admire the altar and watch the banqueting.

The degree of intricacy that the Alcamese bread achieves and the elegance of its decorations, which look as if someone had broken off a piece of Serpotta stuccowork and baked it in the oven to a deep golden brown, are as far as I know unequaled in any other town in Sicily. It reflects the taste for the showy, excessively elaborate and luxurious decoration the Sicilians themselves describe as *spagnuoleggiante*, as if to imply that this were a taste imported from Spain, foreign, nothing to do with that love of vulgar display that the Athenian Greeks derided in the Greeks of Sicily. But in this case, the difficulties of a leavened medium and the simplicity of the souls who shape it are such that even this elegant elaboration of the tradition shares the particular naïve charm of the plainer designs and cruder execution found elsewhere on the island.

This year I am traveling in the opposite direction from Alcamo. Maria Vica has invited me to accompany her to see the *virgineddi* at Làscari, the little hill town near Cefalù where she teaches an adult education course. We have an appointment to meet one of her students in front of the school at eleven-thirty. The nineteenth falls on a Saturday, which makes it easier for everyone to take a holiday, and it is warm and sunny, perhaps a present from the saint for me: I am forty-two years old today.

As we drive east along the coast, Maria Vica tells me what she knows about the ritual we are to witness. Local tradition requires the Lascaroti to fulfill their vows to Saint Joseph by offering dinner to all comers on the nineteenth. Today's dinner is a revival, as this is the first time in fifteen years that someone in Làscari has "done the *virgineddi*," as they call it, much to the excitement and interest of the younger generation, who will be participating in a rite they have heard about but never seen. We are to note that this hiatus confers a special authenticity on the day: the young have not had the opportunity to become blasé, and the ancient simplicity has as yet no modern overlay.

Our host is a mason, who is fulfilling a vow made to Saint Joseph last spring, when his son was driving in the Targa Florio, one of the oldest automobile races in Italy, run on the twisting mountain roads nearby. During the race rumor reached the town that the son had been killed in a crash. The mason prayed to Saint Joseph to make it not be true, promising him in return to do the *virgineddi*.

We leave the *autostrada* at Bonfornello and drive a few miles into the foothills of the Madonie Mountains, whose peaks high above us are white with the last spring snows, *l'ultima varva di San Giuseppe*—"Saint Joseph's last beard," as they were once called. The hills themselves are brilliant green and yellow, terrace upon terrace of lemon groves. Làscari is tucked into the side of one of these hills, and for the Lascaroti the lemons are gold indeed: almost every family owns some groves and this, plus the echoes of nearby Cefalù's booming tourist trade, has made Làscari a wealthy town by Sicilian standards.

Maria Vica's student, a young housewife named Maria Teresa, is waiting for us outside the school, which lies on the outskirts of the town at the lower level. Following her directions we drive up through the town to a square on the upper edge, along narrow cobbled streets that rise at unbelievable angles, as if whoever built them was trying to find out just where the breaking point between the force of friction and the force of gravity lay. Having never had much faith in the force of friction anyway, I have no time at all to look at the town as I will the car upward in first gear with a devout prayer to Saint Joseph that we not meet anyone coming down.

At last we pull up onto a large open space looking out over a ravine to the lemon terraces, with newly built three- and four-story houses on the hillside that the town is slowly climbing, and behind us the steep drop of the road we drove up on and the rooftops of Làscari descending below. The mason lives in a house he built himself, one of the many similar unfinished and unstuccoed houses that ring the towns throughout Sicily, where the growth of the house follows the growth of the family resources, each added or completed story marking a successful harvest or the return of an emigrant with a pocketful of Swiss francs or German marks.

The garage that occupies the whole of the mason's ground floor has been given over to the saint, who surveys the room from the back wall where his portrait hangs above a very simple altar, a sheet pinned against the wall and decorated with columns and flowers cut out of colored tinfoil, ringed with candles and flowers. Two enormous trestle tables, surrounded by a motley collection of chairs and benches and covered with tablecloths, with bottles of wine and water, baskets of bread, and plates filled with quartered oranges, are set to accommodate at least sixty people. Clustered around a makeshift stove under the stairs are some thirty giant pots and pans, which Mimma, another housewife-student and one of the dozen women who are responsible for serving the meal, uncovers one by one to show us the contents: pasta and beans, rice and beans, pasta with green cauliflower, and *'gliotta*, salt cod cooked with broccoli and fresh sprigs of wild fennel. Hidden away on the stairs are more loaves of homemade bread and baskets of *cassateddi di San Giuseppe*, small crescent-shaped cases of fried pastry that for this occasion have a filling of boiled chickpeas mashed up together with sugar, cinnamon, and chocolate.

Everything is ready to go; we await only the blessing of the priest, who will be along as soon as the twelve o'clock mass is over. A small crowd is slowly accumulating in the square, knots of people perching on the benches and leaning on the railings to enjoy the sun easing slowly down into their bones. It will be a while yet before the sun is strong enough to chase away the winter's damp: tufa, the porous local stone with which most houses in western Sicily are built, is a sponge that soaks up the winter rains and squeezes them out again into creeping mold and dark damp patches that ooze a fine white foam, into chilblains and rheumatism. It is almost always colder inside than out in Sicily, and although the Sicilians claim to be very much afraid of the unsalubrious effects of sunshine in wintertime, few of them can resist baking in the first rays strong enough to reach the marrow and knead out the knots in their hunched-up shoulders.

Music swells from below, and, with the purple plumes of their caps swaying in time to the music, the town band marches over the crest of the hill and into the square. They must have very special practice sessions in Làscari, for it is no mean feat to blow a trumpet while marching up that slope. The musicians are, perhaps necessarily, a youthful bunch, with lots of young girls, a recent conquest for Sicilian womanhood. After a pause for a gay brass polka in front of the mason's house they march off again, and presently a car draws up, an elderly priest clutching a stole in one hand hops out with as much agility as his cassock permits, disappears within, and in no time flat is out again and away.

It turns out that we will eat in shifts; the first to be served are the children, an enormous flock all under twelve and highly polished and combed. Maria Vica and I push through the crowd at the door to watch them as they eat, long rows of gleaming black eyes and broad smiles, their behavior just ever so slightly subdued by the occasion. How exciting it must be for a child to find himself suddenly living the memories of his grandparents, to have his mother's stories about "when I was a little girl" come alive. The aproned women squeeze back and forth between the tables, balancing full plates and brandishing ladles. We are in the way, so we move out into the sun again.

A small group gathers around us, all Maria Vica's students, almost all related to each other, all here at least to watch if not to eat at Saint Joseph's table. We press them for information and find that they are very clear about the rules that govern this celebration but have never given any thought to their significance. Each dish is crucial and unalterable: you must have both pasta with beans *and* rice with beans; the pasta with cauliflower must be followed by the *'gliotta*. The oranges are always served cut into quarters—no, someone says, sometimes they were cut into thirds, for Father, Son, and Holy Ghost. The bread must be baked at home and the pastries filled with chick-peas.

"Do you remember when Mrs. What's-her-name did the

virgineddi and served pasta with tomato sauce?" asks someone, adding with disgust, "It was just like going out to dinner at a restaurant!"

We continue to ask why, urging them to consider, but none of them is aware of any connection between the menu for the *virgineddi* and harvest concerns, nor can they enlighten us further as to the significance of the orange quarters. The best they can do is to elaborate their own mythology, based on poverty and quite unconvincing in a town of such relative wealth. The beans and the chick-peas are the food of the poor, and Saint Joseph was poor; the oranges had to come from Palermo and were served cut up in quarters to make them stretch farther.

A minor explosion shakes the crowd as the children burst out from between the legs of the grown-ups, clutching their *cassateddi* and chasing each other about, most literally full of beans. It is the teen-agers' turn now, and there are enough of them too to fill up the long tables, this combination of tradition and novelty being attractive enough to compete successfully with jukebox and motor scooter.

One of the students tells us that there will be another altar next year; no sooner had the son been miraculously saved than the mason himself fell from the scaffolding of a house he was working on. The scaffolding was evidently high enough to allow him time to invoke the saint while falling, and he found himself at the bottom with no bones broken and another dinner for two hundred plus on his hands.

And, someone else adds, this very morning the police visited his present construction site and took down a statement "five kilometers long" about all the building regulations that were being broken. So if San Giuseppe has any pull at town hall, the mason may be good for a third round.

At last it is the turn of the adults, and we squeeze in together with young men in their twenties and gray-haired grandmothers. The women who are serving eat at this shift too, jumping up and down between one mouthful and another to press upon us more pasta, more beans, more rice from the seemingly bottomless pots and pans. The food is very simply cooked and, except for the fennel in the *'gliotta,* has very little seasoning, but it is amazingly good, particularly in view of the quantity and the long wait in the pots. But, then, this is one of the great merits of Sicilian cooking: the basic ingredients are usually so good, the oil so pure, the vegetables so fresh and so intense in flavor, that they can stand on their own merits.

Mindful of the long drive home I am going slowly, but ladle after ladle of food disappears from the plates around me amidst much hilarity and complacent teasing directed at the size of the young men's appetites. The dialect here is very different from the Alcamese dialect I am accustomed to, and the jokes are mostly allusions that Maria Vica and I can't catch, but we find ourselves laughing with the others nonetheless, caught up in the embrace of the group's affectionate good humor. It is, I later realize, a unique moment in my Sicilian experience, a pure and uncontaminated expression of peasant society, outside of and indifferent to the institutions, for the perfunctory blessing of the priest and the participation of the band are mere services, individually contracted for. Except for the distant patronage of the saint looking down from his altar on the back wall, there are no protagonists; I never manage to determine which of the faces surrounding me belong to the mason and his immediate family. It is a rite consumed in the moment of its happening and for the benefit of the participants: no *pro loco* committee orchestrates the ritual, no tourists observe it (for Maria Vica and I are there as participants by virtue of her role in the community), and, most amazing of all, no photographer immortalizes the various moments for an album to lie in the *salotto* next to the family wedding and First Communion pictures. Tomorrow it will exist only in the collective memory of this neighborhood.

When everyone has had his fill and beyond, the baskets of *cassateddi* are brought out. Full as I am, I cannot resist trying the chick-pea filling, which has an earthy, spicy taste akin in spirit, if not in actual flavor or texture, to pumpkin pie filling, and is less dry and clogging than one might expect. We are given large paper plates towering with *cassateddi* to take home with us, and I will have fun when I get there challenging the family to guess what the basic ingredient is (no one succeeds). As we take our leave the women are again at work, clearing and resetting the table for the next shift, the last, which is reserved for the band. I can't imagine how there can be anything left for them to eat, a worrying thought, as they must have worked up quite an appetite tootling up and down these steep streets all morning.

A pensive silence accompanies us for the first part of the drive home, until a few remarks reveal that we are both following, from our different standpoints, the same line of thought. Maria Vica, a new sort of Sicilian woman, living alone and supporting herself (her family now lives in Rome), and I, expatriate wife and mother, are both fascinated by the close-knit community whose ritual we have shared, where everyone is related or at least acquainted, and the boundaries between nuclear family, extended family, and neighborhood overlap and entwine. Despite the lack of privacy and the tyranny of rigid norms of behavior over which the whole community vigils, we cannot forget the faces of the children and the obvious ease with which they navigate the early years of life, cradled by so many benevolent but variegated attentions. I am fascinated by the logistics too: the ease with which Maria Vica's student-housewives have disencumbered themselves of their family duties for the day seems an unbelievable luxury to me.

The organization of Sicilian society postulates the infinite availability of the family. Women can work—and often must work, since a single salary is rarely adequate to support a family—because a grandmother is there to take care of the babies. Elementary schools can malfunction in double or triple shifts for a maximum of four hours a day, because there is always someone at home to make lunch, to help out with the homework the teacher hasn't had time to explain, and, among the middle class, to invest the money and the chauffeuring effort necessary for providing the sports, the music, the art, etc., that the schools don't supply. Hospitals can get by with token nursing because there is always some relative available to sit up nights, to handle bedpans, and spoon-feed the incapacitated. The very rhythm of the day, in which all the stores and offices close from one to four and everybody goes home for a three-course meal, requires someone to be in the kitchen practically all day long.

My in-laws have always been too far away or too ill to be of more than marginal assistance, so until my children grew into some degree of independence I had to negotiate for every minute of time alone, for the briefest leave of absence, to a degree quite incomprehensible to my American friends, who have no doubt wondered why I have not managed to become more liberated. This is not without its advantages. The tangle of Sicilian family relationships and duties, however reassuring it may be as a safety net in time of emergency, is also a snare that can cripple the more fragile members of the family. Excluded by circumstance from all but the most limited participation, I am an ambivalent spectator of the Sicilian family, most often critical, as when I watch my friends struggling to free themselves of its constrictions, but sometimes wistful, as when, today, seen in a certain light, the grass at Làscari looks very green indeed.

Lu jorno di la Nunziata
Nesci lu scursuni sutta la balata.

On the day of the Annunciation
The lizard comes out from under the stone.

It is hot enough to bring out all the hibernating beasts: three days of scirocco have warmed the air, and the young girls have blossomed in the pinks and greens and yellows of this spring's fashions. Except for lizards, however, the Annunciation doesn't seem to be a very important day, although in the past Sicily's year began on March 25, and it wasn't until 1603 that the Spanish viceroy ordered that New Year's Day be moved to January 1. Another Spanish overlay—how much more coherent it would be to have the year begin with the Annunciation and the spring equinox.

The Annunciation comes exactly nine months to the day before Christmas, something I had never given any thought to until I was expecting Natalia. It was almost time for the baby to be born, and I was speculating together with Giuseppina, the cleaning woman who worked for me then, as to whether or not it would be a good idea to go away for the weekend.

"When's your time up?" she asked.

"It will be exactly nine months on Sunday."

"Oh, you can go, then. Only the Madonna gives birth at exactly nine months."

Giuseppina was a true daughter of old Palermo: she had run off at thirteen with a sailor in a *fuitina*, the "little flight" or elopement with which Sicilian couples overcome parental opposition by creating a situation in which honor can be repaired only by marriage. Her first baby was born two days after her fourteenth birthday, and as she went into labor she still believed that the midwife would have to cut a hole in her side to get the baby out. Now, after some thirteen pregnancies, she had nine children and twenty-three grandchildren, and she laughed to confess that she couldn't remember all their names.

Giuseppina had her own particular calendar. By about mid-February she would start putting things off: no use cleaning that *now*, we'll just have to do it all over again for Easter. A token flurry of activity at Eastertime, and then: no use scouring those pans *now*; fresh tomatoes will be coming on the market soon; there's nothing for shining up an aluminum pan like making tomato sauce in it!

Unfortunately Giuseppina also stole, an irresistible urge that had nothing to do with need or class envy; by chance I later learned that she even stole from the other members of the cleaning squad at the town hall where she worked in the afternoons. I turned a blind eye as long as I could and then had to fire her, a very melodramatic scene in which she creaked down onto her knees, clasped

her hands over her very ample bosom, and declared her innocence in ringing tones.

"I swear to you by . . . by . . . *Porca miseria*, there aren't
even any saints to swear by in this household!"

🌿 Natalia has been wrestling with flu again, and we decide to
stay in Palermo over Saturday and just drive out to Bosco for the
day on Palm Sunday. On Saturday evening Tonino reports unusual activity in front of the church that stands in the middle of
our piazza. An enterprising flower seller is trying to steal a march
on the competition by wiring his palm branches onto the church
railings. All week the flower sellers have been busy preparing these
branches; you could see them sitting by their stalls on the street
corners, patiently plaiting the leaves of each frond into intricate
shapes. A big group of men have been occupying a part of Piazza
San Domenico, sitting in a circle and chatting as they work, their
finished products displayed for sale on the railings around the statue
of the Immaculate Conception. The flower stalls themselves have
been breathtaking this week, every street corner a landscape of
color stretching from the pink clouds of peach blossoms down
through mountains of tulips and iris and carnations to a great pool
of yellow and purple freesias flowing over onto the street.

Palm Sunday dawns hot and sunny. The church railing has
miraculously flowered in the night, the white iron bars bearing
yellow-green palm fronds, each one at least a yard high, with its
leaves carefully braided into loops and frills, triangles and circles,
and sporting a large pompom bow of satiny ribbon, colorful if
slightly off-key. The competition is undaunted by such industry,
however, and the street in front of the church is filled with Vespa
pickups that bristle with palm fronds and olive branches, the latter tied with red ribbons or dipped into gold and silver paint.

The countryside through which we drive on our way to Bosco

is dressed for spring as well: soft green now clothes the almond groves on the mountainsides above Terrasini, but the peach orchards are pink with flowers. The yellow daffodils have left the garden to the narcissus, small clusters tucked in here and there to surprise me each spring with their delicacy.

I begin to sing of lovely-haired Demeter, the goddess august,
of her and her slender-ankled daughter whom Zeus,
far-seeing and loud-thundering, gave to Aidoneus to abduct.
Away from her mother of the golden sword and the splendid fruit
she played with the full-bosomed daughters of Okeanos,
gathering flowers, roses, crocuses, and beautiful violets
all over a soft meadow; irises, too, and hyacinths she picked,
and narcissus, which Gaia, pleasing the All-receiver,
made blossom there, by the will of Zeus, for a girl with a flower's
    beauty.
A lure it was, wondrous and radiant, and a marvel to be seen by
    immortal gods and mortal men.
A hundred stems of sweet-smelling blossoms
grew from its roots. The wide sky above
and the whole earth and the briny swell of the sea laughed.
She was dazzled and reached out with both hands at once
to take the pretty bauble; Earth with its wide roads gaped
and then over the Nysian field the lord and All-receiver,
the many-named son of Kronos, sprang out upon her with his
    immortal horses.
Against her will he seized her and on his golden chariot
carried her away as she wailed; and she raised a shrill cry,
calling upon father Kronides, the highest and the best.
None of the immortals or of mortal men heard
her voice, not even the olive trees bearing splendid fruit.

From "To Demeter," in *The Homeric Hymns*

In *The Golden Honeycomb*, which is in most respects a lovely book about Sicily, Vincent Cronin says that "Persephone's wish to pluck the fantastic flower is every man's search for illicit or excessive happiness." I strongly disagree with his interpretation, which seems to me to reflect a very male-chauvinist view of female sexuality, and I fail to understand how anyone could find anything excessive or illicit in the pale precision of a narcissus.

The temperature drops again in the night, and Holy Week is cold and penitential, with clouds dampening the bright colors of the flower stalls. The Communist city councilor from Brancaccio is beaten up on his way home one night. After the bomb went off in the commissariat, the city council decided to hold a symbolic session there, the first one in history to take place outside of city hall, during which this man, elected in the Brancaccio district, made a courageous speech denouncing the Mafia in very explicit terms. He is now wearing a plaster cast for his pains.

From the other side of the island the radio reports a different sort of violence: Etna is erupting. A new crater less than a mile down from the peak on the southern flank is spewing forth gases and lava in a roiling red river that crunches and burns everything that lies in its path. Etna is considered a good-natured volcano, since her eruptions are seldom precipitate or explosive; the lava that boils up and over with considerable frequency often exhausts itself on the barren upper slopes, and even when it does reach the lower regions, destroying houses and vineyards, it is inexorable but slow, allowing the inhabitants to stand and watch as the smoking red tide devours home and harvest. The television news programs show spectacular nighttime shots of the incandescent lava pouring through the darkness as from some celestial crucible.

With the *autostrada* finally completed, Catania is only two and a half hours away by car, and we could go, as many will over the Easter holidays, to see the volcano erupting. Yet somehow it still seems as distant as it did when only winding, ill-kept roads gutted with potholes meandered across the center of the island, another world quite foreign to western Sicily. The eastern Sicilians themselves are very insistent on distinguishing between the two halves of the island; they feel themselves to be Greek as opposed to Arab, commercially enterprising as opposed to parasitic, honest as opposed to mafioso—although recent events seem to deny this last distinction, since it is now thought that the order to kill dalla Chiesa came from Catania.

I have been too little to the east to judge these finer points; for me it is Etna that makes the difference.

> . . . Etna, that wicked witch, resting her thick white snow under heaven, and slowly, slowly rolling her orange-colored smoke. They called her the Pillar of Heaven, the Greeks. It seems wrong at first, for she trails up in a long, magical, flexible line from the sea's edge to her blunt cone, and does not seem tall. She seems rather low, under heaven. But as one knows her better, oh, awe and wizardry! Remote under heaven, aloof, so near, yet never with us. The painters try to paint her, and the photographers to photograph her, in vain. Because why? Because the near ridges, with their olives and white houses, these are with us. Because the river-bed, and Naxos under the lemon groves, Greek Naxos deep under dark-leaved, many-fruited lemon groves, Etna's skirts and skirt-bottoms, these are still our world, our own world. Even the high villages among the oaks on Etna. But Etna herself, Etna of the snow and secret changing winds, witch-like under heaven, slowly rolling her orange smoke and giving sometimes a breath of rose-red flame, then I must look away from the earth, into the ether, into the low empyrean. And there, in that remote region, Etna is alone.

> D. H. Lawrence, *Sea and Sardinia*

Etna as a world apart embraces more than Lawrence perhaps could see from Taormina: even the lower slopes are unique, the vineyards and fruit orchards lush in the rich volcanic soil, strung together by narrow roads that wind through the small towns and underneath high walls, past gates offering a glimpse of aging villas, the brightly colored and unpretentious villas of the Catanese nobility, nestled in luxuriant gardens, shaded by tall chestnuts and spreading magnolias and perfumed by magnificent gardenias and camelias, which will have no part of western Sicily's lime-heavy soil. And then the woods, the tall pine forest of Linguaglossa singing in the wind on the northern slope, the chestnut and oak forests that turn golden in the late spring when the robinia trees let down their cascades of bloom and the Etnean gorse, grown to the height of small trees, threads its long and wiry branches with yellow blossoms. As it climbs the vegetation changes latitude, from Mediterranean to Nordic, and forms an ecosystem apart, with flowers and butterflies found nowhere else in the world. But the green is slashed by ribbons of purple-black lava: ever shorter and sparser, the plants creep up toward the upper slopes, fighting to win back the land that has been coated and burned by the lava of past centuries. The first to colonize are the mosses and the lichens, gray-green blotches on the barren slopes like mold on blackberry jam. Beyond that nothing but the long reaches of lava, menacing and lifeless. Or so they seem. I once picked up a piece of lava, up near the Tower of the Philosopher, where the Greek Empedocles is said to have dwelt as a hermit while he studied the volcano. There the big masses have started to crumble, beginning the slow return to soil, but nothing grows, not so much as a thread of green is to be found. Yet there were at least five ladybugs on the piece of lava that I held in my hand, and bending nearer to the ground I saw that there were hundreds of them, struggling over and around the black rocks, tiny red embers of life among the dead coals, infinitesimal animation of a wasteland.

The crater itself smokes incessantly, belching gas and ashes that float down over the mountainside, coating and insulating the snow that has settled in the crevices so that it does not melt even in the heat of the Sicilian summer. This snow was formerly a very profitable monopoly reserved for the archbishop of Catania, who exported it to Italy or sold it for making the ices and sherbets for which Sicily has been famous ever since the Arab occupation. It is snowing now on Etna, and the volcano is hung with mists that glow ominously where the lava is flowing down toward the ski lift and the observatory. Etna's magma comes from very deep in the bowels of the earth, and there is no way of telling how long it will continue to flow or how much damage it will do.

❧ On Wednesday school closes for the short Easter vacation, and that afternoon I put Natalia on the plane for Milan, where she will spend Easter with her cousin Martina. Natalia is exploiting her last month of paying half fare before she turns twelve at the beginning of May, and the rest of us are spending Easter at Bosco. Late Thursday morning Francesco and I drive out, much discouraged by the weather, which is gray and sepulchral. All morning a strange cloud hangs low over the city, a thick brown murk such as Zeus might whip up to hide some extramarital escapade. Suddenly it dissolves into big, muddy drops of rain that fall for only a few minutes but leave a fine brown film everywhere, thick enough to render the windshield opaque. We cannot decide whether this is dust blown up from the Sahara—the scirocco often bears us gifts of this nature—or volcanic ash that has wafted across the island from Etna.

Easter vacation is always somewhat of a battle for me: I must attempt to reconcile the exquisite pleasures of being in Bosco in the spring with the temptation of the innumerable processions and strange rites that fill the Sicilian Holy Week. And then attempt to reconcile my choices with the desires of the rest of the family. Even as we head for Bosco today I deplore that still another year is passing without my being able to watch the women of Palermo "doing the sepulchers," making the rounds of the churches on Maundy Thursday carrying their *lavureddi*, the pots of wheat and lentils that have been sprouted in the dark. These pots, decorated with ribbons and flowers and filled with dark soil against which the colorless sprouts gleam pale and funereal, are descendants of the Gardens of Adonis, which the Greek women prepared to cast upon the sea during the annual festival marking the death and rebirth of the youth beloved of Aphrodite.

Good Friday is still gray and cold, but a sharp wind moves the clouds along before they can become a menace to the processions that will be winding their way about the towns throughout the island. The most famous of these is the procession of the Misteri at Tràpani, which is nearing its four-hundredth birthday. Tràpani is the westernmost port of Sicily, and at the end of the sixteenth century, at the height of the Spanish domination, it was a very wealthy city, deriving its income not only from the trade with Spain but also from the production of sea salt, from tuna fishing, and above all from the coral that was fished from the offshore reefs and wrought by artisans and goldsmiths of consummate craftsmanship. The guilds were rich and flourishing and welcomed the Good Friday procession decreed by the Spanish authorities as a chance to display both their devotion and their wealth. Through the centuries the various guilds, orders, and confraternities have vied for the privilege of carrying through the streets the twenty huge set pieces that represent the scenes of the Passion, contending the best bands, the most spectacular floral decorations, the heftiest porters.

The procession starts at three in the afternoon and continues, with a brief pause for mass at eight in the evening, until eight the next morning, threading endlessly through the broad avenues and the narrow alleyways of the city, changing in character and growing in emotional intensity as the day wears on. In the afternoon, rays of sunlight breaking through the clouds dance on the street vendors and their gaily decorated stalls, sparkle on the polished instruments of the bands—twelve in all—that are interspersed along the procession, and bounce off the baby carriages, the cones of ice cream, and the cones of pumpkin seeds, as each family strolls along in an air of spring finery and festivity that is out of step with the slow swaying and the sorrowful faces of the statues.

At the end of the day, darkness obscures these extraneous elements. The children are sent off, tardily and reluctantly, to bed, the traffic noises die out, the big-windowed tourist buses carry away the swarms of French- and German-chattering tourists whose pastel-colored summer clothes stand out against the dark wools the Sicilians are still wearing. In the daylight the clustering spectators betrayed the whereabouts of the procession; now, in the night, the ear can follow its passage. The tableaux pass slowly; the wailing strains of one funeral dirge have not yet died out before the muffled drums and mourning brass of the next band come into hearing, echoing along the close-packed houses of the old town, whose whitewashed walls gleam in the distant intervals of the streetlights. Every few minutes a wooden clapper cuts through the music with sharp tones, the procession halts, another rattle and the porters crouch down until the platform on which Christ is stumbling under the weight of the cross rests on its own legs. On the platform, banked in flowers and surrounded by candles, the life-size Christ of polychromed wood, whose linen and plaster robes were swelling and breathing as the platform advanced, falls lifeless, a mere statue holding up a piece of wood again, as it surrenders all animation to the porters, who flex their shoulders under their blue smocks and stretch their necks, making the red pompoms on their blue berets wobble. Cracking a quiet joke or two, they down a quick glass of wine at the tavern on the opposite sidewalk, and then the clapper sounds again and the porters move back to take their places by the two long and hefty poles that stick out in front and in back of the platform, adjusting the little cushions they wear on the shoulder that carries the heavy weight of the pole. There are five men to each corner, crouched and waiting until the sound of the clapper, when as one man they straighten up and launch themselves into the *annaccata*, the "rocking," a synchronized lurching shuffle. Each group has its own clapper, sounded by the leader; their harsh clacking ricochets down the narrow streets as the statues come to life again, wracked by pain and contorted by suffering, and take up their stately progress, swaying from side to side and gathering solemnity from the wavering candlelight and the lonely sounds of the bands in the half-empty streets. The Crucifixion passes, and the Deposition. Another band, another halt to rest. The flowers that carpet the platforms are beginning to wilt, their heads bending and shaking more and more as the tiredness and the wine combine to exasperate the porters' dance. The great coffin with the body of the dead

Christ passes. Then a slow ripple of gathering emotion breaks over the onlookers, drowning their chatter and bringing the women to their knees, fingers fluttering across their breast and to their lips in the sign of the cross, as they see the last and solitary figure, the Addolorata, the sorrowing Mother. The black velvet of the enormous cloak that enfolds her emerges from the darkness, embroidered by the flickering light of dozens of candles that reflect in the crystal teardrops on her pale cheeks and in the dim pool of white carnations about her feet.

. . . the street and the squares [have become] the theater for that great drama, whose elements are betrayal, murder, the sorrow of a mother.

But is it truly the sorrow of the Son of God made Man that is relived, in the towns of Sicily, on Good Friday? Or is it not instead the drama of man, simply man; betrayed by his neighbor, assassinated by the law? Or, in the end, is it even this? Is it not simply the drama of a mother, the drama of the Addolorata?

Beyond any doubt, in these representations one can feel that, more than the Christ himself, it is the figure of Maria Addolorata that touches and moves. Christ, from the moment of his capture, is already in death. And the dead are dead, as all the proverbs say, counseling peace, resignation, *omertà*. But the mother is alive: sorrowing, closed in the black mantle of her pain, transfixed, moaning; image and symbol of all mothers. The true drama is hers: earthly and of this flesh. Thus it is not the drama of sacrifice and human redemption; but that of the pain of being alive, of our obscure visceral dismay when confronted with death, of the closed and perennial mourning of the living.

Leonardo Sciascia, "Feste religiose in Sicilia,"
in *La corda pazza: scrittori e cose della Sicilia*

Chapter Six

Nothing of my childhood Easters has survived the passage across the Atlantic to my present state of agnosticism, into an age when hats are a matter of fashion rather than breeding, and a land where Easter egg dyes and jelly beans are not available. Thus unencumbered, I have fallen very easily into the pattern established my very first year here, when Tonino and I cut short a trip to Tràpani and Selinunte in order to return to Alcamo early Easter morning, to be with his family. And for twenty years our Easters have been that, first at Alcamo and then at Bosco: the heavy dinner at noon; chocolate Easter eggs with a cheap surprise inside until I desecrated even this small ritual, discovering that for the same amount of money I could get twice the weight in chocolate bars and a nice and welcome present as well; the marzipan lambs with tinfoil halos and red paper banners that my mother-in-law produces annually in the hopes, I think, that they might exercise some miraculous power of conversion over her heathen grandchildren. (The first time, when Francesco was just two, Tonino and Turi managed to hollow out the lamb completely before Francesco caught them picking at it from the back and realized that it was edible.)

That first year, however, leafing through the guidebook as we hurried back to Alcamo, I read about an Easter procession in Castelvetrano that I have yearned to see ever since. My chance has now come: a heavy cold has confined my mother-in-law to her Palermo nursing home, so two bars of Swiss chocolate and some drawing pens wrapped up in an egg-shaped package suffice to take care of family custom, and early on Easter morning we are off to see the *Aurora*.

This name is misleading, according to Claudia, a friend whose family comes from Castelvetrano, since dawn comes and goes long before the action begins, but Castelvetrano is on the southern coast, directly below Alcamo, and it will take us about three-quarters of an hour to cross the island.

Nature has orchestrated the feast day to perfection. The wind has gone elsewhere, taking the clouds with it, and as we drive down the hill toward the highway, the early-morning sun rises on a world of soft new green and lemon yellow, on pink peach blossoms and the clustering white of the late-blooming, green-leafed pear trees. We enter the *autostrada* at Alcamo and drive south, swooping above the valleys and skimming the hilltops on long, curving viaducts, twentieth-century colonnades that look out over vineyards that around Alcamo have just *sparato*, as the Sicilians say, just shot into leaf in the sudden, explosive Sicilian spring, and then on to the lusher green of the wheat fields in the interior. Here and there as we go farther south a field of sulla, a legumi-nous plant cultivated for fodder, is in bloom, a blanket of rich carmine blossoms spread out on the green wheat. We are driving down the Belice Valley, through the heart of the earthquake zone: morning mists, rising in the morning sun, reveal crumbled towns and shoddy barracks.

Soon the smell of salt indicates that we are nearing the sea again. The southern coast is low, sweeping, open to the sea that pene-trates inland in an intermingling of dunes and fields and low bluffs quite different from what we are used to in the north, where the sea is a backdrop for the dramatic contours of the land, but re-mains quite distinct from it. There are no tides to speak of in the Mediterranean, and somehow on the northern coast one knows this at a glance, while to the south such an ebb and flow remains a possibility.

It is barely half past eight when we park the car in a small side street of Castelvetrano and continue by foot to the main square. The sun is not yet high enough to find its way into the streets and warm the air, and the bars are just opening. We are hungry after our drive, and when a young boy passes, balancing on his head a huge tray covered with a white cloth, we immediately swing round like the needle on a compass and follow him to the bar where, it turns out, he is delivering freshly fried *arancine*, the rice croquettes.

By the time we have wiped the last grains of rice from our chins, the square is beginning to fill up with people. It isn't really a square at all, but a long, narrow rectangle, slightly bent at the halfway point, where Claudia has advised us to take up our stand. There are a fair number of tourists, brought here by guidebooks or guided tours, but the bulk of the crowd is local, all dressed up and very excited. Next to us a family of emigrants home for the holiday is particularly resplendent, the husband's black and white brocade jacket and matching tie an unmistakable symptom of the way the somber good taste of the Sicilian peasant goes berserk in a foreign climate. The emigrant returns from abroad in loud checks and phosphorescent socks that are immediately labeled *americanate* no matter where they have been purchased.

The *banditori*, the town criers, arrive, the likes of which I have not seen for years. When I lived in Partinico there was still a town crier there, who would stroll through the streets announcing his arrival with a long roll on his drum and then shouting out his messages in thick, garbled dialect and long, drawn-out groans, of which I never understood a single word. These three limit themselves to their instruments, large drums slung from bands around their necks and balanced on their bellies; taking up a position a short distance from the others, as if in solitary command of the piazza, each one beats out in turn a passionate call for attention, vying with his rivals in the velocity of the rolls, the fury of the crescendos, the sharpness of the final rat-a-tats.

In white gloves and white pith helmets, the town police begin to carve a central path through the crowd for the length of the piazza. As soon as the way is clear, a group of majorettes step out, followed by the town banners and then the band, which strikes up a sprightly Sousa sort of tune. Gone are the funeral marches, the dirges, and the requiems; today is for resurrection and rejoicing. The crowd is excited, necks crane, peering to see what is happening at either end of the piazza, which is by now completely filled with people. Small children, piggyback, float above the sea of heads, while the privileged look down upon us from the surrounding balconies.

"Look, there she is! There she is! She's coming!" Everyone is pointing to the northern end of the piazza, where the statue of the Madonna has suddenly appeared, wrapped up in a black cloak and carried on the shoulders of a dozen men. Immediately all heads swing southward to discover in the distance the risen Christ just entering the piazza at the other end. The two statues halt just out of sight of each other, separated by some three hundred feet of curving square and excited onlookers. The Madonna is accompanied by an angel, half the size and weight of the larger statues and mounted on a much smaller platform. The crowd tenses and swells forward; the policemen spread their arms to keep open the path. A shout, and the angel charges down the piazza on the shoulders of a dozen young boys, bobbing and swaying precariously in his agitation. He arrives at the feet of the risen Christ, pauses to catch his breath, and in a few minutes races back again with the glad tidings. Tidings that are not believed: three times this polychromed plaster ambassador is hurtled back and forth across the piazza, faster and faster as the delighted crowd urges the runners on to greater and greater effort.

A roll of drums, some new music, and the big statues begin to move. The crowd falls silent. Mary and Jesus draw toward each other, their slow, shuffling progress full of doubt and hesitation. Might it be? Could it be true? The pace quickens. When they have come halfway, they catch sight of each other, the bearers break into a run, the two statues sweep together and pull up sharply just in time to avoid collision, the momentum bringing their heads together in a brief embrace. Mary's black cloak drops away to reveal a mantle of flowered brocade, and the falling folds release a flight of snow-white doves that wheel and circle over the scene of such rejoicing.

Tonino and I sheepishly discover tears in each other's eyes. It was so real. The emotion that was released together with the doves was so intense, the longing for just such an encounter so palpable. Mary and Jesus, Demeter and Persephone, black-veiled mother and murdered child, release from mourning.

🌿 Beyond the vague intention of ending up at Prizzi to see the devils dance on Easter afternoon, we have no set itinerary for the rest of the day and decide to drive east along the southern coast, turning or stopping at whim. And whim soon declares itself: only a short distance from Castelvetrano there are road signs indicating the turnoff for Selinunte, and it seems sinful not to make a stop when we have all the time in the world.

Selinunte is to me the least accessible of the Greek sites I have seen in Sicily. The bare bones of a city sacked by man and toppled by earthquake lie in careless heaps on low cliffs overlooking the sea, building blocks abandoned by some infant Titan who has centuries since outgrown them. They are illegible in their very size, with the tourists clambering over the enormous fluted drums of fallen columns like tiny, multicolored ants. Today it is very crowded; parking is difficult and the air rings with a many-tongued babble and with the nagging claxons of the tourist buses gathering their various broods. We mingle with the crowds, wander through the eastern temples, and stroll along the road that leads down into the river valley and up to the acropolis on the opposite cliff until the heat and the confusion persuade us to turn back.

Selinunte was a revelation the first time I came, exactly twenty years ago yesterday. Apart from Tonino and me there were no more than a dozen people here, and even these disappeared, swallowed up by the vast sweep of sea and plain and the immoderate proportions of the ruins. We sat for hours on some stones and stared out across sea and centuries, the sea of flowers in the foreground no less brilliant than the Mediterranean that sparkled in the distance. The *selinon*, the wild celery that gave the ancient city its name, was submerged by the red of the sulla, the yellow of

mayflowers and mustard, the blue of bugloss and borage, bobbing and trembling under the insistent and noisy prodding of
thousands of bees. It was my first immersion in the Sicilian spring,
in its colors and its perfumes and its heat, a baptism that caught
and held me convert. Today the flowers are still as beautiful, the
sun perhaps even hotter, but the crowd and the confusion drown
out the bees, and the ruins are silent, unable despite their size to
cope with this Lilliputian invasion.

We continue eastward and then turn north on the road for
Caltabellotta, which winds up over the ridge of low mountains
that separates the southern coastal plain east of Selinunte from
the rolling hills of the interior. These mountains are quite barren,
with patches of vineyard or wheat exploiting the rare flat spaces,
an occasional olive or almond tree clinging to the steep and rocky
slopes, and, as closer inspection reveals, a sparse carpeting of the
crouching, grasping plants of arid soil and high altitudes: purple
squill, delicate white clusters of star-of-Bethlehem, the single tiny
yellow-and-brown orchids of the *lutea* family, and the many-
flowered stalks of the *orchis italica*, bristling with minute pink
tentacles.

The village of Caltabellotta lies at the summit of the highest
mountain in this southern ridge, topped only by two great spurs
of rock that thrust up behind it like giant tusks. The streets are
narrow and zigzag steeply up the hillside; a policeman directing
all five cars' worth of traffic instructs us to park the car and continue on foot if we want to see the procession. Of course we do,
so we quickly park and follow the main street up to a point where
it splits, one fork leading farther up a very steep slope, the other
curving down to the right into a tiny piazza. The "procession" is
here—townspeople and bandsmen, their instruments tucked forgotten under their elbows, have gathered in a circle to cheer and
applaud a dancing saint, a life-size plaster statue of the Archangel
Michael, the town's patron. Michael, dressed in the armor of a
Roman legionary, is leaning against a column that has been completely wrapped in purple phlox, with a young laurel tree tied
next to it so that the purple flowers glow against the dark leaves.

As in Tràpani and Castelvetrano, the flower-decked platform that bears the statue is mounted on two poles—in this case very long, thick wooden beams that of themselves must weigh an enormous amount—and requires some thirty hefty young men to carry it. But "carry" is not the right word: they rock and jostle and bounce the statue in the most extraordinary manner, accompanied and encouraged by a crescendo of cheering and clapping from the crowd that presses in around them. Sweat pouring off their faces, the young men push and pull still harder on their poles, and the Archangel rocks and sways and reels in a frenzied dance, until his porters can bear it no longer, the movement subsides into a faint bobbing, and the statue itself seems to pant as the men fight to catch their breath, still holding all the weight on their shoulders.

Bottles of water and beer are passed around, the band recovers its role and starts to play again, and considerable maneuvering is necessary to effect the passage of the statue around the curve and into the main street, where it pauses at the foot of the rise, gathering strength. Meanwhile another statue arrives, a little winged cherub about two feet high, with platform, poles, and porters in proportion: a handful of boys about twelve years old bounce the baby statue about in great excitement, egged on by an amused crowd.

The music dies out, and, at a sign from one of the porters, the drummer sounds a roll. On the final snap of the drumsticks the men charge up the street, running and stumbling with their heavy burden up a slope so steep that the statue seems almost horizontal. The cheers of the onlookers assist them over the top and around the corner, quickly followed by the angel, who bobs gaily and effortlessly up the rise in the wake of his big brother.

We too turn and climb. We have lost the statues, but echoes of their progress parallel to ours reach us at the street corners. A final hike up a street so sheer that the sidewalk is a flight of stairs brings us out onto the Piano della Matrice, the open square of the mother church, unexpectedly spectacular. In front of us a wide checkerboard of cobble and grass slopes gently up to the steps of the Matrice, built by Count Roger after he took Caltabellotta from the Saracens in 1090. The weathered gray stone of the Norman church blends into the sharp-toothed rock that rises abruptly behind it. On the left-hand side of the square stands the chapel of San Michele, its Gothic portal garlanded in laurel branches, and next to it a gate and a stairway carved into the live rock lead off toward the second, bigger pinnacle, ringed by the trees of the town park where the ruins of the Norman castle lie.

Commotion rising from below tells us that Saint Michael is about to make his final assault on the mountain. The last steep rise is rendered more problematical by telephone wires and shop signs, and considerable measuring accompanied by animated discussion is necessary before a strategy can be agreed upon. At last somebody climbs out on a balcony and unties a laundry line, final directions are shouted out, and the group braces itself. Up they come, the initial momentum waning as they scramble up the cobbled street, their boots slipping and straining to find a grip on the polished stones. A final push and they burst into the square, where they bring up sharply, the statue swaying back and forth, evidently in some confusion as to where to go next.

One of the townsmen who has followed the progress of the statue explains to us that the municipal *pro loco* committee has decided that Caltabellotta should cash in on the "Easter in Sicily" tourist boom and has organized a new procession for the afternoon, a version of the Castelvetrano Aurora, but the details have not been thought out all that well, and no one knows whether Michael should spend his lunch hour in the Matrice or in the chapel of San Michele, where the garlands declare a readiness to receive him sooner or later.

After a few false starts and some rather languishing discussion, Michael is carried up the steps and into the dark interior of the Matrice. We start to follow it, but a priest, heretofore absent from the scene, closes the door firmly in our faces. Lunchtime. The Matrice is closed, the chapel is closed, the gate to the castle is closed. The best we can do is climb up some stone steps that lead around behind the Matrice, to discover that the rock is sheltering a miniature Alpine meadow, shaded by pine trees whose sun-warmed resin fills the air and dotted with tiny daisies, the kind whose white petals have had their tips dipped in red. I remember the flowers from a French children's book I had when I was little, and it is surprising yet suitable to find their smiling faces here in the shadow of the Norman walls. The view from the meadow is spectacular: we can look north toward the mountains of Palermo across the whole of Sicily, the hills and valleys flattened from this height into a gentle pool of green, flecked with the white foam of the blossoming fruit trees.

The priest had something, however. Our stomachs call us to more prosaic questions. We discover that Caltabellotta offers a choice of two restaurants, one in the town itself and one just outside, around the back of the peak that rises above the castle ruins. Walking down toward the car we pass the first, which is occupied by a baptismal party and has no free tables. A winding road takes us out of town, past vegetable plots and tiny vineyards, to a huge baroque monastery, this too flanked by a cliff and by a charming restaurant with a trellised terrace. The proprietor is polite and extremely apologetic: a wedding reception is in progress, and there isn't a free chair in the place. Tonino, undaunted or perhaps desperate, asks if they couldn't fix us a little antipasto to go. After a brief wait the obliging host produces three foil-covered plates, a bottle of mineral water, and a round kilo loaf of fragrant, crusty bread. We drive back along the road a little way to a curve that offers space to park and some rocks to sit on. Our plates turn out to hold spicy olives, some slices of *prosciutto crudo* and of a peppery local salame, and two kinds of pecorino cheese, one fresh and mild, the other aged and sharper. With a bag of oranges from the car, the sun warm on our backs, the mountains rolling down at our feet to the southern coast and the sea beyond, where the heat haze clouds the horizon and hides Africa from view, we have as fine an Easter dinner as I have ever eaten.

The drive north to Prizzi, a rapid descent switchbacking down the north side of the mountain to the green valleys we had seen from above, takes us along luxuriant riverbeds, over hills of green wheat, past isolated pear and apple trees in bloom. The hedge-rows are overflowing with flowers, unable to contain such a riot of color, such an exuberance of form and texture. It is difficult to believe that in the space of a few months the velvet softness of the wheat fields, shifting from emerald to chartreuse with the wind, will give way to bristling, colorless stubble; these are the hills that the Lampedusa family cross in the Visconti film of *The Leopard*, in blinding light and smothering dust, their carriages creaking to the shrill song of the locusts.

But the extravagant hand of spring is less and less successful in concealing the poverty of the agriculture the farther north we go. Our destination, the village of Prizzi, is quite high, slapped down on a hill of rocky soil and stunted vegetation with none of the cozy shifting and filling with which most Sicilian towns have accommodated themselves to the bones of the island. The out-skirts of the town are ringed with the usual half-finished houses, fruit of the emigrants' remittances, but once past them the streets are small and close and we are hard put to find a parking space and then to fight our way through the crowds that are thronging toward the center of town, the ranks of the Prizzitani being very much swollen by both foreign and Sicilian tourists. Tonino greets several of his students from the university, then most unexpect-edly a hand claps down on my shoulder. It is Nicolò, a man who served on the school board with me. He is a native of Prizzi, a linesman for the telephone company, and after a period of tech-nical schooling in Milan now lives in Palermo, where, fortified by his northern experience, he has become very active in the local section of the Communist party, in the neighborhood council, the trade union, and the school board. He proved a most unusual and valuable addition to the school board, able and willing to work on two levels in a way that is rare among Sicilians, ready to de-bate the ideological or educational implications of a policy deci-sion and at the same time to fix a light plug or repair a busted slide projector himself rather than trusting to the lengthy mean-derings of the school bureaucracy. But today he is here in Prizzi to be with his family and to see the devils dance.

We are lucky to run into him. We have arrived too late for the distribution of the *cannateddi*, Prizzi's special Easter cakes, but Nicolò carries us off to the Circolo della Caccia, the Hunters' Club, which the Chamber of Commerce has been using as its head-quarters for the occasion, and there he sets various cousins scur-rying around to unearth some last undistributed *cannateddi* for us, oval cakes of biscuit dough braided about an egg.

Cannateddi in hand, we follow Nicolò out again and push our way along the main street, which dips sharply down, then rises again in the distance. Nicolò guides us to the lowest point in the street, where he tells us to stay put, this being a grandstand seat for watching the triumph of Good over Evil. The street is filled with people, strolling, talking, and shouting across from one crowded balcony to another. Here at the bottom we can look up in either direction at a sea of faces. A small and hornèd vortex is descending upon us from the eastern end: the devils are coming, accompanied by the clanking of their chains and the squealing and shouting of a swarm of little boys. There are three masked fig-ures, two devils escorting Death. Death is dressed in yellow, a big, loose-fitting yellow jump suit and a yellow mask of soldered tin covering his whole head in the shape of a skull, in which have been cut eyeholes, a black dent for the nose, and a mouth grin-ning around a few long and crooked teeth. Under his arm is a crossbow with which he menaces the crowd. The devils have rust-colored jump suits, ample enough to accommodate a variety of figures over the years, and their masks are large, flat tin ovals, painted brown, with curved horns, long noses, and tongues stick-ing out from leering mouths. The backs of their heads and shoul-ders are covered by heavy, long-haired goat pelts, black for one, white for the other, a touch of the genuine that is somehow much more menacing than the masks themselves. The multicolored stripes of Adidas sneakers show underneath the baggy trouser legs.

Comfortable shoes are a must for the devils, whose loping, lolloping dance betrays considerable weariness. Well it may, says Nicolò: they have been dancing ever since the hour of the Crucifixion on Friday, chasing about the town making mischief and teasing all they encounter. Nicolò was a devil one year and assures us that the costumes are unbearably hot and heavy, especially on a sunny day like today—the only thing that keeps you going is the wine. Anyone whom Death manages to hit with his crossbow is obliged to stand the devils a round at the nearest tavern, and if Death is a good shot, they all have quite a bit under their jump suits by the end of the day.

There is movement up at either end of the street, and for the second time today we are shoved back against the buildings by white-gloved policemen. The street is long and I can barely make out the Madonna to the east, Christ to the west, and just hear the loudest notes of the band. Down the hill come the forces of Good, two angels in armor, with cardboard wings, red capes, ropes of beads and gilt chains across their breasts, swords in hand, and strange flat-topped helmets that Francesco is quick to notice have been cut out from Alemagna panettone boxes. The devils at first have the best of these bizarre apparitions; a brief skirmish leads to a hasty retreat, and then a counterattack. Back and forth they run and clash and feint as the statues continue their slow but steady descent. The battlefield shrinks as the statues draw nearer, the dance and the swordwork grow more and more frenzied as the devils find themselves hemmed in between the advancing figures, until a last and desperate leap marks the meeting between the risen Christ and the rejoicing Madonna, and Death and the devils fall to earth, vanquished and immobile.

This scene will be repeated four more times this evening, the last time in the dark in the big piazza in front of the Matrice, at the top of the hill. Nicolò urges us to stay, but it is a long way back to Bosco and it is already half past five, so we say good-bye. Drunk with all that we have seen, my cheeks burning from the sun and wind, and my eyes watering, I can hardly take in the landscape we drive through, nor do I notice where we are when

Tonino turns his attention from the road to give me a reproachful glance.

"When I was a boy, I spent all my time *avoiding* processions!"

❧ The next day is Pasquetta, "Little Easter," a day on which the family picnic in the country is as sacred a ritual as the procession is on Easter. This is a tradition that goes back for centuries; the famous "Sicilian Vespers," the revolt that shifted the power structure of the Mediterranean and brought Sicily under Spanish domination, was supposedly touched off on Pasquetta in 1282 when a French soldier insulted a Sicilian girl who was coming out from the Vesper service at the then rural church of Santo Spirito, after having spent the day in the country with her young man and his family.

Until quite recently, Easter Monday morning found the country roads around Alcamo and Partinico full of cart-borne families heading out to the fields for their picnics. The horses were strapped into holiday harness, with bells jingling, brightly colored plumes and woolen pompoms nodding, and the sun flashing on tiny round mirrors. Behind them, balanced on two high wheels and beautifully carved and painted, with gay primary colors depicting the triumphs of Count Roger over the Saracens or of Garibaldi over the Bourbons, the carts themselves were bursting with people: the grandmother in black, sitting stiffly in a straight chair and holding a large black umbrella over her head to keep off the sun, a flock of grandchildren tucked in around her feet, the adults squeezed onto the driver's seat; the family dog, tied to the axle of the cart, ran briskly along behind. (One of the great chestnuts of Sicilian humor is the touring Englishman who stops one of these carts and makes the peasant untie the dog, to the considerable bewilderment of both man and beast.)

This is a rare sight nowadays, since most families have a car to travel in, and many peasants even have a summer house, albeit tiny, by the sea that they prefer on holidays to the scene of their daily labors. But some still choose the countryside: I am out early in the morning, pruning the lavender bushes that border my herb garden, and as I work I can hear the landscape come alive with laughter, with shouting children and calling mothers, the voices traveling a long way in the quiet air. Some cheerful traditionalist has brought a record player that vibrates with the nasal twanging of the *marranzanu*, the iron mouth harp, over and over in a tireless tarantella. Before long I will see thin columns of smoke begin to rise here and there on the hillsides: you need a lot of embers for roasted artichokes, which are obligatory today and marvelous anytime. To achieve this apotheosis of the artichoke, you must grasp it firmly by the stem end and pound it vigorously on a stone until the leaves flatten and open out enough to allow you to poke in toward the heart a large pinch of garlic chopped up fine together with mint, salt, and pepper. Olive oil in generous quantity follows upon the garlic, and the artichoke is then placed on ash-covered coals to roast gently for about forty-five minutes until the tough outer leaves have charred and the tender heart has steamed in its own juice and absorbed the oil and the seasonings in one of the world's happiest marriages.

The whining of the chain saw drowns out the distant music: Tonino and Francesco have decided to tackle the palm and give it the definitive pruning. They cut and saw and chop all morning, carving out with surgical delicacy at least ten large clumps of fronds and almost twice as many little shoots. The final effect is very peculiar: the trunk goes up for about ten feet and ends in a large tuft, just like any proper palm, but halfway up four big branches curve up and out, their scratchy plumes waving to the four points of the compass like a badly smoking candelabrum. I cannot come out and say that I don't like the fruit of so much hard and prickly labor and can only hope that this is a good omen, that having reduced this heraldic device from chaos to mere eccentricity, we will now proceed to operate in like fashion upon ourselves.

I must start early for Palermo, leaving Tonino and Francesco to finish putting the severed palm shoots to root and to close the house, because I have to go via the airport to meet Natalia, who is arriving from Milan. The trip from the airport to Palermo, usually only twenty minutes, is very slow tonight: all Palermo is returning from its Pasquetta picnic in a triple line of slow-moving cars whose red taillights flicker like last embers from the picnic fires. Natalia tells me about her Milanese Easter, rainy and urban, full of movies and nonstop confiding with her cousin. I describe to her our parade of processions and tell her how much I missed having her to share my delight in the wildflowers. After a while we fall silent, tired from our different experiences and mesmerized by the red lights that stop and start in a tedious crawl in front of us. I remember earlier evenings when I came upon the carts creaking back to town, grandmother's umbrella folded, a woolen rug over her shoulders against the night air and sleepy heads propped up against her knees, the oil lantern that swung from the axle throwing a swaying circle of dim light on the asphalt below.

The darkness outside the car windows conceals an endless row of little villas, summer houses that have checkered with red tile and white stucco the empty beaches, stony fields, and olive groves that lay along this piece of coastline when I first came to Sicily. So much has changed, so much is being lost, so much altered in the attempt to conserve it. The quintessential message of the Trà-pani and the Castelvetrano processions has allowed them to survive intact their inclusion in the tourist itinerary, but the pagan exuberance of Caltabellotta is surely doomed to succumb to self-consciousness. Prizzi seems neither here nor there; we had the impression that repeating the ritual now serves more to accommodate tardy tourists than to satisfy different neighborhoods, but perhaps we were suffering from a surfeit of pageantry by the time we got to Prizzi, and watched the devils dance with jaded eyes.

My doubts about the survival of the authentic spirit of the Easter processions are in part quelled the next day when I read the following article in the morning newspaper:

There is Passion and passion!

The traditional Good Friday procession that, even at Leonforte, represents the high point of the Easter ceremonies, was transformed this year into a gigantic free-for-all, which the police and the carabinieri were hard put to control. The coffin of the crucified Christ and the Madonna Addolorata were surrounded by a sea of punches, slaps, and shoves, of shouts and swear words, which paralyzed the long cortege of the faithful. The cause of it all was the dispute that for several years now has divided the senior priest of Leonforte, Father Ragusa, from the confraternities of the "Christo morto" and of the "Addolorata."

The bone of contention is the organization of the Easter week celebrations and in particular of the Friday night procession, which is a very old tradition at Leonforte and attracts a big crowd of tourists and people from the neighboring towns. A further source of tension comes from the new statue of the Madonna Addolorata, made in Malta and shipped to Leonforte, a novelty that has divided the town.

It was clear right from the beginning of the rite that feelings in the church were running high. The priests began to detach the statue of the dead Christ from the cross in order to lay it in the coffin, and this ceremony, which should be carried out in devout silence, was instead accompanied by noisy bickering. The discussion revolved around the statue of the Madonna: which one was to go out of the church, the new one from Malta or the old one? The senior priest tried to cut short the argument and harshly scolded the representatives of the confraternities, but these gave tit for tat, and the shouts could be heard over the singing of the congregation. Finally the procession got under way, but not for long. Some say it was the fault of the priests, who were urging the faithful to step lively and get the procession over with. Some say that the confraternities were responsible because they didn't like how the procession was organized and wouldn't lump it. In any case it ended in a free-for-all: the air around the statues rang with "words that shouldn't be repeated" and the two factions lit into each other.

Conclusions: the police and the carabinieri are preparing their reports, and the opposing factions are organizing a town meeting to determine how the people of Leonforte want their Easter week cel-

ebrations. Meanwhile, the traditional Sunday procession, the "Encounter," has been canceled.

Article by Melo Pontorno in *Il Giornale di Sicilia*, April 4, 1983

🌿 Sicily continues to make the headlines in the national newspapers as well as the local ones: right after Easter the Christian
Democratic party announces the nomination of a woman as mayor
of Palermo. If she is elected, Elda Pucci, the head of the newborn
division of the Children's Hospital and preferred pediatrician to
the upper-middle-class children of Palermo, will be the first woman
to be mayor of a major Italian city.

The news is greeted with equal doses of interest and skepti-
cism. Everyone is startled to see the dam of male supremacy
crumbling at what was supposed to be one of its strongest points,
but few people believe that Dr. Pucci, whose political experience
is limited to three years as a city councilor, can ever be much more
than a puppet of the Demochristian bosses who are trying to create for their party a new image, free from the suspicion of collu-
sion with the Mafia. Dr. Pucci has a record of rigorous and courageous behavior at the hospital but is profuse in her expressions
of admiration and respect for some of her more dubious, if not
infamous, predecessors and fellow party members: either she is
much more naïve than she seems or she is a great deal less sincere. Time will tell—to a delighted audience: nothing constitutes
a more pleasing pastime for the Palermitani than *cortigghiu*, "court
gossip," be it the chattering of the women in a crumbling courtyard of the old city or the sycophantic back scratching that goes
on in the courts of power. One of Palermo's least attractive char-
acteristics is the pleasure it derives from destructive criticism of
anyone who takes an initiative, and in the coming months the city
will be watching avidly for the hair in the egg—the Italian version of the fly in the ointment—and waiting with ill-concealed
amusement for the defeat of its new mayor, who has already been

described by one Palermo intellectual as "a butterfly immobilized upon a pin."

But the attention for Mayor Pucci is short-lived, brushed aside by a spray of bullets. "Massacre in Sicily" reads the headline of a national paper today. Twelve dead and five wounded in twenty-four hours. The body count is evenly divided: six here in Palermo and six in the east between Catania and Gela. Special correspondents arrive from all over Italy to paint a lurid picture of a city rotting in its structures and its morals, permeated by the stench of uncollected garbage and by the arrogance and violence of an economy and a power structure based on heroin and bullets. The authorities and the journalists discover that a woman and her eight children have been sleeping in a car parked outside the one-room house of a married daughter ever since her husband was murdered more than a year ago. Local politicians are arrested on charges of graft and corruption and then released in time to be included in the list of candidates for the coming national elections.

The newspaper articles and the debates on the radio are full of quotes and telephone calls from Palermitani bewailing the horrors of life in this city, as if all its inhabitants felt flattened by the steamroller of Mafia power. Yet in most cases it is hard not to entertain the suspicion that these protests are part of a recital of anguished impotence that requires far less effort than would be necessary to search for an alternative, viable, and constructive way of living in Palermo. Closing an eye here, turning a deaf ear there, most Palermitani have learned to navigate quite comfortably in these foul marshes, or to convince themselves at least that they live on an island within an island. "As long as they are shooting it out between themselves, the more dead the better!"

At the bottom of the front page, day after day, in a basso continuo of rumbling and belching, the news of Etna's eruption continues, keeping pace with the slow but steady descent of the three branches of lava. The ski lift and the observatory have long since been swallowed up, the people who worked there and elsewhere in the tourist industry are jobless, and it is the lower slopes, the scattered villas and summer camps, the vineyards and the fruit orchards, that now constitute the daily sacrifice to the great three-headed red dragon slithering down the mountainside. Three towns lie in the projected path—Nicolosi, Belpasso, and Regalne—and although at its present speed it will be a long time before the lava could reach the first houses, the inhabitants are justifiably uneasy and demand to know what the government intends to do. The government has no idea; among other things, it is against the law to deviate the lava flow in any way, and no one wants the responsibility of deciding where it is to end up. We have the ultimate waste disposal problem.

The debate over Etna offers a peculiar counterpoint to the discussions in the west. If some prefer to see the Mafia as a force of nature, the inevitable expression of human aggressiveness aggravated by historical circumstance, there can be no doubt about Etna. The amoral and impartial violence of the volcano is somehow fascinating and almost refreshing after the morass of moral responsibilities in Palermo. The conservationists are looking on with glee as Etna takes her revenge on the villas and tourist establishments that have violated both nature and the zoning laws. The authorities wring their hands, caught between the lava's descent and the rising anger and impatience of the local population. Meanwhile the latter has decided to put the question into more competent hands. Repeating a ritual that has successfully stopped the flow of past eruptions, they will this afternoon carry the veil of Saint Agatha, virgin, martyr, and protectress of Catania, in procession before the advancing tide of destruction.

This is another procession I am loath to miss, but my presence is required at Bosco. The heat has come, right after Easter, an early and unwelcome accomplice to the drought, and I can no longer put off in anticipation of rain the planting of the corn seed that has arrived from the United States.

Very little corn is grown in Sicily, but strangely enough peddlars hawk corn on the cob on the beach at Mondello, Palermo's fashionable watering spot. It is, however, horrid stuff, cold and clammy cobs of tough boiled orange beads that an American would be ashamed to offer to a pig, so I have hybrid seed flown over from the States—Butter and Cream, Silver Queen, Golden Bantam—paying twice as much for the airmail postage as I do for the seeds themselves. Every year I struggle to explain to Turiddu how to plant it, since he has no experience with corn, but the fact that I am a woman, an American, and a *padrona* far outweighs his lack of experience. So last year I told him to do exactly the opposite of what I wanted and had somewhat more success than in previous years. But wages have gone up and we can no longer afford to pay Turiddu for our caprices; this year I intend to do the planting myself.

If winter works miracles along the upper road to Bosco, spring is the season to take the lower track, tunneling between high green banks that close out the view on either side. In summer this is an avenue of bleached, dust-covered brambles and canes, shady except at noon, the dirt smooth as talcum powder under bare feet, the air humming with insects and heavy with the resinous perfumes of the Mediterranean underbrush. Startled turtle doves and lizards flit in front of the car in the daylight, toads and wild rabbits leap from the headlights at night. But now, in April, we drive between walls of color. Each leg of the road has its own vegetation, and each turn produces a new variation on spring's basic scheme of purple and yellow.

The first stretch cuts in straight from the highway, closed in on either side by a steep hedgerow of blackberries that are just preparing to flower, the first of the pale lavender blossoms overpowered by the white-flecked purple brilliance of the vetch. A bigger, more colorful cousin of the tares that were sown with the wheat in the Biblical parable, the vetch clings to the other plants in the hedgerow, hoisting itself up until the time comes to unfurl its buds, so many tiny purple flowers so perfectly arranged to catch the sun and the passing insects' attention that they glow like royal banners let down for some triumphant passage.

At the end of this first stretch the road runs into the *reggio trazzera*, a royal cart track originally financed and built by Sabaudian good intentions after the unification of Italy, now a muddy morass in winter and a succession of stony ruts and sandy skids in summer. Theoretically, all the farmers who use this road could unite in a consortium and obtain a government contribution to improve and surface it, but in order to make the road wide enough to qualify for state help it would be necessary to persuade the landowners whose fields border on the track to relinquish and donate a strip of land about two feet wide, a task so hopeless that I fear Tonino will never even try, although an improved road is essential if we are ever to live here all year round.

The royal track marks the edge of the plain; through the years a river of traffic and rainwater has dug a bed whose high banks hide from view the flat fields to the north and the gentle slopes leading to the southern hills. Here the germander is in bloom, low bushes of gray-green leaves and gray-blue flowers, and purple star anemones, and rockroses, their crumpled white petals and yellow centers easily confused with those of the true white roses that grow here too. Farther on the wild garlic is bursting into bloom. A cluster of delicate white bells strung from a single stem, wild garlic is a terrible temptation: so lovely to look at, so long-lived once cut, but so overwhelmingly garlic-scented as to make the best-aired room uninhabitable. The street vendors in Palermo pass them off on the unwary; I once heard them being sold as lilies of the valley to an elderly lady, much to the disgust of her chauffeur, who was holding them at arm's length while his mistress paid the bill.

At the foot of the hill we leave the royal track and climb south between low banks and vineyards, where full sunlight brings out vivid colors again: crimson sulla that has escaped from some past planting to sow itself each year along the roadside, more rockroses, fuchsia-colored here, and the strange crook of the honeywort with its dangling yellow-and-purple bells, the intense blue of the bugloss, *erba viperina*, used by the Greeks to cure viper bite, and the purple-blue of the pitch trefoil.

At the top of the rise, beyond the two small houses of our nearest neighbors, our own house comes into view. This is the back door, the working side of Bosco: it is big and bare and graceless from this angle, the windowless walls and big iron door of the *cantina* where the wine is kept seem unwelcoming and un-interesting, and the flower beds are hidden behind a big ramp of earth and stones that serves for loading the tractor onto the truck. We drive past the kitchen door and beyond the house, park the car under the budding mulberry trees, and walk back toward Bosco's frivolous side.

The last of the narcissus, withered and papery, are lost to sight in the brilliance of the freesia, the ranunculi, and the big yellow calendulas. For the first time dark purple spears thrust up from the iris I planted two years ago around three sides of the stone seat that was originally the base of the old wine press. This giant brick of gray travertine is one more instance of my fortuitous landscaping: one might think that its site, on the edge of the road, in the shade of the palm, was the result of careful if rather unin-spired planning. It isn't. That's as far as the bulldozer managed to haul it from the about-to-be-rebuilt *cantina* before the steel cable broke. I feel a great affinity for that stone: surrounded by flowers, we both strive to convey the impression that we are not mere flotsam and jetsam, but that intention brought us to such unexpected shores.

The afternoon is long and warm; I putter about the garden well into the sunset, snipping off the dead heads of the grape hyacinths, discovering the first blossoms on the strawberry plants and on the white musk rose, and smelling the meager flowering of my poor stunted lilac bushes, inappropriate and ill at ease in the Mediterranean setting to which I have constrained them in tribute to the New England garden of my childhood vacations. As the light fades to lavender and dusk I realize that, unheralded and unobserved, there has been a changing of the guard. The swallows are back, chittering and swooping above the eaves in search of their evening meal, while the robins that winter in the almond trees and add their spot of red to the rosebush outside the kitchen window have gone without my noticing, having checked out only with the magpies, elegant scolds who are, together with the crows and the sparrows, our only permanent residents.

A distant mewing call comes from the olives in the valley, announcing the return of the little Athenian owls who used to live in the eaves of the Blundas' roof, which sticks out at a right angle, eye-level to our upstairs corridor windows. We would watch them from the windows, and they would stare back, shifting from foot to foot in a worried dance and clucking angrily at this invasion of their privacy. One flew in the bathroom window one evening; I walked in to find him sitting on the radiator glaring at me, as outraged as if I had caught him with his pants down.

To our great distress the cat ate two of the owls, and now the survivors come no closer than the olive grove, but we can still hear them calling throughout the night. I wait in vain, however, for the return of the falcons who used to nest in the pits and hollows of the stable walls before we rebuilt the house. Sometimes a falcon will still circle lazily overhead on a hot summer's day, but none has found a place to rest in the new house. This is a grave disappointment, for the house's full name, from the *contrada* in which it stands, is Bosco Falconeria, the "Falconry Woods." I fancy that Frederick II, master falconer and author of history's first scientific treatise on hawking, hunted in these hills while he was laying siege to the last rebels who had taken refuge on the mountain behind Alcamo. But the woods have long since been cut down, and the falcons will surely never return to nest in a place as frequently, if intermittently, inhabited as Bosco is now.

The next morning Tonino and Francesco plow the vegetable garden with the big rotary tiller so that Natalia and I can plant the corn, Natalia staking the rows and sprinkling the seed in the furrows that I dig with the hoe. A Sicilian hoe, with its wide forged-iron blade and thick, stubby wooden handle, weighs at least eight pounds and must be brought up over one's head and then down hard with a shove from the lower back muscles, if it is to make any impression at all on the heavy clay soil. In the early days roars of laughter would ring out across the fields as Turiddu Vivona watched me struggling to master the beast, but nowadays I can wield the hoe with what at least looks like ease and effectiveness.

We plant some squash too, more American imports, butter-nut, acorn, and pattypan, whose delicate white scalloping fascinates the Sicilians. But the soil is already very dry, and if Demeter doesn't pull a few strings with the rain god there will be neither corn nor squash at Bosco this summer.

🌱 Wisteria blossoms drip like early grapes from the railings and balconies in Palermo, and Maria Vica and I must visit the Villa de Cordova. At the end of the seventeenth century it became fashionable among the Palermo aristocracy to build splendid villas in the luxuriant orchards and citrus groves that stretched for miles outside the walls of the city, where they could take refuge during the summer from the heat and smells of the city. According to the English historian Denis Mack Smith, more than two hundred of these villas were begun, and the pompous magnificence of their facades—behind which the villa often remained uncompleted—was a major factor in the ultimate bankruptcy of the aristocratic class.

The spreading tide of modern construction on the outskirts of the city has engulfed what remains of these villas; high-rise condominiums dwarf those lying nearer the center, while smaller houses, commercial enterprises, junkyards, and repair shops have encroached upon the more remote, flooding the surrounding parks and invading the stables and the outbuildings. Spare parts and rusting chassis prop up toppling Grecian urns, and laundry flaps on the scraggy remains of exotic shrubbery.

The later villas, the more famous and splendid examples of this fashion, are to be found in Bagheria to the east: Villa Valguarnera, Villa Trabia, Villa Palagonia, this last produced by the warped creativity of a humpbacked prince, who ringed his garden walls with grotesque stone monsters and lined his ballroom with distorting mirrors, so that all his guests appeared crooked too and wherever he looked he could keep a jealous eye on his beautiful young wife.

The villas to the west in the Piano dei Colli are smaller and somewhat simpler, although almost all of them bear the hallmark of the Sicilian baroque, the double staircase that curves up the facade to the piano nobile. The inventiveness of the Sicilian architects lay in the variation with which they were able to treat this theme: each family wanted its staircase to be similar but unique. At the Villa de Cordova the curve of the staircase is repeated in the wisteria vine below it, and Maria Vica and I have a long-standing date to see it at the height of its flowering.

It is already hot at ten o'clock when Maria Vica comes by to pick me up, and a slight haze tempers hue and texture, the perfect light for the lichened walls and lavender flowers that we are to look at. The winding country road that once led past quiet villas to the little fishing village of Sferracavallo is now a major artery for traffic heading to the *autostrada* for western Sicily. The stream of cars whisks us past the big Villa Boscogrande, a fashionable nightclub lodged in the Lampedusa family villa that was the setting for the opening chapter in *The Leopard*, and drivers honk impatiently as we brake to turn left through the Villa de Cordova gateway, the shape of the urn-topped pillars barely discernible under a swathing of tattered ivy.

The charm of the villa lies in its scale, its perfect, intimate, livable proportions. The courtyard where we find ourselves is less than a hundred feet long and half again as wide. A low row of stables encloses it on either side, their flat roofs topped by an openwork stone balustrade that flows around the courtyard from the gate, borders the terrace that runs across the second story of the villa, then sweeps down and around the curving arms of the double staircase. The simple facade above the terrace is broken by shallow pilasters whose rich golden brown stands out against the pale gold of the walls and the mossy gray of the stonework.

The courtyard itself is a tangle of unkempt and faded green: four palm trees droop gray and withered fronds over weedy gravel and leggy thistles. In the central bed a hibiscus bush, unpruned and shapeless, is surrounded by spikes of deep-purple iris and the pale violet flowers of a rambling scented geranium, thus stating in the foreground the range of hue to be admitted within the curve of the staircase, where the thick gray trunk of the wisteria vine echoes exactly the arc of the broad stone banister, swirling up like a spiral of smoke to lose itself in the cloud of lavender flowers suspended in the stairs' embrace, a watery cascade of purples and violets laced with the first tiny leaves of green.

Below the wisteria an arch leads underneath the house to some rear courtyard: a peasant woman with a washtub balanced on her hip peers out at us from the shadows. A pop song from a transistor radio accompanies the hammering noises that come from one of the stables, but the villa itself is closed; the upper windows are boarded up behind their broken panes, and slatted shutters losing their paint bar the lower ones. The structure itself looks sound: surely this villa is not in any danger of falling. Having withstood revolutions and earthquakes it will merely flake away, a sliver of lichened stone here, a sprinkle of plaster dust there, neglect nibbling at the marble and sanding down the stucco.

The sun that filters through the overcast floods the courtyard with the same warm, nostalgic glow that lights Lampedusa's memoirs of his childhood in the villa of Santa Margherita Belice, *Places of My Infancy*. To see these villas in this light is to be exempted from mental acrobatics; it blocks out the gray winter of their present decay, the contempt with which Sicily treats her past; it tempers the harsh glare of a Sicilian summer sun baking the vast feudal holdings, three-quarters of the island, that were milked dry to build such mansions, each penny that could be squeezed from starving peasant labor invested in pomp and luxury rather than in roads, new crops, irrigation. I am grateful for such an exemption: it is too much of an effort to juggle all at once these other seasons together with the exquisite taste and loveliness of the flower-lit facade before me now and to keep all three aloft in some coherent construct.

Maria Vica has something else to show me, a recent discovery she is eager to share. We leave the Villa de Cordova and make our way to Acquasanta, a little fishing village hidden in the westernmost corner of the Bay of Palermo in the shadow of Villa Igea, Palermo's most glamorous hotel. The narrow strip of land between sea and steep mountain has offered little foothold for the city's advance, and despite considerable new construction, Acquasanta retains the character of a village.

We park the car in the piazza, a square swaying with tall, sparse palms that look out over a little port cluttered with pleasure boats, a few magnificent yachts, and dozens of brightly striped fishing dinghies. Maria Vica leads me into an alleyway, around and behind a turn-of-the-century house with two doors leading, according to the words carved over their lintels, to hot baths and cold baths. We follow the alley down into a courtyard half filled by a voluminous tangle of vines, wisteria, and bougainvillea knotted together by white rambler roses, which have escaped the pruning shears of the Villa Igea gardeners and tumbled over the hotel wall. A little two-storied house occupies one side of the courtyard, its facade proclaiming in faded letters "Establishment for Mineral Baths: Sacerdoti Pandolfo Bros."

The upper windows of this house are shuttered, but some sort of life goes on downstairs: an old man in an undershirt is repairing a motorbike inside the front door, a young woman in slippers flaps out of the house and up the alley, then comes back shortly with a can of Coke in hand, giving only a quick, uninterested glance at my attempts to focus my camera in this narrow space. What interests me lies to the right of the house, where six feet of railing and a gate mark a passageway that tunnels under the second story of the house and opens on a little ravine, where natural rock and sunlight are visible, thick foliage and a faint tinkle testifying to a vestige of the thermal waters.

Maria Vica has brought me here to look at the tiles that cover the walls of this passageway, hand-painted majolica squares each bearing a grape leaf and a generous bunch of purple grapes, whose tendrils twist and link from tile to tile, encasing the walls in a network of curving branches and purple clusters, a naïve echo of the wisteria we have seen so much of this morning. On the wall opposite the gate a large marble plaque reads:

THIS MINERAL WATER
CONSIDERED SALUTARY BY THE ANCIENTS
WAS EMPLOYED FOR THE REBELLIOUS OBSTRUCTIONS OF THE BOWELS
AGAINST CHRONIC RHEUMATISM GOUT GALLSTONES PROSTATE ETC.
SCIENCE, HAVING THEN STUDIED ITS CHEMICAL QUALITIES,
SAID TO IT: SULPHATE, MAGNESIAC, FERRUGINOUS!
THUS CONFIRMING ITS THERAPEUTIC ACTION
IN THE AFORESAID MALADIES.
CLINICAL EXPERIENCE SANCTIONED ITS EMPLOYMENT
WITH REPEATED PROVEN SUCCESS.
PATIENTS PRAISED ITS EFFICACY
FOR THE BENEFITS THEY DERIVED.
ITS DIVULGATION FOR THE GOOD OF HUMANITY WAS PROMOTED
BY IMPORTANT AND ILLUSTRIOUS CITIZENS
BY MERITORIOUS AND INDUSTRIOUS DOCTORS.
IN HOMAGE
THE JURY OF THE NATIONAL EXPOSITION OF PALERMO
GAVE IT A MOST DESERVED AWARD.
JUNE 7, 1892

From one courtyard to another we have jumped almost two centuries. The innocent faith in science, industry, and progress carved into this piece of marble has nothing to do with the weary sophistication of the Villa de Cordova. We are fully into the last splendid blossoming of the city, the Belle Epoque, when the huge industrial fortunes of the Florios, of the Whitakers and the Inghams, English merchants of Marsala wine, joined with the dwindling fortunes of the aristocracy to finance Palermo's last great moment of architectural glory, the villas and the town houses designed by the Art Nouveau architect Ernesto Basile. It is the period of the Teatro Massimo, whose stage is second in size in Europe only to that of the Paris Opéra, and of the Villa Igea next door, whose halls, frescoed with maidens wading through water lilies and carved into sinuous floral designs, welcomed the royalty of all Europe, kings and kaisers, who considered Palermo to be a watering spot of the greatest gaiety and opulence.

The First World War, which was soon to extinguish this last brief blaze, seems to have smothered taste as well. After the pretentious monumentality of the Fascist epoch, pure unadulterated ugliness has taken over, "modern" cement and stucco blocks that rapidly age and discolor into uniform dreariness, whimsical villas afflicted with wrought iron and tile on which even the most luxuriant landscaping cannot confer charm. Not that the means are lacking: if Palermo ranks seventieth among Italian cities in per capita income, it holds seventh place for per capita consumption, a mysterious discrepancy that can be explained only by heroin, graft, and tax evasion. But licit or illicit, it all flows into the status symbols of mass consumption: BMW cars, Gucci luggage, *Les Must* de Cartier.

Maria Vica and I still have some time to spare before we return to our respective duties, and we decide to continue our drive out past Villa Igea and along the narrow road that runs between the cliffs of Monte Pellegrino and the sea. We are leaving Palermo behind us: the city gives way to summer beach houses, the sun burns through the haze and lights up the sparkling sea, the glistening white of the stucco, the bright crimson and fuchsia of the bougainvillea, the tropic green of palms and banana plants in exotic backyards. Two-thirds of the way around the mountain we arrive at the beach of Mondello. The broad, tree-lined streets are peaceful now in the spring noon, the little houses with their gingerbread turrets and neo-Pompeian swags, Belle Epoque scaled down to a bourgeois pocketbook, mostly shuttered still; the beach itself, a wide cove between two mountains, is still free of cabins and crowds, with only a student or two skipping school to lie in the sun and a few hardy German tourists actually swimming. We drive on past the Bathing Establishment, a vast, ivory-colored wedding cake standing on piles in the water, and the little fishing port, crowded with seafood restaurants and stalls selling boiled octopus, raw mussels, or dark purple sea urchins that taste of iodine.

The sight of the sea and the smell of the clean air tell me that I am ready to turn my back on Palermo, on its opulent history and present decay. I want landscapes bleached clean by the sea and the sun, the illusion of classical simplicity, the pungent smells and sounds of the Sicilian summer.

🌿 The first tastes of summer, like vegetables out of season, come dear. The next weekend is a long one, since Monday the twenty-fifth is a holiday commemorating the liberation of Rome from the German troops, but we cannot make use of it as I would like. The delivery of some new furniture becomes the occasion for a domestic revolution: like a dog that gets up and circles about on his bed before settling down to sleep again, every so often we move ourselves about in the hopes of accommodating ourselves more comfortably to the cramped dimensions of our Palermo apartment. Saturday and Sunday find us painting walls and shifting furniture despite the sun outside the windows.

I have convinced everyone, however, that the proper reward for all this hard work is a trip to Erice. Or at least almost everyone: Francesco, just turned fifteen, has lost interest in family outings, so it is Natalia, Tonino, and I who set off on Monday morning.

The mountains that form an almost unbroken chain from the Straits of Messina west along the northern coast of Sicily run past Palermo, swing round the gulfs of Carini and Castellammare, and then reach out to Capo San Vito, the western tip of the island, whose abrupt outline and winking lighthouse we can see from Bosco. The southern shore is much flatter, however, a long coastal plain that ranges from the Arab near Tràpani, Marsala, and Mazzara to the Greek of Selinunte, Agrigento, and Gela. This plain, which is very broad in its western tract, is broken only at the beginning, where Mount Erice rises to guard the port of Trà-pani. Erice is a smallish mountain, really, only 2,454 feet high, but the improbability of its position, all alone at the edge of the sea, gives an impression of greater height. And of great mystery: this is one of the most sacred spots of the Mediterranean, sacred long before man had discovered the means of recording and transmitting the reasons for this reverence.

Actually, Erice was never Greek: it belonged to the Elymians, who together with the Sicels and the Sicans inhabited Sicily when the Greeks began to colonize the island in the eighth century B.C. Very little is known about these peoples, neither when nor from where they came to Sicily, but the Elymians are the most myste-rious of all; the one distinct trait that can be ascribed to them is a remarkable capacity to absorb more complex cultures, whether it be the Greek, as in the Elymian city of Segesta, or the Cartha-ginian, as in Erice.

The lack of factual information about the origins of Erice is compensated for by a great abundance of myth, which traces its founding back to the very beginning of creation, when the Titans revolted against their father, Uranus. Cronus castrated his father with a sickle and threw both sickle (hence the name Sicily) and genitals into the sea off Cape Drepanum (Tràpani). To mark the spot where her ancestor's genitals fell, Aphrodite rose from the waves in a cockleshell chariot and created the mountain of Erice, claiming it as her own. It was here that the goddess brought Butes, the Argonaut, when he succumbed to the sirens' song and threw himself into the sea, and here that she bore him a son, Eryx, who gave the mountain its name.

The Carthaginians worshiped Aphrodite here in the guise of Astarte: each spring a flock of white doves was released toward North Africa and the sister shrine of Sicca Veneria. After nine days the flock would return with a red dove in the lead, Astarte, symbol of fertility, whose return signaled the reawakening of nature. The Greeks arriving in Sicily also took up the worship of Aphrodite at Erice. When Daedalus, unlike his unfortunate son,

Icarus, managed to escape successfully from Crete by means of the wax-and-feather wings and fly safely to Sicily, he entered the service of Kokalos, king of the Sicans, and is said to have forged a magnificent golden honeycomb as an offering to her shrine there.

The Romans maintained the cult and the shrine, especially after the Sibyl advised seeking the help of Venus Erycina during the Second Punic War, but the Elymian town appears to have been abandoned until the advent of the Saracens, who built a fortress on an outcropping connected to the bulk of the mountain by a narrow bridge of rock. This practically invincible citadel was besieged by Count Roger in 1077 and only fell thanks to the intervention of Saint Julian, who loosed a pack of hounds on the unfortunate infidels. (From then on the mountain was known as Monte San Giuliano until Mussolini restored its classical name.) After this Erice became a medieval town, and nothing of its classical heritage remains today, except for a length of Punic wall and perhaps something in the faces of its women, to whom Ibn Jubayr, true to character even in the very last entry in his diary before he set sail from Tràpani to Spain, attributes "the fame of being the most beautiful on the island—may Allah soon deliver them as slaves to the Muslims."

The feast of Aphrodite Erycina was celebrated on the twenty-third of April: I have come as close as I can, and she is showing us her appreciation by giving us an absolutely perfect day. We speed across western Sicily under a cloudless sky, and the red carpet of sulla flowers is out to welcome us as we drive along an avenue of golden fireworks, the bright flowering of the acacia trees that line the *autostrada*. As we take the turnoff west, the temple of Segesta floats briefly above us before we are sucked into the dark of a long tunnel and spewed forth onto the plain of Tràpani, gently rolling hills of green wheat and red sulla, the chartreuse of the burgeoning vineyards and the warm rust of bare fields waiting to break out in a rash of bright yellow melons.

Erice beckons us all the way with its dark green slopes and its ragged crest of castle towers. Just before Tràpani we circle round to take the road up the northern flank, around switchbacks and hairpin turns that swing us back and forth, like a slide projector gone haywire, now a dazzling view straight down to the bay of Bonagìa, sparkling azure and turquoise before the distant purple mountains of the Cape, and then back to the slope we are climbing, cool shady pine forests carpeted with swatches of color, with borage and calendula, with thick pink clusters of *Fedia cornucopiae*, and solitary scarlet dots of asparagus pea. Here and there the dark green of the pines is interrupted by the brilliant fuchsia blush of the flowering Judas tree. There is no room to park the car, fortunately, or I should forsake Aphrodite and be off like a truffle hound, snuffling through the underbrush in pursuit of Flora.

At the end of its climb, the road circles round to the south of the summit and finishes in a broad piazza filled with cars and tourist buses, which with the town at its back looks out over an almost vertical drop to the plain twenty-four hundred feet below. If it were an absolutely clear day we could see Africa, but as usual the horizon is veiled over by haze and we have to be content with the nearer checkerboard of brown and green fields edged by the uneven line of the Sicilian coast skirting the Stagnone, the lagoon of Marsala where the small island of Mothya, once a thriving Phoenician port, is just visible. Land fades gradually and geometrically to water across the grid of the *saline*, the ancient salt flats with their windmills, tiny from this distance. To the west the Egadi Islands float in the haze, the dark, humpbacked turtles of Levanzo, Marittimo, and Favignana, and at our feet the city of Tràpani stretches the long arms of its breakwaters into the blue.

Beneath the low stone parapet that borders the piazza, the mountain has hung out all its banners to welcome back Astarte, to celebrate Aphrodite: yellow, orange, celeste, and midnight blue; mayflowers, calendulas, borage, and purple vetch; great bolts of silk unrolling as they fall.

It is almost noon when we head into the warren of narrow streets, but we have no fixed itinerary to respect other than a visit to the fourteenth-century Matrice with its carved portal and intricate rose window, the purchase of Erice's special almond cakes in a pastry shop just off the main square, and then, after lunch, the castle. Erice is a town to wander in; its charm is one of scale and contrast. Tiny streets patterned with gray cobbles wind among low houses, stark peasant dwellings, or little palaces with baby baroque facades that testify to former wealth, and innumerable abandoned churches, boarded up and crumbling. The streets themselves are silent and empty; low voices and the ring of a child's laughter come through the gates that allow a glimpse of sheltered courtyards, short flights of stairs, fruit trees, and carefully tended flowerpots. The life of the town is hidden from the public eye, played out behind the walls of these green and flowering court-yards, seemingly isolated yet linked one to another by a sense of community that shows itself in the absolute cleanliness of the streets, the neatly clipped box hedges and well-pruned trees in the public gardens, the well-kept appearance of the houses, even those a much-diminished population has left empty.

The cool gray stones, half hidden by thick mantles of dark and polished ivy, are the outward armor of reserve and civic pride, shadowy and impenetrable, unlike the yellow limestone and the whitewashed plaster of the plains below that seethe and overflow, spilling out people and garbage and laundry and passions and noise into hot and dusty streets.

We walk along the western edge, where the flowers have crept up from the pine forests to attack the old Punic walls, huge blocks of stone that are all that remains of Erice's Carthaginian era. They drip with green, the colored tide advances, tunneling between the stones and dancing triumphantly along the top of the wall. We squeeze sideways through a narrow arched passage that likes to think itself the narrowest street in Europe and peer into the courtyards, each of us picking the house we would most like to live in, the play-house scale of so much of the town an invitation to such games. And finally, prompted by the growlings of our stomachs, we chart a zigzag course back to the southern side and the Taverna Re Aceste.

Each time I come back to this restaurant I'm afraid it won't be as good as I remember, and each time I am relieved to find it unchanged, neither the famous luxury restaurant that in any case would lie beyond our means and interest nor the rustic Sicilian cooking, excellent ingredients in simple combinations, that I would seek elsewhere. This is food for Erice, subtle, mysterious seasoning, intimations of flavoring prepared with pride and restraint.

Replete with *risotto alla marinara*, *rigatoni all'Ericina*, and grilled shrimp, we roll gently down the path that leads to the castle, not the Castello Pepoli, which is nineteenth-century neo-Gothic, but the real Castello di Venere, the Saracen and then Norman fortress, built at the very edge of the rock. Its walls supposedly enclose the site of Aphrodite's temple, but there is nothing left of that to see. In fact the castle itself has rather little to offer, and its appeal lies in leaning over the walls and parapets to enjoy the spectacular view.

I prefer to focus closer, however, to stick my nose right up to the castle walls and discover the world of tiny plants that cling to the stones and fill the crevices, a dwarf vegetation growing in a thimbleful of earth: camomile, grape hyacinths, feathery tufts of fennel, and an infinite variety of stonecrop, the succulent plants that appear to live on nothing, their fat-leaved branches bursting into miniature stars of pink, lavender, and white. And then, most appropriate here, a slightly bigger succulent whose smooth circular leaves dented in the middle have earned it the name Venus's-navelwort—*ombelico di Venere* in Italian. A square foot of these walls in spring equals an entire field in the richness and the variety of color and texture, and I am perfectly happy to peer close, forgetting the larger setting.

On our way home we stop at the farm. Bosco too is doing its best: the iris are magnificent, the clematis in the courtyard has its first flowers, and the air around the gate is heavy with the scent of the *zàgara*, the waxy white flowers of the lemon tree. Natalia picks an armful of wild gladiola, the elongated and intensely pink blossoms smaller and much more elegant than their cultivated cousins, while I pick artichokes and spinach.

Despite the beauty of the day and the abundance of blossom, I feel discouraged. Bosco looks neglected; the grass that was so green and lovely a few weeks ago is out of control, while the nasturtiums under the rosebush are stunted and spindly for want of watering. A truck clanks and clatters up the hill, and Mr. Amato climbs down to say hello. He has a load of oil drums filled with water: he and his cousin are setting out melon seedlings, and the soil is so dry they have to truck in water and ladle it out around each plant. He has had luck with the melons planted from seed here, almost all of which have germinated, but none of his tomatoes has come up.

A curled leaf, a withered flower, a yellowed spear of grass— these are the first intimations that we are already, prematurely, past the peak, that the sun so pleasant on our bare arms today has set to its long slow task of leaching out all color and coolness from the earth, that Sicily is exhausting its riches in the exuberance of a spendthrift spring, a brave front of color that will soon give way to the bare-bones economy of summer, the husbanding of moisture and the tilling of dust.

Chapter Seven

❧ That we should speak about the "merry" month of May, set our kindergarten classes to making May baskets, and entertain innocent images of village lads and lasses courting around the Maypole is evidence of very selective transmission. We have forgotten that May, the month of the hawthorn tree, was sacred to Artemis, the Virgin Huntress, the Lady of the Wild Things. It was a month of enforced chastity, during which no weddings were allowed in either Athens or Rome, and even when it was over the goddess was propitiated by carrying hawthorn torches in the wedding processions and by putting hawthorn leaves in the cradles of newborn babies.

The hawthorn itself shares in May's ambivalence. Because of its perfume, suggestive of female sexuality, the Turks consider the hawthorn flower an erotic symbol, but in northern Europe the hawthorn belongs to witches (which says quite a bit about different cultural attitudes toward women), and it was thought that if hawthorn branches were brought into a house, someone in the household would die. As for Sicily, in this matter at least the Levantine appears to neutralize the Norman, which is fortunate, considering how much we depend upon the red-berried hawthorn branches to decorate the house at Christmas.

The Church has encompassed these traditions by dedicating the month of May to the Virgin Mary and preaching the observance of chastity in her honor, just as it has tried to appropriate May Day as Labor Day by making it the feast of Saint Joseph the Laborer, so that now, throughout the towns of Italy, the trade unions parade in the morning behind tractors and red banners, and in the afternoon the ACLI, the Catholic Workers' Association, carry out the statue of San Giuseppe.

Although the Maypole can be found in northern Italy, according to the Sicilian ethnographer Giuseppe Pitré, there is no evidence that it has ever been used in Sicily. In many parts of the island, however, it was customary for the women to decorate themselves and their houses with *fiori di maggio*, mayflowers, the gaudy crown daisies that invade the roadsides and the fallow lands in shoulder-high stands of cadmium yellow. These flowers were also useful for an appealingly restful form of spring cleaning; on May Day the housewives would throw a bunch under the bed while reciting what can be loosely translated as:

> Flowers of May, flowers of May,
> Make the bedbugs go away!

These older traditions would seem to have been replaced by a new one, intermittent and sinister, reflecting the darker side of the month of May. For Sicily, May Day is now above all the commemoration of the massacre of Portella della Ginestra in 1947, when the famous bandit Salvatore Giuliano, popular hero become tool of the allied reactionary and Mafia forces, opened fire with an automatic rifle on a group of peasants and workers and their families who were holding a May Day picnic. And last year on the eve of the holiday, Pio La Torre, the regional secretary of the Communist party, and his driver were gunned down in the street on their way to the party offices.

At the various commemorative services that are being held this year, everyone is talking about the latest manifestation of the arrogance and power of the Mafia, the just-released newspaper story about Cardinal Pappalardo's Easter visit to the Ucciardone, the old Bourbon fortress that serves Palermo as a jail. As at Christmas, the cardinal had intended to say mass in the main courtyard and then visit with the prisoners. But the mafiosi do not appreciate the position the cardinal has been taking in his sermons, and they have decided to make this known. Not one of the 1,025 prisoners left his cell to attend the service; after an hour's wait the cardinal returned to the Curia without having performed the rite. In case the message was not clear enough, the next day all the bosses and their henchmen turned out to hear the jail chaplain say the regular Sunday mass.

❧ Last year we paid our respects to May's double nature by interrupting the long weekend in the country to come back into Palermo for Pio La Torre's funeral, since we wished to be present at the close of a long history of courageous battles, in which La Torre had frequently risked his life and now finally lost. He began his career in postwar Sicily as a trade union organizer and a leader in the land reform movement, marching at the head of the peasants who went out to occupy the great feudal *latifondi*. Unlike some fifty or more colleagues who were shot down in those terrible years, La Torre survived the opposition of the landowning classes and of the Mafia and was called north to work in Rome. He returned to Sicily only a few years ago as regional secretary of his party, and became a leader in the anti-Mafia battle and a promoter of the Sicilian peace movement.

The Italian government has chosen to install its allotment of 112 Cruise missiles at Comiso, a small town on the coastal plain of southeastern Sicily, in an area that has evolved remarkably over the past twenty years thanks to the creation of agricultural cooperatives specializing in greenhouse production of early fruit and vegetables. For the most part this has been a collective conquest, and the resulting wealth has been distributed fairly equitably, without causing drastic disruptions in the traditional fabric of life there. But now Comiso faces a triple invasion: the several thousand American soldiers who have begun to arrive, bringing their dollar economy with them; the European peace movement that is camped out there with its rainbow flags and often startling customs; and the Mafia, which is buying up land in the area as fast as it can, recycling its illicit earnings in the rich local agriculture and preparing to conquer the 300 billion lire's worth of building contracts and the market for drugs and prostitution the military base represents. Within the movement to block the installation of the Cruise at Comiso, La Torre was the first to call attention to this potential marriage between missiles and Mafia, an insight that is thought to have cost him his life.

The funeral procession assembled outside the Porta Nuova, behind the Royal Palace, and by the time the last red flags had filed under the gate, the hearse had gone down the Corso, turned at the Quattro Canti, followed the Via Maqueda past the opera, and was approaching Piazza Politeama, where the speeches were to take place. La Torre was accompanied on his last march by those who had marched with him in Sicily, gone on strike in the north, demonstrated at Comiso. A ribbon of red banners stretched as far as the eye could see, linking together the most disparate groups in a pageant of contemporary Italian history: subdued and dignified delegations from the left-wing administrations of Milan, Florence, and Bologna; blue-overalled workers from the factories and steel mills of Turin, Taranto, and Bagnoli, weary from a night's train ride, occasionally breaking into a hoarse rendering of the "Internazionale"; the flamboyant youth of the left and of the peace movement, promising with clenched fist and chanted slogan to carry on the fight. Dark islands in the current, the delegations from the towns of Sicily marched, black-suited policemen carrying the municipal standards and *contadini*, La Torre's companions in the march on the land, old now, shoulders bent, the napes of their necks creased and brown above their starched white shirt collars, weeping silently.

🌿 This year May Day falls on a Sunday, depriving us of a holiday but giving us a good occasion for a private spring rite, a feast we hold every year at Bosco for a few of Tonino's friends and colleagues. I call it a feast for want of a better word: picnic, cook-out, or barbecue would sound too urban, or at best suburban, if used in such an agrarian context, and there is more than a little of the spring propitiary orgy in the amount of food and wine that is consumed.

The five men—a teacher, a farmer, a government inspector, and two technicians—who come with their respective families are all involved in some way in agriculture, and all of them have their roots in the land as well. With the exception of the farmer, they are the first generation to have reached higher education in families belonging mostly to the *burgisi*, the intermediate class of small farmers owning and working their own land, who in the complicated hierarchy of rural Sicily were neither peasants nor yet quite middle class. Each one, even those who live in Palermo, has at least a small piece of land in his hometown, some olives, the odd fruit tree, the little vegetable plot worked by an obliging uncle, monument to that Italian dedication to the homegrown and the genuine, which has supplied much of today's menu, from the boiled fava beans to the artichokes we are about to roast.

Enzo and Nicola set the children to shelling fava beans, Giuseppina and Vita pound open the artichokes to receive the mint and garlic I am chopping up. Considerable controversy accompanies the preparation of the meat—*castrato*, castrated goat, for which the Sicilians have an inexplicable passion. It must be atavistic, a hangover from some ancient age in which the sacrifice of a castrated goat was a rare and festive opportunity to eat meat, since nothing less could explain this taste for gamy mouthfuls that are difficult to chew and impossible to digest.

Should we make the classic *ammogghiu* marinade—abundant garlic pounded up with ripe peeled tomatoes, salt, and olive oil—or use lemon juice with oregano? Should we put it on before the slices go on the fire or spoon it over the already roasted meat? Alcamo, Tràpani, Partinico, Prizzi, and Chiusa Sclafani are represented (New York has nothing to contribute), and their various customs are compared and weighed before we decide, as we always have, on a side dish of *ammogghiu* for those who want it. As Pina pounds up the garlic, she informs me that my mortar and pestle of hand-blown French glass is very inefficient, and I remind her laughingly that for two years now she has promised to bring me a better one.

Our feast does, however, resemble an American barbecue in the way that men who hardly ever put hand to pot become expert cooks at the mere sight of an open fire, which in this case they are lighting out at the edge of the garden, igniting a huge tangle of vine branches put aside from the winter's pruning for just such an occasion. It roars up in a rapid blaze, then subsides into the ash-covered coals necessary for the artichokes' slow roasting. Tonino and Nicola are cleaning off the discarded bedsprings that have proved to be the perfect grill for large quantities of meat (we baptized them with sausages for sixty—linkless three-foot Sicilian sausages in skewered coils), and Enzo and Tommaso carry out the courtyard table and set it in the shade of the mulberry trees. By this time the fava beans are cooked, and we slide unawares into eating, popping bean after irresistible bean into our mouths and washing them down with wine as we stand around waiting for the meat to cook.

There is as always much more food than we can possibly eat, but everyone makes a valiant effort, and the strong white Bosco wine does much to extend the advisable limits. The trays of pastry that Pina and Anna bring out at the end, fancy store-bought cakes and homemade *cassateddi* filled with sweet ricotta, are greeted by groans of despair.

"Ah," says Andrea, "my uncle always used to say that pastries are like the cardinal at Easter. The cathedral is so packed with people come for High Mass there isn't a spare centimeter to move in, but as soon as the cardinal appears, a pathway opens miraculously to make room for him to pass."

Under the influence of the wine, the conversation takes a May Day turn, a bawdy Fellinian recollection of postwar provincial boyhood, the world of *Amarcord*, of making do, of getting by on big ambitions and no cash, or, as someone succinctly puts it, of jerking off on soda pop while dreaming of women and champagne.

Maudlin from a surfeit of wine, food, and memories, the men stagger as far as the almond trees, where they collapse in the grass to bewail the disappointments of age and the weight of family responsibilities, or so Francesco, a sober but very amused initiate, later reports; while the women—the real ones, the chains and fetters, with not a Gradisca among us—putter around cleaning up.

In northern Italy Sunday lunch in a country tavern has become a ritual search for an antidote to a week of fast foods and industrial menus:

> The Sunday drive outside the city becomes a voyage in time in search of roots, of irremediably lost origins; an attempt to recuperate through the mediation of the dinner table (talisman and magic object) slices of the past by techniques of cooking that are impossible in the city; to recuperate with the magic help of soups and stews by now mythical in urban households, a universe of lost smells and flavors that restores—in an illusory fashion, as with all drugged liturgies inevitably destined to alter the relationship of time and space—the ghost of a lost culture: a striking mass phenomenon solicited by a sharp hunger, cultural rather than physiological, a valuable testimony for investigating society's unconscious mechanisms.
>
> A double nutritional track has by now become diffuse, a culinary double helix, in which to the quick, light modern cooking, frozen and even precooked . . . is contrasted Sunday's gastronomic flight to the most intransigent country traditions, rustic and aboriginal.
>
> Piero Camporesi, *Alimentazione, folclore, società*

But in Sicily we are still one stage earlier. The people who come to Bosco today are still holding on to the substance as well as the memory of an earlier culture, which they struggle daily and at great cost to accommodate to modern urban life, attempting to reconcile slow cooking to office hours, rushing through city traffic to shell their homegrown peas, dedicating their afternoon off to a trip back to the *paese* to stock up on wine, oil, and fresh vegetables. Bosco is an artificial setting, perhaps, restored by a nostalgic professor and an American expatriate, but today it has offered the opportunity for a collective return, grass roots to sink back into under the shade of an almond tree.

And, for at least some of our guests, an opportunity to forget most pressing worries: with us today is the man from Alcamo who received the threatening phone calls. He and his wife have just begun to go out again, and rumor has it that "the question is settled," although we do not know how. In the meantime bombs have gone off in three different beach houses at Alcamo Marina, and other people we know are being threatened. But it appears that one can learn to live with this possibility too, to remove it to the category of random and senseless dangers like mugging, cancer, or nuclear war that for Western man have come to replace the fear of famine or plague or barbarian invasions.

꙰ We have hardly had time to digest this first dose of *castrato* before we must tuck into another one. One of Tonino's colleagues at the university has invited the entire Institute of Agrarian Economics and its assorted families for a *mangiata* of ricotta and *castrato* at his family sheep farm outside of Tràpani.

The Italian language and its various dialects are rich in words for eating one's bellyful—*mangiata, abbuffata, scorpacciata, panzata*—for which I am hard put to find an English equivalent. "Blow out" and "splurge" are not specific enough: the Italian words have behind them the weight of centuries of hunger interrupted only by famine. To eat all one wants and more, in one glorious and wasteful feed, is to consecrate the feast day by distinguishing it from the careful measuring out of the daily bread.

This Saturday's banquet does not honor any recurrent feast but is a simple act of hospitality. The guests range from the senior professors and their wives, of a generation in which only the upper classes aspired to university teaching, through the junior professors, some from middle-class families like Tonino's, others having made enormous jumps (for instance, his colleague from a small town who as a boy was often asked by his teachers what he thought he, the son of a barber, was doing at the classical lyceum), and then to the technicians and secretaries and the janitor, a Palermitano from the San Pietro *mandamento*, irremediably urban in this rural setting.

Our host is the younger son of an aristocratic family whose sheep farm is housed in buildings that, to judge by their architecture, must have been part of a rural resettlement scheme launched in the fifties, an attempt to avoid the confiscation of undercultivated lands under the land reform law. Like almost all attempts to promote such resettlement, the scheme was unsuccessful, because most of western Sicily's peasant population, accustomed to urban life after centuries of being driven to the towns by Saracens, bandits, pirates, and malaria mosquitoes, has steadfastly refused to live on their farms. The long-empty buildings are now being slowly transformed into a modern sheep farm, with milking machines, refrigerated storage tanks, and rooms for cheese processing.

The count and countess are there to greet us on our arrival, which has been timed to coincide with the curdling of the ricotta from the morning's milking. We are immediately ushered in to watch the head shepherd stirring and ladling out platefuls of hot ricotta floating in its whey. He is using a big copper cauldron like that of the shepherds at Bosco, and the smell of the ricotta is the same, but all likeness ends there. The fire comes from an enormous gas burner, and the walls and floor of the room are covered with gleaming white tiles.

The farm is at the center of a shallow bowl between soft hills covered with pasturage, green grass and red sulla stretching out in all directions to the horizon, where, to the west, the dark crest of Erice rises over the rim. We walk out to see the artificial lake and to admire the flocks of Maltese goats. A far cry from Sicily's usual grubby, Roman-nosed beasts, these have long, silky white wool, black faces streaked with white on the nose, and long and languid black ears that curve down below their cheekbones and curl up at the tips, giving them the air of a 1930s movie star. We wade knee-deep through flowers, sulla, bugloss, lavender thistles, and the yellow-throated, blue-rimmed *convolvulus siculus*, to watch the harvest combine mowing the sulla, its great blades cutting through the stand of flowers like a paddle steamer on a red sea.

Dinner arrives by car, prepared elsewhere by the peasant couple who runs the family's estates. The countess apologizes over and over again for the preparations, which are necessarily makeshift here where only the shepherd and his flock are in permanent residence and no one has ever served a meal for thirty before, but we find them charming: on the cement platform under a high tin roof where the sheep gather for shelter from the winter rains, an enormous table has been hammered together from two-by-fours expressly for the occasion. Gay checkered tablecloths cover its length, and big baskets of yellow daisies are placed at intervals. Bowls of olives, slabs of fresh sheep cheese, and slices of freshly baked bread flavored with fennel seeds keep us going until the car comes, laden with pizza *arianata*, a specialty of the Tràpani region made with pecorino, oil, onions, and abundant oregano, then huge pans of *castrato* roasted together with tomatoes, potatoes, and onions in the same wood-fired oven that cooked the pizzas; sausages of chopped *castrato* mixed with pork and seasoned with rosemary; big bowls of tomato salad; and finally, enormous trays of *cassateddi*, their sweet ricotta filling deliciously sharpened by a little grated lemon rind.

Abundant wine quickly washes away any awkwardness, and laughter drowns out the remote tinkling of sheep's bells and the buzz of the insects in the wildflowers. The farmer and his wife jump up and down from their seats near the other peasants at one end of the great table in order to press a little more of this and just one more of that on us. The farmer is a thin, weathered man, perhaps in his late forties, with brilliant blue eyes and a smile of seraphic gentleness. The count's eldest son has much to say in praise of his abilities, both as a farmer and in keeping the accounts, in helping him out in his law office and drawing up deeds and wills as if he had had legal training. The young aristocrat speaks of the peasant with the greatest admiration and just a hint of surprise.

The head shepherd is also much admired by the company, a caricature of the *omo di panza*, the "man with a belly" who knows how to defend his honor and hold his tongue. He is indeed a man with a belly, an amazing tight drum that balances immobile over his belt, and his eyes slant slightly, impassive and observant in the shadow of his cap, giving him the air of a Sicilian buddha. Someone comments on his economy of motion, and the farmer, passing at that moment with a platter in his hand, laughs.

"He's a real shepherd, that one. If he wants to eat snails for his supper, he just props himself up in the middle of the field and waits for the snails to crawl up his crook!"

We are undone by the quantities of food we have put away, and by the news of a minor tragedy: they have forgotten to bring the coffee. Abject apologies from the farmer and the countess are still being brushed aside when a large Mercedes pulls into the farmyard. An equally large gray-haired man well laden with gold rings and gold ID bracelets gets out. It is the village baker in whose oven all this has come to pass, and he is brandishing aloft an enormous thermos jug.

"Look," he says proudly, "perfect timing! Piping hot coffee just when you are ready for it." Refusing an invitation to join us, he gives a courteous bow and drives off.

Intending to stop off at Bosco on our way back to Palermo, Tonino and I avoid the *autostrada* and follow the old road that climbs over a ridge, leaving the flat lands of Tràpani behind it, and drops suddenly into the valley—lush, tree-shaded, and unexpected—that leads to Segesta. I will be coming back here tomorrow, but right now I hardly notice the temple's triangular pediment hovering in the dip of a hill as we drive by. I am busy wondering about class, words, and collective guilt.

"Do you really want to use the word 'peasant'?" my friend Claudia asked when she read the first chapters of this journal. Claudia is a first-generation American who swam against the current, coming back to visit Sicily on a Fulbright scholarship and staying to marry a distant cousin. While she shares none of my historical guilt about blacks and Indians in America ("we were on the receiving end too"), I seem to approach the European peasantry with greater ease than Claudia or many of my middle-class Sicilian friends.

It's true that "peasant" is a loaded word in English, much more so than the Italian *contadino*, which is very matter-of-fact, even anthropological, as in *cultura contadina*, peasant society. The disparaging sense that "peasant" can have in English is more often reserved to *villano*, the worker of the Roman *villa*, which implies the uncouth and the oafish.

"Turiddu is a proper *villano!*" Tonino exclaims with annoyance. "Having raged and fumed and carried on yesterday about how lousy our sulphur pump was, this morning he discovered that it does work after all and now he's taken it home with him!"

Or maybe it's just Americans who have trouble with the word "peasant," apologetic as they often are when forced to speak in terms of class. An eight-year-old American who was visiting us once asked me what the word meant, and it was difficult for me to explain it in terms that a little boy from southern California could understand. In any case it is a problem that is rapidly resolving itself: Turiddu Vivona and the Pirrello brothers grew up in a peasant society, in a subsistence-level struggle for survival, of which the next generation, their sons and daughters, does not possess even the memory.

🌿 It is a pleasant relief the next day to start out on an expedition that is neither anthropological nor gastronomical, but a feast for the eyes alone; I have promised to accompany a visiting American professor to Segesta. I am always delighted when someone gives me an excuse to go to Segesta, since close as it is, I never get there under my own steam, and yet I love it almost above any other place in Sicily.

The remains of the ancient city straddle the low ridge of hills that separates the plain of Castellammare from the flat lands of Tràpani. We must take exactly the same route out along the *autostrada* that Tonino and I followed yesterday, but the weather has changed, altering the landscape as well. The scirocco is blowing, spreading a veil of dusty yellow light, fading out the colors of the wildflowers that were so gay in yesterday's sun and whipping the acacia blossoms, now withered to a dull mustard. On the viaducts the car trembles and shudders as I struggle to keep us on course, and the rooks hovering about the ruins of the castle of Calatubo swoop and surf on the sudden gusts.

The theater comes into view first, clinging to the brow of its hill, the semicircle of walls that embrace the cavea breaking the skyline like a laurel crown. The eye runs down the slope to the west, caught by the play of this rugged, stony ridge and the smooth flow of the grassy plain that cradles the temple. The *autostrada* sweeps around a curve, rises, falls, always in sight of the temple, and then dives underground, bringing us out just a few short turns from the parking lot, so full of tour buses that it is not easy to find room for our car.

Like Erice, the city of Segesta belonged to the Elymians, but here the predominating influence was Greek rather than Carthaginian. The Segestans adopted the Greek alphabet to inscribe their pottery and were so successful at absorbing the Greek culture that they were allowed the unusual privilege of contracting marriage with Greek citizens. The vulnerability of their city's position forced them to rely on diplomacy for their defense, playing off Carthaginians against Greeks and Athenians against Syracusans in a quest for allies to support them in their continual border controversies with the city of Selinunte to the south. In 416, when Selinunte turned to Syracuse for aid, Segesta called upon Athens. In order to impress the Athenian delegation come to negotiate an alliance, the Segestans borrowed all the gold and silver plates and goblets that Erice could lend them and set them out in turn, together with their own, in each house in which the delegation was entertained. The Athenians were very impressed by the immense wealth of a city where every family ate off gold, and they voted to support the Segestan cause.

Even if we had no other record, the temple alone would be ample testimony to how the Elymian culture fused with the Greek, for it is a splendid example of Greek Doric architecture. It represents one more of the many mysteries surrounding the Elymian people, in that it is not a complete structure but consists simply in a flat base ringed by a peristasis of thirty columns. For a long time archeologists believed that the temple was complete as it now stands, a simple garland of columns to honor some more ancient altar or sanctuary, with no roof or inner cella ever planned, but recent studies indicate that further building was contemplated. It has even been suggested that its construction was hurriedly undertaken to impress the Athenian delegation and abandoned once it had served its purpose.

It is inconceivable to me that such base circumstances could ever give birth to the perfection of Segesta, or hasty planning bring about such a felicitous marriage of building to landscape. Whatever the reason, I like to think that it was left unfinished, that the warm gold of its stone never knew the gaudy paint and plaster so difficult to reconcile with the classical Greece I have imagined since childhood.

We climb up toward the temple along a path lined with giant agave plants, out of place in these surroundings, and with much more appropriate myrtle trees. As we draw closer, the temple, perfect from afar, gives up its imperfections: the weathering of centuries of rain and wind upon stone has honed and riddled the columns, carving the vein of the limestone into the rough bark of an organic, living structure. And indeed it breathes with life, as big tufts of white flowers reach out from the metope in a wind-tossed dance, and the swallows nesting between the capitals chitter gaily among themselves.

It is not known to whom the temple was dedicated. If flowers were any clue, they would say Aphrodite: I find Venus's navel and love-in-the-mist in profusion about its steps. On the other hand, Cicero tells us that the Segestans had a famous statue of Artemis, which was carried off first by the Carthaginians and then again by the hated Roman governor, Verres.

> The figure, draped in a long robe, was of great size and height, but in spite of its dimensions, it well suggested the youthful grace of the maiden, with quiver hung from one shoulder, bow in the left hand, and the right hand holding forth a blazing torch. . . . No story is better known throughout Sicily than that of how, when Diana was being borne out of the town, all the matrons and maidens of Segesta flocked to the spot, anointed her with perfumes, covered her with garlands and flowers, and burning incense and spices escorted her to the frontier of her land.
>
> Cicero, *The Verrine Orations*

And it is Artemis' tree that grows on the other hill, a hawthorn that sticks up from the low scrub, its flowering over now. We pass it on our way to look down over the semicircular steps of the amphitheater to the stage, with its splendid backdrop of mountains, sky, and sea. The theater is beautifully preserved, even to the backrests on the highest row of seats, an arc of armchairs waiting for the chorus to file onstage. In the summer the theater is still used, and we have seen Aristophanes here and Pirandello, and even the National Ballet Company of Senegal, whose leaping black dancers were more at home in this dramatic landscape than one might have thought. An elderly shepherd is now wandering through the theater gathering herbs to sell to the tourists, little bunches of wild oregano, the healing herb that Heracles discovered when he descended to Hades. Wild oregano culled from the steps of the Greek theater at Segesta would be a charming souvenir, but to get it past the U.S. Customs would be a labor equal to that of outwitting Cerberus.

We drive back down the narrow road to the temple through fields of stones and thistles where once the city of Segesta stood, now empty except for low stone sheds and stone-walled sheep pens that seem to grow out of the bedrock itself. As we ease our way around the hairpin turns, the constantly shifting perspective on the temple across the narrow valley underlines the essential, exceptional equilibrium of this structure, so solid, so deeply rooted to its hill, yet so close to the ideal of harmony that it almost seems to levitate, otherworldly, poised just above the earth on some divine and invisible hand.

🌿 An aberration of my inquiring mind prompts me to stay up all the following Friday night to watch the dynamiting of Etna on television. All the world has turned its eyes toward Sicily tonight, and at 4:00 a.m. I uncharitably wonder if the continual postponing hasn't something to do with hitting prime time in America. The actual explosion, when the dynamite charges break down the petrified banks of the lava flow and the incandescent magma spills into the artificial channel created by two weeks of furious bulldozing, is an anticlimax. The accompanying uproar has been much more entertaining, a proper cautionary tale about how things get done in Italy, with the bandying about of legal and political responsibilities, the ecological outrage, and the romantic blond Viking, a Swedish explosives expert, called in much to the resentment of the local technicians.

After this all-night stand, I am ready for a restful Sunday, puttering among my plants and tending my own oregano. The herb garden is a piece of Bosco for which I feel a particular affection, perhaps because it is all my own creation. When the house was rebuilt, the masons raised a retaining wall along the path that leads from the road to the gate and filled the space behind it with some earth and a lot of rubble. By dint of much mulching and composting I have made this into an herb garden, and it has responded gratefully, forgiving me the ignorance that comes of being both city slicker and amateur scholar, and the errors this combination has bred, not the least of which are the shadows of the trees that grow there, the oleander, the lemon, and the pomegranate. Fortunately Sicily can compensate for my ignorance, since partial shade here is tantamount to full sun in a more temperate climate.

The wild fennel was there to begin with, its tall stems growing up six feet or more each summer, bearing the umbrella-shaped clusters of seeds that were used by the Egyptians as an aid in fasting and chewed on by the Roman legionaries to quell their hunger pangs as they marched across the empire. The stems dry to a brittle gray, forming the hollow stalk inside which Prometheus hid the embers of fire he had stolen from the gods to bring to man. Fennel is a symbol of success: it wishes my garden well, as do the camomile (for patience) and the borage (bringer of courage), which grow wild about its edges.

I have a much-traveled assortment of herbs. The oregano—"joy of the mountain" in Greek—was a present from the Pirrello brothers. Many of the others we acquired by raiding the house at Finocchio: the silvery sage, for example, and the laurel bushes that will shield us from lightning and witches.

Rosemary, *ros marinus*, "dew of the sea," will not grow in the gardens of the wicked, but it grows in mine, a cutting from the enormous bush that grows seven feet tall at Finocchio, belying the English legend that rosemary grows to the height of Christ in thirty-three years and then will grow thicker but no higher. Rosemary is for remembrance: Greek students would wear it in garlands to help their memory while studying for exams. I have offered to make one for Francesco, but he will have none of his mother's whimsy.

The mint, from my mother-in-law's garden by the sea, is an ambivalent herb, both aphrodisiac and abortive. Minthe was Hades' mistress before Persephone arrived, and she made such a fuss about having her bed usurped that Hades got fed up and turned her into a mint plant and condemned her to sterility. Chastity, on the other hand, can be encouraged by the lavender, grown from prunings gathered on the university campus in Palermo, and the thyme comes from farther still, two wild plants, one from the woods around Caltanisseta and one that grew on a bank of pine trees, looking out from the shores of Puglia toward Greece.

Still other herbs have flown the ocean in seed packets ordered from America: coriander and marjoram because I couldn't find them here, despite the fact that the Greeks knew and loved them well, especially marjoram, whose sweet smell came from the touch of Aphrodite, the first to cultivate this herb; and then tansy, hyssop, and pennyroyal because I loved the Shakespearean ring of their names, little suspecting that "tansy" comes from *athanatos*, "immortality," the quality it conferred on Ganymede, or that a potion of water, barley meal, and pennyroyal was the first food tasted by Demeter when she took refuge at Eleusis after the rape of her daughter. It became the ritual food at the Eleusinian Mysteries, symbolizing "the transition from sorrow and fasting to joy and festivity." Or that hyssop grows wild in Sicily and was strewn before the statue of Demeter in the spring processions at Enna.

I must confess that in the ignorant enthusiasm of my first year at Bosco I even ordered a packet of borage seeds. Tonino, puzzled by what was sprouting in the carefully tended flats on our balcony in Palermo, kept mumbling that it looked like *burrania* to him!

The herb garden is at its most beautiful now; the lavender is just lengthening into bud, and its tall spears do not yet hide the smaller plants, the thyme and the hyssop, the mint and the sage, all flowering in varied hues of pale purple, mixed with the white of the rosemary. Spiky flower stalks thrust up from the Venus's navel tucked in between the stones of the wall, and the trailing ivy geranium pours down effusions of pink. Spread above all this are the first pink buds of the oleander and the yellow fruit of the lemon and the bright scarlet of the long-lasting pomegranate flowers, which glow among the leaves. Even the pomegranate in the courtyard has two flowers—its first—this year, and the quinces near the kitchen door are full of delicate pink-and-white blossoms that rest their porcelain petals on the mossy green leaves. The quince, like the pomegranate, prefers to wait for foliage to frame its flowers, but these are as fragile as their colors and will shortly blow away, while the pomegranates go on for weeks, new buds still opening when the first flowers have already swollen into fruit.

🌿 The needs of industrial production that beat out the measure of our days have moved Ascension Day to Sunday, reducing to little more than a picnic in the country what was once the night of universal benediction, when field and crops, man and beast received the divine blessing, the grain descended into the wheat stems, and incurable illness miraculously disappeared.

If we pass from the fields to the seashore, we will find even more curious spectacles. It is a dogma of popular faith that at midnight on Ascension the salt water of the sea becomes fresh, and as fresh water becomes holy; and from this a series of prodigies derives. People afflicted by all types of skin disease run to the sea and full of enthusiasm and faith they throw themselves in, almost certain of being cured. . . .

Nor is this only for man, or for the sick. The owners of sheep, cows, goats, mules, and horses, in order to preserve them in good health or to cure any disease they might have, are accustomed to bathe them at that very hour, or during the night. It is a beautiful sight to behold each shepherd or cowherd or goatherd or muleteer drive down from the mountains, from the fields and the stables whatever he has of oxen and cows, sheep and goats, and beasts of burden, with their horns and heads decorated with multicolored silk scarves and all manner of bells hanging from their necks, which with the irregular gait of the various animals give out a confused and clamorous sound. More often than not in Palermo these ablutions are accompanied by the joyful sounds of the musical band, by the songs and dances of the herdsmen, who for joy give great leaps and abandon themselves to unaccustomed frolics. As they come out of the blessed bath, every ill has disappeared and the udders of the female beasts are swollen with milk.

Giuseppe Pitrè, *Spettacoli e feste popolari siciliani*

Despite the lack of rain, which is drying the wild grasses and gilding the wheat so soon, the signs of universal benediction are all about us. At either side of the fork in the lower road the wheat fields have been invaded by poppies, hundreds of daubs of pure color, so red they hurt the eye and dance like spots on the retina, making me wonder how people saw poppies before the French Impressionists painted them. The Greeks saw in their blood-red color a promise of resurrection: these too, like the pomegranates, are sacred to Persephone.

Farther along the road the wild roses are in bloom, more of them than I remember from other years, their white petals so close one to another as to hide the foliage underneath. In the garden I have so far limited myself to the roses I have inherited, the fragile white musk rose that sprawls over a piece of the garden near the quinces, shedding its petals quickly, then slowly maturing bright red rose hips, and the tea rose in shades of yellow and pale pink, which has been here for close to a century if the thickness of the trunk is any clue, and blossoms all year round in turgid, many-petaled buds that often rot before they open. Roses represent too much of a challenge, something to be tackled when everything else is accomplished and I have won my stripes, and I have taken warning from what happened to Prince Fabrizio:

> The Paul Neyron roses, whose cuttings he had himself bought in Paris, had degenerated; first stimulated, then enfeebled by the strong and languid pull of the Sicilian earth, burned by apocalyptic Julys, they had changed into things like flesh-colored cabbages, obscene and distilling a dense, almost indecent scent which no French horticulturist would have dared for. The Prince put one under his nose and seemed to be sniffing the thigh of a dancer from the Opéra.
>
> G. Tomasi di Lampedusa, *The Leopard*

Above all the benediction has fallen on the fruit trees: no April storm has torn the flowers prematurely from their stems, and the plum and the pear, the peach and the apricot trees are heavy with ripening fruit. Even the citruses are studded with tiny dark green balls. The olives are in flower, microscopic white blossoms that are almost invisible from a distance, but so abundant this year that the white stands out against the silver-gray, and hundreds of bunches of yellowish fuzz drip from the grapevines. The irony of such an abundance when there is no water to swell and mature the fruit is more than one can bear to contemplate.

We take heart from the medlar trees that are covered with orange-yellow fruit waiting to be taken back to Palermo by the basketful. Eating a medlar entails a long run for a short slide: there is only a thin layer of sweet, tangy flesh between the skin and the shiny brown seeds the size of a slightly flattened marble, so that small mountains of skin and seeds accumulate on our plates at the end of dinner. The Everest that Tonino's grandfather would produce in his passion for medlars is legendary in the Simeti household, while Tonino has passed on to Francesco his own childhood taste for shooting the smooth-skinned seeds across the room with thumb and forefinger. At least once each spring, dinner degenerates into outright warfare, with Natalia and me pretending to be above such nonsense while taking surreptitious aim at the men who circle the table carrying their munitions in a glass of water to make them squirt better. The rule is that they must sweep up afterward, but now and then throughout the summer and into fall the odd medlar pit will roll out from under the furniture.

The white mulberries are plentiful too, and ripe in time for Ascension Day. The Sicilian dialect has the same word for mulberry (*gelso* in Italian) and for Ascension—*scéusa*—a coincidence commemorated by the Palermitani, who always made a point of stopping under a mulberry tree on their Ascension Day outings. The mulberry is one of the rare fruits in Sicily that have no owner: anyone has the right to pick and eat as many as he wants.

The cultivation of the white mulberry and the raising of its attendant silkworms spread from China to Europe around about 700 B.C. and was particularly encouraged in Sicily by the Arabs and the Normans, but nowadays the black mulberry is more common, since its dark red fruits, which the Greeks thought had acquired their color only after Pyramus and Thisbe bled to death under a white mulberry, have much more juice and flavor than the white ones. The two grow side by side in front of the house at Bosco, a shady place to park the car in summertime, and the fruit of the white mulberry ripens first, darkening from white to pale mauve and tasting, for all that it is insipid and too sweet, like summer.

❧ The balance between the lush and the parched tips a little further each week as we slide slowly toward the summer solstice. The wheat is pale gold, rippled with waves of dark shadows and topped with the bleached foam of the wild oats, which reach above the wheat and circle its shores, shedding their spikelets on all who pass: at the end of the day our shoes and socks and pant legs are full of the bristling heads. The children love to do battle with them, since they cling obstinately wherever they land, but I find them slightly sinister. As I ease them out of my stockings, I can't help remembering that they were found in the trouser cuffs of Aldo Moro after the Red Brigades abandoned his body, an unlikely clue to the whereabouts of the murdered statesman's prison that somehow brings home to me with great immediacy the horror and the brutality of that whole affair.

The wild grasses growing about the house, a luxuriant if shaggy lawn just a few weeks ago, have gone to seed as well, bleached and unkempt despite our Sunday scything, and the plants in the courtyard are suffering from their once-a-week-only watering. This is the time of year when it is hardest to reconcile myself to our split life: the harsher light discloses the extent to which the dust and cobwebs have accumulated over the winter; spring garden projects wither for lack of care and water, like the corn on which Demeter has just plain turned her back; ideas and plans for the four short summer months flower in my head with the same hopeless, foredoomed abundance that burdens the olive trees.

Despite the accumulation of chores and despite the flats of

pepper, tomato, and eggplant seedlings that have come with us from Palermo, we take off the last Sunday morning in May to go to Gibellina. Summer is getting an extra shove from the scirocco, which has sent the temperature up to 104 degrees in the shade, an irritable, petulant wind that rattles the windowpanes and slams the doors behind it, leaving us restless and headachy, glad to get in the car and go, but so distracted that we miss the proper exit from the *autostrada* and have to double back along a winding country road. This is earthquake country; you feel it subconsciously before you can put a name to what is wrong with the landscape: all the old farmhouses are missing. Here and there a jagged shard of stonework points a reminder that a world was shattered here, but the only buildings intact are new. We drive by the outskirts of Montevago, all recent and still-shiny stucco, low apartment houses and fancy villas. The oldest houses are the barracks, their regimentation barely discernible under the patina of fifteen years, time enough to acquire individuality with a lean-to, a picket fence, a rambling rose.

We are headed toward Gibellina Nuova, the new town across the valley from the ruins of the old, destined to total destruction by its faulty subsoil. Apart from the geological necessity of complete relocation, the reconstruction of Gibellina has followed an unusual course thanks to the town's mayor, Ludovico Corrao, a wealthy lawyer from Alcamo, ex-senator and patron of the arts. One feature of this has been the establishment of a small museum housed in a traditional farmhouse, a rare survivor. According to a brochure available in three languages, the museum has as its aims

> those of collecting and preserving material evidence of the rustic history and culture of the inhabitants of the Valley, as well as that of making possible the widest and most correct utilization of this heritage.
>
> In a territorial entity that has experienced, as a result of the violent earthquake of 1968, a sudden and total annihilation of its urban structures and thus the rapid and inevitable transformation of living

conditions and traditional productive activities, the collection and the safeguarding of this material assumes for the entire community the precise meaning of the recovery of its historical and cultural identity, which is either threatened or swept away.

Today we are not going to the museum itself but to a special show at the local high school. Dedicated to "Crafts and Trades in the Belice Valley," it is an exhibition of tools belonging to the ancient crafts sustaining peasant agriculture that are fast disappearing.

The tools are immensely evocative, worn with use, their wooden handles black and shiny from what the cook of my childhood used to call "elbow grease," but the iron is often rusty and the wood riddled with dry rot. Among the many handmade tools for making other tools by hand, there is the proper instrument for every cut, for every blow or stitch, differing just in the thickness or curve of the blade, in the size of the last, in the weight of the mallet.

They are grouped according to the craftsmen who used them, each one labeled with the fine, rugged names of the Sicilian dialect and accompanied by explanations and photographs that show how the tool was used. The very names of the trades themselves have a strong, sweaty taste to them: the *conzapeddi* (tanner); the *scarparu* (cobbler); the *crivaru*, who made sieves, wooden rings of different sizes, like tambourines, on which meshes of wire or pierced metal or woven leather cords in varying textures were stretched taut to winnow and grade wheat, olives, beans, and other crops. The *vardaru* made the harnesses and the packsaddles for the mules and horses, and the blacksmith, or *firraru*, shod them and forged the blades for hoe and plow.

The woodworkers—*mastru d'ascia* means literally "master of the ax"—were divided into two categories, *d'òpira rossa* and *d'òpira fina*. The carpenter "of large works" built the carts and wooden plows and presses, while the cabinetmaker created the "fine works," the tables and chests and wardrobes that furnished the peasant dwellings. Lastly the *vuttaru*, the *bottaio*, made the wine casks; and the *stagninu*, or tinsmith, hammered out the pots, pans, funnels, and measuring vessels for us in kitchen and wine cellar.

The simple arrangements of wood and metal, of tool and end product, evoke the texture and weave of the rural economy, just as the exhibition of bread and pastries, put on two years ago, illustrated the liturgical calendar that had occasioned them. Last year's show, dedicated to weaving, traced the life cycle of the peasants in the embroidered baptismal dresses, the nuptial bed-spreads, the tightly woven sheets destined, in the end, to become shrouds. In keeping with its content, the current show has been put together with a straightforward, pragmatic approach, refresh-ingly free of the semiotic embellishments that cluttered up the other two.

It's the same problem again, how to look at the peasant world. A certain part of Palermo has rediscovered its roots and crowds the openings of these shows at Gibellina or flocks to the new Museum of Marionettes to see the traditional Opera dei Pupi (now that many of the old puppeteers have closed down for want of an audience and sold off their puppets to antique dealers). We ourselves have carefully preserved at Bosco all the old tools and farm implements that were stashed away there, and if these were actually part of Tonino's childhood, I don't know what to make of the two outsize wooden bellows that he scavenged from an abandoned blacksmith's forge. Figuratively, that is; literally they serve to fill up one end of the cavernous living room that we cannot yet afford to furnish properly.

The museum, in its flyer, claims to take "a definite stand against possible representations and exploitations of the romantic-aesthetic type that have been proposed of the popular world and rustic civ-ilization and are still widespread." I try to too, by following the advice of a Sicilian friend of mine who is quite fierce on the sub-ject: every time I look admiringly at the *zappa da gramigna*, the short-handled hoe for digging out crabgrass, I force myself to vi-sualize the old *contadini* who walk around the streets of Alcamo with their chins at waist height, permanently bent double by a lifetime of wielding it.

And when I read about the newly discovered wonders of the Mediterranean diet, I remember the annual food budget for the family of a day laborer from Marsala that I once copied out of the report of a parliamentary commission that investigated the condition of the southern peasantry in 1910:

Wheat (50 bushels)	£350.00
Fava beans (8 bushels)	28.00
Oil (about 4 gallons)	16.00
Wine (none is consumed)	0.00
Vinegar	0.30
Salt	0.50
Potatoes (none)	0.00
Meat (only at Carnival)	3.00
Fresh fish (2 or 3 times a year)	1.50
Salt fish (once or twice a month)	1.80
Cheese and dairy products (none)	0.00
Vegetables (cauliflower, onions, etc.)	2.50
Total	£403.60

When you consider that in 1910 a lira could buy what an American can buy today with $1.17 and therefore that $472 had to feed a family of seven for a year, you realize that the main ingredient in the original Mediterranean diet was hunger.

Today the Sicilian *contadini* chew their way through a leathery *bistecca* almost every evening, the daily consumption of meat being the most important symbol of their newly acquired prosperity. (In the city, to say that something has no substance or foundation in fact, you say that it is "all smoke and no roast": the poor but pretentious Palermitani used to beg a scrap of fat from the butcher to put on the fire, in the hopes that the smell of roasting meat would linger outside their door, making them seem more prosperous.) This change in diet, which has taken place during the time that I have been in Sicily, implies a general improvement in the standard of living that is, of course, entirely praiseworthy, and if the destruction of the coherent and close-knit culture that is on exhibit at the Gibellina high school is the price of such an improvement, surely no one can object. There was probably never any possibility that peasant culture could survive in Western Europe side by side with modern industrial culture, and it was probably not so much the inherent attractions of the modern that decreed its death as it was the distortions that centuries of exploitation and suffering had produced in the peasant culture itself. Yet it seems sad to me that our contemporary society has so little in the way of a viable alternative to offer to this transitional generation, who often can find no more valid investment for their new prosperity than elaborate kitchens and fancy furniture that they cannot bring themselves to use.

When we leave the exhibit it is almost one, Sunday dinner time, the only hour I have ever driven through Gibellina Nuova, although each time I come I promise myself to return on a weekday, during business hours, to see if the town comes alive. The bulk of the town is well planned, with double rows of two-storied houses, each with a garden and a garage facing the street side, and a tree-shaded pedestrian mall in the middle, where the inhabitants are supposed to re-create the street life of the old village, the children playing, the women sitting in front of their doors, backs turned to the street for propriety's sake, and chatting as they shell their beans or bend over their embroidery hoops, the men gathered about the gaping hood of a car, young boys playing soccer or tinkering with bicycles, a cobbler straddling his narrow bench and hammering on his last. But the streets and malls of Gibellina are always deserted when I drive through, save for a few men clustered in front of the bar for a last aperitif before going home to dinner. The strange humpbacked and glass-walled bus station designed by the sculptor Consagra always seems at the same stage of incompletion, weeds grow about the base of the sculptures that Corrao has persuaded various Italian artists, my brother-in-law among them, to donate toward the reconstruction. As we leave the town we drive under an enormous concrete star that arches over the road, this too designed by Consagra, a gateway to the town intended, I suppose, to indicate some transition from empty field to empty street that otherwise would escape our notice. But maybe I am being unfair, and twenty years in Palermo have made a *disfattista* out of me, an "undoer" who only likes to indulge in destructive criticism. Maybe Gibellina is merely out to lunch right now, and there is a thread of continuity I cannot see between the worn and cared-for tools in the exhibit and the abstract sculptures in the piazzas.

We hurry home to our lunch and to the seedlings waiting to be planted. Ever since a power failure forced me to throw out fifteen trays of eggplant Parmesan, I have given up trying to grow enough vegetables to freeze for the winter, but each year we try to have enough eggplants, peppers, and string beans for the summer, and Mr. Amato has had such bad luck with his tomatoes that I am hastily putting in a few of my own. His melons are coming along beautifully, though; the rows of little green tufts march down the hill and across the valley floor with martial regularity.

Unexpectedly the wind stops. Bent over to hoe and dig I haven't been noticing the weather, but I realize now that the scirocco is no longer breathing hotly down my neck. The air, dried out by the desert wind, hangs still and listless like a dusty curtain, then, with a sudden rustle, it is riven by a cold damp current from the north. The change in temperature is abrupt and the dark clouds that have been piling up silently on the horizon come scudding across the sea in great dark shadows. The seagulls follow them inland, wheeling and wailing high above us in an unfamiliar clamor, and just as he did in Virgil's time, "the raven calls for rain, that wretched bird."

As we head back to Palermo, a few large drops gather the dust and splash it onto our windshield.

"Perhaps we'll get a really good rain," I say, thinking wistfully of my thirsty garden.

"It'll do a lot of damage."

"Why?"

"The olive and grape flowers are setting into fruit right now; a good storm could knock them all off."

It's always like that for a farmer: the rain never comes at the right moment or in the right quantity, the sun is either too hot or too weak, the wind ill timed or ill measured. Each meteorological event, each change in the weather or in the marketplace must be exorcised and disarmed by gloomy forecasts: beware of entertaining even the suspicion of a good harvest fetching a good price. But perhaps such relentless pessimism is the necessary counterweight to the profound faith and optimism required of one who hangs his livelihood on something as small and perishable as a seed.

III SUMMER

The summer solstice coincides, in
the Mediterranean world, with a fervor
of activity: it is the time of the wheat
harvest, the time to gather the fruit of
one's labor, the time of serene navigation
upon an ordinarily tranquil sea.

Franco Cardini,
I giorni del sacro: il libro delle feste

BOSCO

Chapter Eight

🌿 A half day of rain, a brief interlude of cool weather, then June arrives, hot and heavy with summer, pregnant with the tastes and smells of pleasures to come. The children drag themselves through the last tormenting days of school, the textbook pages dancing before their eyes unabsorbed, and teachers and students alike complain of the absurdity of making Sicily adhere to a national academic calendar ending in mid-June, when nothing can be achieved after the end of May in this climate. Francesco goes off in the morning, his book bag bulging with towel and bathing suit, ready to head for the beach at Mondello as soon as classes are out, while Natalia, young yet for such an adolescent gathering, languishes about the apartment licking ice cream cones.

From the moment we enter the *autostrada* and see the lanes of flowering oleander bushes stretching pink, white, and red ahead of us, the weekend is a summer in microcosm: long hours of watering, Sunday morning at the beach, a trip with basket in hand to gather fruit, even the first canning of the season, since the sour cherries are ripe enough to make the cherry syrup that, diluted with ice water, will cool us off when the heat comes in earnest.

Natalia and I set out to pick the cherries, which grow down in the lowest part of the farm. We walk down between Mr. Amato's melons, whose single tufts have shot out long feelers toward one another, and swollen into broad stripes dotted with yellow flowers that hide tiny melons under the canopy of their leaves. We pass the citrus grove, where next year's grapefruit hang like dark green golf balls from the trees, and stop to give a gentle squeeze to the peaches, not quite ripe yet. Beyond the fallow field where the drought has killed all but four or five of the trees that were our attempt to start an avocado plantation, the red grapes run along a ridge. We turn here, skirting the rim of a bank that is thick with brambles and hawthorn trees, with bushy heather and *'ddisa*, the tough *ampelodisa* grass with long plumes that is used to tie up the grapevines.

Turiddu has been at work this past week, a big bunch of *'ddisa*, first dried and then soaked in water to make it pliable, tucked into his belt. Embracing each vine in turn, he gently gathers up the long branches that wave curly-fingered tendrils at the sun, pulls them carefully together to form a protective blanket about the newborn bunches of grapes, and with one deft motion extracts two or three blades of *'ddisa* from his belt, wraps them around the vine, twists and tucks in the ends. His hands are so horny and callused that they hardly feel the sharp edges of the grass that tear and scratch at our bare legs as Natalia and I brush by.

At the bottom of the path we enter another world, an island lifted from another climate, where even on the hottest day the air is cool and damp, and the light filters down pale green and gentle. Here, where four adjoining farms meet, an underground spring feeds three wells and a miniature marsh. Two of the wells are on our land, the new one with a concrete wellhead built a few years ago to replace the old one that caved in during the earthquake and now sits in the shade of the cherry trees, a ring of mossy stones and a few feet of water housing a family of enormous toads.

Behind them the canes grow seven or eight feet high, clustering about a few alder trees and stitched together by brambles, wild grapevines, and morning glories into an almost impenetrable wall that hides the third well, of old stone, dark green and mysterious, and shields the little swamp with the bulrushes and then circles the big pit of long-forgotten origin, this year barely covered with slimy green water, where Francesco and Natalia used to hunt tadpoles in the spring. Huge saucers of white sway among the canes, Queen Anne's lace grown to giant proportions in the damp soil.

"Speaking with all modesty," Natalia reminds me proudly

each year, "*I* was the one to teach you that these are really wild carrots."

There is no cave that I know of, yet Pan never seems far off. Whether it is the witches' hawthorn, or the alders—the tree of the fourth month, the tree of Orpheus, which grew in a ring around the island of Circe—or the reeds that belong to the twelfth month, when they whisper that the year is ending and death approaching, I do not know, but there is often some other presence near the wells. It is not always just my imagination: one afternoon I felt someone looking at me, and glancing around and up I discovered a marsh rat, crouched in the crook of a cane leaf, swaying back and forth in the wind like a sailor in a crow's nest as he stared down at me, black eyes sharp and wary over quivering whiskers.

Today the presence is withdrawn. The reeds and canes are still and silent in the late-afternoon calm, and the slanting sunlight illumines the red translucence of the ripe cherries. We stoop to slide beneath the low-hanging branches until we are standing inside a tent of dark green glossy leaves, lacy against a brilliant azure sky and lit by a thousand little lanterns glowing red, and we laugh for the pure pleasure of such a harvest.

Our neighbors' fields of grain are ripe and rustling, and the wild oats have dried to a white haze that floats above the wheat like smoke in the sunlight. An artichoke, unharvested from the plant that Turiddu was moved to put in the middle of the herb garden, has opened to a flower, the leaves a purple spiky crown around the choke, which has grown long and silky and turned a brilliant cornflower blue. The first harvest of oregano, hanging from the rafters in the *palmento*, perfumes the kitchen with its pungent aroma, and at suppertime a young mantis, no more than an inch and a half long, flies into the kitchen and kneels on the rim of Tonino's wineglass. Summer's troops are on the move: the daddy longlegs know no seasons, but now the mosquitoes are gathering to attack, and the mercurial centipedelike horrors that we have baptized "ugly bedfellows," the moths that tap on the kitchen door in the evenings, and the tiny, foolish dragonflies that end up in the salad bowl, to be fished out gingerly by my tender-hearted children and have their oily wings blotted dry with paper napkins. Least welcome of all, the first flies have come to hover and dive, their loops and spins spelling out a warning of the swarms to come.

But the countryside slips into summer much more easily than I do: her winter clothes dry up or rot where they fall, whereas mine have to be put away in mothballs, and new ones bought, and dentists and medical certificates seen to, and the apartment closed for the summer, and the materials assembled for all my summer projects. The rites of passage are unusually complicated this year, as I must accompany the children to Rome, to put Francesco on a plane for America, and then to take Natalia to a three-week camp near Paestum. The idea of going to camp in the shadow of a Greek temple seems strange to someone accustomed to associate camp with the Adirondacks, but even more mind-boggling is the flood tide of forms and instructions that arrive from the American hosteling group with which Francesco will be doing a bike tour: after all these years of Italian improvisation, such superorganization staggers me.

It is not only the complicated preparations that cost me so much sleep, however, or the fact that this is the first time one of my children is going away so far and for so long. As I weed the courtyard the morning before we leave, my fingers occupied but my thoughts free to poke and pry, I suddenly realize that it is Francesco's destination that weighs upon me. For all that I thought I had made definitive and lasting peace with myself about having left America, I have been unconsciously investing Francesco with a terrible ambassadorship: to like America (and therefore me), to be liked there (and thereby justify my choice).

Francesco is uneasy too—loath to leave his friends and worried that his English is not good enough to get him through the summer. More or less bilingual when he was learning to talk, he discovered at age two and a half that all the children around him spoke Italian, and he became very angry with me, standing up in his crib and glowering when I came in to get him up in the morning.

"*Non si dice* good morning, *si dice CIAO!*"

In the long intervals between our rare visits to America he would lose his English, remembering only what he needed to squeak by in school without studying, and only in the past two years has he been making a serious effort to regain his fluency.

Francesco is almost five foot eleven, and despite his leanness looks a lot like me, even to the shape of his head. (A Palermo neurologist, called in to examine the children at the pretentious private school where Francesco went to kindergarten, exclaimed at first sight: "Look at that narrow skull! Either this child is mentally deficient or he has Anglo-Saxon blood!") His height and his intellectual curiosity are misleading, however; at fifteen he is less sure of himself than he seems, and like his mother is plagued by ambivalence. Being different from his friends, finding a part of the American image abroad that he can identify with, reconciling the conflicting indications of home and society, and at the same time charting his own path in the enormous space allowed him by his father, whose only expectations are that his children develop a sense of responsibility and respect for other people—these are all problems for Francesco in a way that they will never be, I suspect, for Natalia. And in a few days' time, when I kiss him good-bye in front of the passport control desk at Fiumicino and watch him stride off without hesitation, I will be full of pride for this good-looking and seemingly self-possessed young man, and full of admiration too, as I remember another morning ten years earlier, when we accompanied Francesco to have his tonsils removed. He had seemed quite tranquil and convinced by our explanations, but as we got out of the car in front of the hospital entrance, he suddenly took off down the street, his short legs pumping up and down as fast as they could. I am sure that Francesco is controlling at fifteen much the same urge that he gave in to at five.

We leave Palermo on the thirteenth, Saint Anthony's Day, and I punctually forget to wish Tonino Happy Onomastica—the Italian custom of celebrating the day of the saint one is named after is one custom I just can't fit my mind around. Saint Anthony is the patron of the wheat harvest and, I have just discovered, of Palermo drivers. Faced with the impossible task of parking anywhere near the center of town, one has only to say:

> *Sant'Antoninu, vestutu di velluto,*
> *Fammi trovare un posto fotuto!*

> Little Saint Anthony, all dressed in velvet,
> Help me to find some damned parking spot!

Today the children and I leave harvest and car and Tonino in Saint Anthony's care and board the train for Rome. We are well supplied with reading material for the twelve-hour trip, but the majority of the travelers come equipped only with bananas and bottles of mineral water and settle down to sleep in their seats or strike up a conversation with their neighbors. My Anglo-Saxon reserve, or shyness, usually keeps me from joining in, but I often eavesdrop behind the protective shield of newspaper or paperback and occasionally learn some startling information, such as the explanation I once overheard of how the balance of nature was threatened.

"Now, the earth turns on an axis, see, and this axis isn't quite straight, it's a little tilted, like so." The speaker was illustrating his story with gestures, as any proper Sicilian would, one hand held up with palm and fingers slightly inclined, while the other hand began to dart back and forth from one side of the upright hand to the other.

"Now, you take all this construction, digging out quarries here and building up these great heavy skyscrapers there, it's ruining the balance, it is. If we aren't careful, the earth's going to start tilting more and more, and all of a sudden—bang! The whole thing's going to fall right over."

This time we have the compartment to ourselves, and as the train, a *rapido*, rushes northward, I give Francesco a last English lesson on sprockets and chain rings, inner tubes and handlebars, and try to remember for his benefit how the pay telephones in America work. It gets cooler and cooler as we go north. In the fields of Calabria the poppies are still in full bloom, much to the children's surprise.

"The season comes later here."

"Backwards, these Calabresi!" Tongue in cheek, but only up to a point, Francesco is tinged with the Sicilian conviction that the Calabrians are far more underdeveloped and ignorant than the islanders, just as a Calabrian woman I travel with on the return journey will explain the rowdy behavior of some young men in the next compartment by saying that they must be Sicilians.

❧ The trip back is very different. I have to deliver Natalia at eight on Sunday morning to Agropoli, a small railway station near the camp, where she is to join up with the main contingent of campers, including her cousin Martina, as they arrive on the sleeper from Milan. An hour or so later the Treno del Sole is due to stop here and will take me directly to Palermo. I have been welcoming the chance to ride the "Train of the Sun," the daily express between Turin and Palermo, which in the fifties and sixties carried tens of thousands of Sicilian emigrants southward, on vacation from the assembly lines of the Fiat and its related industries. Books and songs have been written about this particular train, about the families that boarded it in Turin, wrapped in woolen shawls against the Alpine climate, their belongings strapped into cardboard suitcases and bulging paper parcels, and about their arrival at the southern stations where their entire village was waiting, come to welcome them home from their great adventure and reenfold them in its web. I used to be amused at the melodramatic scenes that accompanied such departures and returns, the crowds, the weeping and the waving of damp handkerchiefs, the fainting lady, invariably stout, being propped up and vigorously fanned, until Claudia reprimanded me.

"I get so damn mad when I see people laugh!" she said fiercely. "They have no idea of the pain involved, the tearing out of roots and the rending of hearts. Family is all most of these people have ever had, and to see it split apart is dreadful!"

But it appears that there has been a strike near Turin, and the Treno del Sole is three hours behind schedule, so I board a local that will take me to a big station farther south where I can catch the *rapido* coming down from Rome.

All of one carriage long, the local train has hardly time to gather speed before it must slow down again at the next tiny station, and so by fits and starts it bears me down along the Campanian and the Lucanian coast to Maratea, like a leaf propelled by a breeze across a stagnant pond. These jerking, halting windows open on a world other than that glimpsed from the hurrying, indifferent *rapido*.

Half of the passengers are railway men, hoping to get home for Sunday dinner, boarding, jumping off, leaning out to exchange a crack or a bit of gossip at each station. The other passengers either know each other or discover after ten minutes of conversation that there is some mutual connection. I board together with an elderly woman, long since emigrated to Val d'Aosta, who has brought her little granddaughter south for a seaside vacation. We enter a compartment occupied by a young student, who turns out to be the nephew of the brother-in-law of a woman to whose second cousin this grandmother from Val d'Aosta was engaged for six years.

Each station looks like the last and like the next; SALA D'ATTESA Ia CLASSE written in marble letters from the Fascist era, RITIRATA and USCITA all stamped in tin at some central headquarters, even the same carefully tended zinnias and marigolds growing in the flower beds and the same bougainvillea vine growing on the fence. No doubt the seeds are traded up and down the line. The student yells out the window to a friend climbing down from the other end of the carriage, hails someone else boarding at the next station, finally shakes hands with the grandmother and with me, wishes us a good journey, and gets off himself.

An express roars past us headed north, and our solitary carriage shudders and sways in the wind, then resumes its own rhythm, its wheels clicking and clacketing like steel needles knitting up the rent, stitching up the holes that speed, emigration, and the passage of the modern world have torn in the fabric of the South.

A little boy, playing ball in front of a house stuccoed in the faded wine color the Italian government has deemed appropriate to station masters and road menders, looks up as we pull in and waves to the blue-suited, black-satcheled conductor who jumps down. I wonder what this delicate equilibrium between the restless, open-horizoned speed of the *rapido* and the shabby familiarity of the local will produce in him, where the eddy and tug of this current moving through the still waters of the South will pull him. In Sicily these same wine-red houses have produced writers like Elio Vittorini, Salvatore Quasimodo, Danilo Dolci.

I am almost sorry to leave the local at Maratea, and I enjoy the hour's wait in the sun on the little platform. It is hard to orient oneself out of sight of the sea; someone has hung up an old shutter on the other side of the tracks and stenciled on it "Battipaglia" with an arrow pointing north. I noticed the other half of the shutter doing the same service at the last station.

Once aboard the *rapido* I am swept into another dimension of time, restless and eager to get home, lowering my book at frequent intervals to check on our progress and catch the first familiar glimpse of the dark hills of Messina beyond the Straits and peering through the haze in vain for a look at Etna, still tiredly drooling lava after almost three months. It is all familiar now, the fried *arancine* eaten at the bar on the ferryboat, the long wait at Messina, leaning out the window to buy a lemon ice from the little boy in the white jacket at the station of Sant'Agata Militello, the new cars lined up outside the Fiat assembly plant at Termini, the proud villas of Bagheria that appear in the opening shots of

The Leopard, cleverly isolated by the movie camera from their surrounding slums, and then the wooded slope of Monte Grifone soaring up from the squalid outskirts of Palermo.

Even too familiar. While I was in Rome, the captain of the carabinieri at Monreale was shot down, together with the two men in his escort, as he was getting out of the car in front of his fiancée's house. He had come down from the north to replace Captain Basile, who was killed a few years ago as he was walking hand in hand with his wife and small daughters down Monreale's main street on the evening of the local festa.

When I call Maria Vica to tell her that I am back, she has just come from paying a visit to the captain's fiancée, who is a friend of hers, a girl from northern Italy who had followed her young man south when he was posted to Sicily.

"I felt so ashamed for Sicily. I'm thinking of leaving Palermo. There is no hope for Sicily—she told me that during the funeral the children in the street outside the church were playing at being mafiosi and shooting down the policemen. You're lucky, Mary, at least you have Bosco to go to."

Maria Vica is holding up to me the mirror of my own illusions, and today I am happy to believe in them, anxious to assemble the last bits and pieces of packing and shopping and be gone. I have missed so much in the ten short days I have been away. The fields around Bosco have been drained of their golden sea of grain and dredged by the harvesting machines into spiraling rings of yellow stubble and pale blond chaff. As I drive up the hill, the dog trotting happily behind the overloaded car and the cat balancing on my shoulder to peer eagerly through the windshield, I can see a big combine circling the crest of the next hill over, the driver standing high up on his platform like a captain on the bridge, the machine spewing out a wake of straw bales behind it and pausing to pour into the waiting truck a cascade of wheat that glistens and sparkles in the sunlight.

I am sorry not to have heard the whining and clacking of its careful navigation around the nearer fields, not to have watched the spears of wheat falling to the wide blades, or to have climbed up on the truck to plunge my hands down into the warm and powdery smoothness of the grains slithering against my skin. But I am sorrier still never to have seen the old harvest, with the long line of reapers strung out across the hillside, their sickles rising and falling in unison. For every seven reapers there was a gatherer, who followed behind them, gathering the severed stalks into the fork of a stick by means of a blunt-edged sickle and then tying them into a sheaf with a blade of '*ddisa* from the bunch hanging at his belt. The arms of the reapers moved to the rhythm of the songs, always sacred at harvest time, that they sang, each verse ending in:

> Praise be and thanks
> To the Holy Sacrament!
> Praise be and thanks
> Every hour and every moment!

Or they followed the playing of drummers and bagpipes hired by the landowner to step up the pace with lively music.

Five times in the course of the day, which went from dawn to dusk, the line would break up to eat, and still more often it would halt "to pass the saint," to hand from reaper to reaper the barrel of wine that would quench their thirst and replenish their flagging energy.

Then the flattest part of the field was smoothed into a threshing floor where a pair of mules were driven round and round to trample the ears of wheat with their hooves and break off the grains as the peasants stirred and tossed the wheat with pitchforks. More hymns accompanied this endless circling, cries of encouragement to the mules alternating with prayers to all the saints to invoke their blessing on an abundant harvest. Later still a different sort of chant, droning and solitary, urged forward the long string of pack mules, eight mules to each driver, that carried the harvest back to town.

The Romans too had music at their harvest:

See that your country folk adore the goddess:
For her let milk and honey flow, and wine,
And lead the sacrificial victims round the crops
Three times, to bring good fortune, let a chorus
Follow the procession, singing hymns
To Ceres, ask her blessings on their homes;
Let no one lay his sickle to the grain
Until, with festive oak wreath of his brow,
He honors Ceres' name in dance and song.

Virgil, *The Georgics*

Alcamo, however, has long since abandoned Ceres for Santa Maria dei Miracoli, its patroness, whose worship goes back to June of 1547, when the Madonna appeared to some women who were washing their clothes in the millstream that ran along the northern edge of town. As the Blessed Virgin disappeared into the bushes, some stones rolled down into the water with a splash. One drop of water fell on the lips of a mute, who instantly found her voice, while another woman recovered the use of an arm that had long been paralyzed. When a crowd gathered the next day, more stones fell, causing more miraculous cures, and when the men cut down the brambles from where the stones had come, they found an image of the Madonna attached to the wall of the mill. A church was built around the image, and each year its discovery is celebrated in a three-day feast culminating in the procession of the twenty-first of June in which a statue of the saint is carried about the town.

Like many Sicilian festivals, Santa Maria dei Miracoli has had its ups and downs. In the early nineteenth century it was a very extravagant affair, and the procession was preceded on the second day by the exhibition of the triumphal cart, a small-scale version of the famous wagon of Saint Rosalia used for the Festino in Palermo, and on the first day by horse races, the so-called *corse dei barbari.*

The triumphal cart went out of use in the 1860s, swept away by the wave of anticlericalism that followed in Garibaldi's wake, but the horse races, dangerous hell-for-leather rides up the Corso, continued into the twentieth century. Pitré describes an ex-voto painting hanging in the sanctuary of Santa Maria dei Miracoli, dated 1883, which shows the racing horses galloping out of control into the middle of the town band. Miraculously not one of the musicians was injured, and the band repaired forthwith to the sanctuary to give thanks.

The races were revived some years ago, with wooden transepts erected all along the Corso and a thick layer of sand spread underfoot, which would then blow back and forth with the scirocco for the rest of the summer. All through the spring one could see beautiful, nervy, and well-groomed horses being exercised on country roads—the modern miracle of the festa being how certain people acquired the money to indulge in such an expensive hobby—and on the day of the races an enormous crowd would gather from all the towns around.

The horses ran four at a time, the whole length of the Corso, from Porta Palermo to Porta Tràpani, and only a small percentage of the crowd got to see the finish. The rest of the people, like the Simeti family hanging over their balcony railings halfway up the Corso, would watch the horses gallop past but would know who had won only when the triumphant jockey rode back down the Corso in the back of a truck, brandishing his prize, a wooden eagle glistening with silver paint.

It was more fun to watch the crowd itself. Those who had no access to a balcony would begin to gather hours before the races began: old grandfathers bent double scuttling out from the side streets and dragging little chairs, which they would set up on the curb right behind the transepts so as to be sure of a good view; little boys staking out the lampposts they would shinny up as soon as the action started; families purchasing a generous supply of *semenza* before occupying their piece of sidewalk.

In my mother-in-law's house both the *salotto* and the master bedroom open onto the Corso, so we had two large balconies on which to offer hospitality, and on race and procession days they were always alarmingly crowded, my mother-in-law carefully piloting her various nieces and cousins onto the bedroom balcony, while reserving the less intimate *salotto* for the Pirrellos, the Vivonas, and for Genoveffa, a maid who had long since retired but reappeared once a year to hug and kiss everyone and watch the races, wrapped in an enormous black shawl and surrounded by an even larger flock of grandchildren.

This year, however, Alcamo has been deprived of its races once more. It appears that this custom, which is not limited to Alcamo, has come to involve the prestige of rival Mafia clans, and the races held a few months ago for the festa of Monreale ended in knifings and bloodshed, causing the prefect of Palermo to ban them throughout western Sicily. There is much discontent among the horse owners, and the townspeople have had to make do with the procession, the fireworks, the traveling fun fair, and the usual influx of torrone and toy sellers.

All this is over by the time that I arrive at Bosco on the twenty-third, and the Alcamesi, exhausted by three days of festivities, hardly notice that Midsummer's Night has come. Midsummer is the middle age, the moment of greatest vigor, and if the days begin to shorten we will nonetheless have light enough and more to spare in the blazing months to come, before the waning of the year and the onset of old age and decay begin to weigh on us. We have forgotten the death of the sacred king, who was chosen at midwinter to be the consort of the Great Goddess and put to death at the summer solstice in the shadow of the oak, most sacred of all the trees, which rules this month. All the oracular powers of the oak have been transferred to Saint John the Baptist, whose feast day falls on the twenty-fourth, when young girls throughout the island used to question the saint about the husband that the future held in store for them: either by throwing an apple into the street and waiting to see who would pick it up or by throwing molten wax or lead into water and observing the shape into which it solidified. (A T-shaped piece could mean a hammer or a hoe, conveniently allowing one's fancy room to choose among a cobbler, a carpenter, and a *contadino!*)

This melting pot of traditions is nowhere stronger than at

Marsala, where the church of Saint John the Baptist was built over a well that marked the seat of the Sibyl of the Roman city of Lilybaeum. Pitrè quotes the Marchese di Villabianca's description of an odd medieval custom that was observed on the saint's day:

> . . . a superstitious abuse that was practiced in the underground crypt, where people were leached by barbers; and the bleedings were of such great numbers that at times they could be counted at more than four hundred.

Giuseppi Pitrè, Spettacoli e feste popolari siciliani

and elsewhere Pitrè speaks of

> the *cara Sibilla*, who to the simple people of Marsala has become a beneficent genie, a sort of fairy who brings fortune to whom she chooses . . . [and] is to be invoked at noon on the 24th of June . . .

Giuseppe Pitrè, Feste patronali in Sicilia

There is none of all this at Alcamo—or so I thought. On the twenty-fifth Tonino and I must telephone to my sister's in New York to wish Francesco well on the eve of his departure for the bicycle tour, and we decide to make the call from Alcamo Marina, the long strip of beach where the Alcamesi have their summer houses. They were late in discovering the sea: the Simetis' villa, one of the first to be built, dates only from 1936. According to Sciascia, Sicilian towns turn their backs on the sea, "capable only of carrying away the emigrants and disembarking the invaders," and this is almost true, despite its name, of Alcamo Marina. When I first spent summers there, before Bosco was rebuilt, it still had the air of a tentative approach, a knot of houses around the old tuna fishery, and then beach running for several miles beside the railroad tracks and the provincial highway. Beyond these, the houses dotting the narrow strip of flat land were still spaced out by pieces of vineyard. Now row upon row of villas and small apartment buildings sit cheek by jowl, nudging and elbowing each other in an attempt to get whatever view of the sea the house in front allows, or clamber up the ridge behind, clinging perilously to the sandy slope, where the better view comes at the price of a longer walk to the beach. Having banished all danger of solitary converse with the sea, the Alcamesi can now take up their normal life, noisy and crowded, the afternoon visits followed by the evening *passeggiata* either on foot with the baby carriage or by car, up and down the main road in such force that on weekend afternoons all traffic comes to a standstill, except for the swarm of Vespas and motorcycles that weave in and out of the stationary lanes of cars.

In June and September it is pleasant here, however, with the bulk of the houses closed and shuttered and the festoons of shells and seaweed still stretched out along the beach where the winter storms have thrown them. Here and there an open window, a thread of smoke from a barbecue, a beach towel hung out to dry indicate the early arrival of an enthusiast, and elsewhere workmen are hurrying to finish a new house or repair an old one before the season starts. As we drive along, Tonino points out to me a black smudge on the wall of one house, the twisted metal shutters of another, where the wear and tear of winter weather have given way to the ravages of the Mafia.

We have left time for a quick swim before the call must go through, and we head toward the beach, which is hidden from view until we cross the last row of houses. At two-thirty in the afternoon there is no human presence to break the long white line of sand that stretches from Castellammare in the west more than ten kilometers east to Balestrate. But the beach is not empty. Standing up some seven feet high against the sea and sky is a cross of green canes, decorated with pink oleander flowers and yellow euphorbia, a garland of flowering oleander branches hanging from each arm. It sticks up out of the sand, a solitary priest stretching its arms northward. Robed in Mediterranean vegetation, its origins are otherworldly: in fact a small crayoned Swedish flag is fastened to the top.

Back at Bosco, I rush to Sir James Frazer, and sure enough,

in a quote from a source unidentified in the abridged edition, *The Golden Bough* tells me that I have seen a Maypole, which in Sweden is set up on the Eve of Saint John.

> This consists of a straight and tall spruce-pine tree, stripped of its branches. "At times hoops and at others pieces of wood, placed crosswise, are attached to it at intervals; whilst at others it is provided with bows, representing, so to say, a man with his arms akimbo. From top to bottom not only the 'Maj Stång' (Maypole) itself, but the hoops, bows, etc., are ornamented with leaves, flowers, slips of various cloth, gilt egg-shells, etc.; and on top of it is a large vane, or it may be a flag."

I later learn that this expatriate Maj Stång was the work of a Swedish family who have rented a house on the beach for the month of June, who even brought with them cans of pickled herrings and boiled potatoes, the traditional fare for the Eve of Saint John. But this rational explanation does not remove the memory of how my blood ran cold to see the Maypole standing there, or shake my conviction that I have received some private oracle.

This first swim in the shadow of the Maypole brings a desire for more, and the next week Tonino takes a morning off to drive with me along the coast west of Castellammare, where the mountains fall abruptly into the sea, and a small road picks its way along the steep slope, suspended halfway between the little village of Scopello, hidden from view by a rock outcropping and a Spanish watchtower, and the Scopello *tonnara*, the tuna fishery that crouches below on the water's edge. As we descend the dirt path from the road, we can see the *tonnara* spread out below us at the apex of a tiny cove, shut off to the east by an arm of low cliffs and to the west by the Faraglioni, tall and jagged masses of stone that thrust up from the sea, their crests bristling with prickly pears and agave plants. One of the Faraglioni is topped by another watchtower, which some lucky person has restored to use as the world's most beautiful beachhouse.

Directly below are the ancient buildings of the *tonnara*, the cobble and cement slide that leads down to the water from the low boat sheds with their wide-arched doors, the narrow-windowed barracks where the *tonnaroti*, the fishermen, sleep while the tuna are running, and to the west the flaking chalky-pink stucco of the complex that houses the owner's apartments, the chapel, and the storerooms, all disposed about a courtyard shaded by an overgrown fig tree. The buildings nestle in the arc of the bay, exploiting with great economy the thin margin of flat land before the mountainside begins to climb, and appearing to grow out of the rock rather than to be built over it.

The waters of Scopello are cool, deep, and limpid, shifting from turquoise to azure as the sea bottom changes from sand to eelgrass, blending slowly into the intense blue of the distance, where we can see the black boats of the *tonnara* dismantling the nets. The season is ending now. The tuna come in May and June to lay their eggs in the warm waters off the northern coast of Sicily, and the catching of them is supposed to be, for the strong-stomached, one of the most fascinating spectacles that Sicily has to offer, repeating with unfaltering fidelity the rites and rules that were brought here by the Arabs more than a thousand years ago.

Nets mended and boats caulked, the crew begins its work in April when the long, low wooden boats are brought down to the water's edge and the fishermen fold in the huge nets with care so that they will feed out smoothly and quickly when they are being set. Following the orders of the head fisherman, who is still addressed by the Arabic title of *rais*, the crew works to the rhythm of a chant which at the end of each net becomes a prayer to the Virgin that the net may be filled with a good catch.

The *tonnara* proper is an enormous rectangle formed by huge cords that are floated by corks and stretched taut by forged iron anchors eight feet tall. Nets drop down vertically from the cords to the sea bottom to form a long corridor, the shore end of which is open to admit the fish. More nets, placed crosswise along the length of this corridor, can be raised or lowered to create a series of chambers through which the *tonnaroti* force the fish toward the closed end of the corridor, known as the "death chamber."

Once this elaborate mechanism is set up, the long wait begins (it was not rare in the past for the statues of the *tonnara*'s patron saint to get a dunking if the fish were slow in coming). When at last the lookouts announce the arrival of a school of tuna, the boats drive the fish into the mouth of the trap and then gather round the "death chamber." The *raìs* waits till the nets are full to order the closing of the doors, and then the *tonnaroti* begin the slow pulling in on the ropes, leaning and heaving to the beat of the *cialoma*. Each verse of this ancient chantey begins and ends with the cry *"Aimola! Aimola!"* which some say derives from *"Allah! Che muoia!*—Allah! May it die!"

The pace of the chant quickens as the great fish come to the surface, crazed by the tightening nets, thrashing their power-ful tails in an attempt to clear a space for themselves with blows that maim their neighbors and send sprays of bloody water fif-teen feet into the air. The boats close in around the mass of heav-ing, shining, bleeding, thrashing dark gray bodies, and at a com-mand from the *raìs*, the *mattanza*, the slaughter, begins, as the fishermen spear the frenzied fish with long-handled harpoons and drag their dying bodies into the boats. The sea churns with foam and blood and the air throbs with the splashing and the shouting and the relentless, quickening beat of the *cialoma*.

I have never quite been able to decide whether I really want to see the *mattanza* or not and am not displeased today to find that the sea has washed away all traces of blood. Nor have the summer crowds arrived: we float lazily in the cool water in soli-tary peace, interrupted only by bits and snatches of song and laughter that waft in from the distant boats and by the cries of the seagulls searching for the last remnants of the slaughter.

🌿 "Halcyon" is a word that belongs to the winter solstice, "a bird fabled by the ancients to breed in a floating nest on the sea at the winter solstice, and to charm the wind and the waves into calm for that purpose," but there is no better word that I can borrow to describe the days that follow on the solstice of summer. Tonino goes off to Palermo each morning early, and I am alone in the house till dark, with only the dog and the cat, the chattering sparrows, and the buzzing insects for company. I put away my watch and arrange my day at whim, reading, writing, and cleaning the house for the friends and family that July will bring. Even cleaning is almost pleasant when there is no telephone to ring while I wage war on spiders from the top of a ladder, and no one for whom I must interrupt everything to prepare a meal. There are moments, while washing the endless stretches of terracotta tiling or dusting the plows and the bellows, when I wonder why we didn't decide to build something small, modern, and practical after the earthquake, instead of resurrecting this beloved but unwieldy behemoth, but like the daddy longlegs before my broom, discouragement is routed by the satisfaction of awakening the gleam of copper, old wood, and tile.

If I am hot, I cool off in the garden, hose in hand, watering and watching the sunlight ring its changes of the landscape. Forthright and industrious in the morning, it freshens the olives and the vineyards, a good housewife plumping up her pillows, only to flatten them out again at noon and deprive them of their color. An element of drama creeps across the hillsides toward six o'clock, as the slanting rays pencil lines of black shadow behind the grapevines, add inches onto the melon plants, intensify the red of the soil and the emerald of the fruit trees. All this art is erased when the sun drops into the sea near Capo San Vito, leaving only the lighthouse to twinkle on the horizon, and a lavender haze falls, a giant cobweb strung from the gray-blue mountains in the west to the reddish purple peaks of the east, resting on the hilltops and sagging into the valleys.

If I am hungry, ten paces to the right of the kitchen door will take me to the *perazzoli*, tiny pears an inch in diameter, a concentrate of flavor that grows in bright yellow bunches on a young tree near the quinces. Or I can turn left to the mulberry trees. The black mulberries are ripe now and bursting with crimson juice that trickles down your arm when you reach up to pick them, delight of children who feign mortal accidents and flourish bloodstained fingers before their mother's horrified eyes. If I want something more substantial, the figs are waiting for me down in the valley, the early ones, dark purple sacks of honey dangling from the branches, and the peaches yield in ripeness beneath my touch. If I feel industrious, I can slither down the steep hill to the *casette di Zu Natale*, two little stone huts that nestle into the hillside as if inhabited by hobbits, part of a piece of adjoining land that we bought from a *contadino* who had grown too old to work it. In front of the bigger hut a rich orange carpet is spread out, apricots that at the least breath of wind drop gently onto a soft bed of dried grass and lie there, waiting for me to gather them and turn them into jam.

If I am lonely I stick my head out and greet Mr. Amato in his comings and goings or hail Turiddu as he comes into the *cantina* for another load of copper sulphate to spray on the grape vines, to fight off the fungi that heavy dew has encouraged. Mr. Amato is pleased with his *novara*, although he tells me he has given up on one piece of land:

"I've seeded it with tomatoes four times, but nothing has come up. You need a little shove from the soil too."

Calm and careful, Mr. Amato offers a contrast to Turiddu's volatile nature. He is also very generous: each time I proudly gather a first meager handful of string beans from my vines, he appears with a plastic bag bulging with beans from *his* vines.

"Per Lei, signora."

And yesterday he arrived with two fine *cucuzze*. The *cucuzza*, the same from which the *cucuzzata* used to fill pastries is made, is a particularly Sicilian squash. A long, smooth, pale green cylinder, it grows in a comma or a curlicue if the vine is left on the ground, or straight as a ruler and as much as five feet long when trained on a trellis. In the absence of any flavor of its own, it has an amazing capacity for absorbing and neutralizing any other taste. Hence the proverb *"Consatala come vuoi, sempre cucuzza è*—Flavor it as you will, it's always *cucuzza,"* which applies to anything intrinsically insipid or uninteresting. A person who answers this description is said to have a *cucuzza* head.

Cucuzza is nonetheless held in high esteem. A mainstay of the summer diet, it occupies a very high slot in the hierarchy the Sicilians have devised in their endless preoccupation with the workings of their innards, a topic that, far from being banished from polite conversation, is preferred for the dinner table.

Cucuzza is *fresca*, the ultimate in "cool" food. This has nothing to do with the temperature at which it is served but indicates its effect on the bowels. Like lettuce, chicory, dandelion greens, and endive, *cucuzza* refreshes, while cabbage, broccoli, cauliflower, and artichokes are "hot" and irritate. Spinach and chard are in between, not quite condemned but suspect enough to make them rare visitors to my mother-in-law's table. A friend of my brother-in-law's tried to seminate panic at Alcamo Marina one summer by spreading the rumor that *cucuzza* has been found to be bad for the liver. Tradition won out, but not before one dreadful quake of doubt had menaced the very foundations of the local domestic economy.

In return for the *cucuzze* I have promised to give Mr. Amato some of my parsley seed as soon as it has ripened enough to be harvested and put away for resowing on Saint Francis' Day at the beginning of October. It was indeed enviable parsley, not at all like the parsley in my favorite Sicilian proverb, which is used, with a resigned shrug of the shoulders, to indicate something or someone who has seen better times: *"C'era beddu lu pitrusinu, c'iì lu 'attu e ci pisciò*—It wasn't such beautiful parsley in the first place, and then the cat went and peed on it."* But I wish it would hurry up and finish going to seed; having grown to staggering heights it hides from sight the flower beds beyond it.

The herb garden is hidden too, by a sea of flowering lavender, the long spears bobbing and dancing under a multicolored regatta, the white jibs of the cabbage moths, the striped spinnakers of the swallowtails, the bumblebees, and the huge and furry purple wasps. I have decided to leave the flowers on the plants for all to enjoy; last year's harvest still hangs from the rafters of the *palmento* waiting for someone to make it into sachets, and often there is another flowering in the fall.

For the better part of the day I am happy to be a hermit. I have spread my books and file cards on the table in the guest-house while it is still free of tenants, and I work there or pace the courtyard with lined pad in hand, pausing to breathe in the sweet smell of the wild mint that I have trodden underfoot or to admire the grapevine that sags under the weight of a thousand rock-hard grapelets ("And at zero cost!" says Tonino wistfully. "What did you do, some two minutes' worth of pruning?") or the pomegranate tree on which each of the two flowers has set to fruit. When inspiration comes, I stretch out with it on a deck chair in the sun, or swing with my sources in the hammock under the porch roof.

Although the courtyard at Bosco is closed to the world beyond, it is of itself a microcosm. One has only to tune one's senses down to its proportions, to adjust one's focus: the grasshopper sitting next to my foot flexes his powerful hind legs for flight; three ants drag a worm across the stubble left by my diligent weeding, their route, filled with useless detours and unnecessary climbs, revealing the lack of intelligence behind a seemingly rational endeavor. The erratic flight of a yellow-winged butterfly, thus confined, becomes a careful exploration of possibilities, beginning with the scarlet bougainvillea, then the orange and crimson of the geraniums, then the last of the purple clematis lingering among the leaves of the Virginia creeper, while discarding the mere green of the succulents, the spiky yuccas, the potted kumquat tree. On the sun-warmed cobblestones lizards keep their immobile watch, heads raised to spit out a tongue and gather in a fly, and as dusk falls the geckos creep out to take up their posts beside the wall lamps.

Sounds, too, wash over the courtyard walls: the waxing and waning hum of a tractor, the pitiful cry of a sparrow fallen prey to the cat's patrols, occasionally the motor of a passing car that obliges me to peer out the gate to see who is using our road. One morning I hear fire, a greedy, sinister sound like the snapping and cracking of a thousand tiny bones. Someone has fired the stubble in the Blundas' wheat field, but I can see no one, and, alarmed, I call Tonino, who fortunately is working at home this morning.

"No, they'll be down in the valley somewhere. It's not hot enough for spontaneous combustion, and the Blundas aren't the sort to start a fire and then go away and leave it."

But I am not reassured. It is a windy day, a poor choice for firing stubble, and the flames dance and crackle, leaping in frenzy to reach the tall grass along the road. Cinders blow in the window onto the table where I am working, and the acrid smell of burning straw calls me back to the door again and again. The roar of the fire is so loud that I do not hear the knocking of Nino Di Giovanni, the elderly *contadino* who lives just down the road, come to call Tonino for help in putting out the flames that are threatening his olive trees.

In half an hour they manage to extinguish the blaze, working up the hill along the flickering orange line and beating on the flames with green branches. Two days later Mr. Blunda stops by to thank Tonino. He is convinced that the fire was set by a farmer of dubious repute who lives just a little north of us on the next hill over. Blunda had told this man that he intended to plow a firebreak around the field before firing it himself, but the man has a grudge against our local shepherds and wanted to prevent them from pasturing their sheep in the stubble, as Blunda had given them permission to do.

The smell of smoke comes often in the days that follow, and columns of gray pulse skyward from the valleys and the hillsides as one by one the harvested fields are fired in order to destroy the seeds of the wild oats and the other weeds that infest the grain. I am always quick to try to locate the source of the smoke or the crackle: the piles of firewood waiting to be sawn and the dried grass about the house make me uneasy, nor do I like sitting in the line of fire between the shepherds and their enemies.

Following on the heels of the fire come more reassuring sounds, the rattle, squeak, and roar of the giant tractors with their one monolithic plow blade, hastening to deep-plow the fields now, before the sun hardens the claylike soil to granite, so that they will be ready in October, as soon as the *vendemmia* is over and the grapes are in, to begin the cycle anew.

Chapter Nine

❧ With wristwatch and appointment book put aside, I hardly notice that June has faded into July, bringing closer and closer the moment when Natalia's return will catapult me back into time. I am reminded only in the evenings, when I climb into bed and see the clock radio I had the unfortunate idea of borrowing from Francesco during his absence, flashing out the passing minutes at me, its red digital numbers crazed by our uneven rural power supply. The digital clock is surely the quintessential symbol of our modern sense of time, announcing relentlessly the irrevocable end of each minute, abolishing the sense of cycle, death and re-birth, that is implicit in the rotating hands of the traditional timepiece, which mark the beginning in the very moment in which they indicate the end.

Natalia is due home on the seventh; Turi is driving down from Milan and picking the girls up on his way south. Our brief paren-thesis of peace comes to a close that evening with the sound of a car coming up the hill, its motor barely audible under the excited blowing of the horn. When we open the door, summer bursts in on us like butterflies as two tanned and laughing young ladies in brightly colored bathing suits rush in and fling their arms about our necks, at least three inches taller and three years older than the little girls I left on the station platform at Agropoli.

It takes only a day or two for the usual pattern to establish itself, as I begin to shuttle the girls back and forth between Bosco and the beach. Ostensibly, Natalia resides with us at Bosco and Martina at Alcamo Marina with her father and her grandmother; in fact they will spend only two or three nights apart in the next two months. We spend most mornings on the beach, but I return thankfully to Bosco after lunch, glad to escape the confusion and the traffic that have overtaken Alcamo Marina now that the season is in full swing. The roaring of the motorcycles and the whistling of the trains at the level crossing flood the house despite the oleander bushes that Turi has planted along the front fence, a bone of generational contention, since they prevent my mother-in-law from seeing who is walking past, with whom, and in which direction. The round of visits has begun, cousins and nieces and nephews, dragging with them reluctant grandchildren, or bringing new fiancés to be presented, come to pay their respects to Mrs. Simeti, who is the only survivor of her generation in the family. She is too old now to scold us still for not returning all these visits, for being "Turks," unsociable and ill mannered. I have always been delighted by this lingering if imprecise trace of the island's history in its dialect, and great is my pleasure one day to hear my mother-in-law, disoriented by her transfer from the nursing home to the beach and startled to find pasta on the table when she was expecting breakfast, complain about her state of mental confusion.

"*Mi sento pigghiata dai turchi!*—I feel as if I had been carried off by the Turks!"

The complement of this use of "Turk" is the Sicilian's habit of using *cristiano*, "Christian," as a generic word for human being.

I remember the Sicilian woman-servant of a gentleman of my acquaintance, coming into the room one day, and taking away the key to a back door. On being asked what she wanted with it, she replied that she was going to let out the Christians, meaning only two old women who were her visitors.

William Irvine, *Letters on Sicily*

The same traveler who wrote this home to London in the early nineteenth century reports another delightful instance of Sicilian categorizing, this time apropos of the English, whom the Sicilians

have always admired greatly, their Protestant heresy notwithstanding.

> I remember an old woman looking with the jealousy of poverty and
> age at a young English officer, who was passing by on horseback,
> handsomely accoutred. "Ah!" said she, "for all his lace he goes to
> hell." A priest standing by reproved her presumption, by calling her
> a beast,—a favorite Italian phrase,—"*Che siete bestia*"—"as for the
> Turks," continued he, "they certainly go to hell, but nobody knows
> where the English go."

History has made the Sicilian dialect almost a language apart,
so great is the legacy of the Greeks, the Arabs, the French, and
the Spanish. The dialect is full of marvelous metaphors, strong
and vivid and with a rude vitality that has long since been ironed
out of Italian, for centuries a literary, official language more often
than a spoken one. My mother-in-law, for example, an insomniac
of many years' standing, would complain enviously about how
easily her husband slept: "*Ha il sonno attaccato col laccio*—He has
sleep tied on with a string," and in my mind would appear a soft,
quilted cloud, like a balloon tied on by string to the bedpost, which
at a gentle tug from my father-in-law would slowly descend to
envelop him in sleep.

The dialect has a rich range of epithets as well, covering the
spectrum from sworn enmity to momentary hostility in a traffic
jam. My husband tends to disparage Palermo drivers as *scricchia-
panelli*, "*panelli*-chompers," reserving the true Sicilian offense, *cornutu*, for graver occasions. *Cornutu* means having horns, cuckold
and therefore dishonored, and when said without a smile is about
as much of an offense as one might need, but Tonino prefers to
embroider, as in *cornutu abbiveratu*, an "irrigated cuckold," who
thanks to watering has grown particularly long and flourishing
horns, or *chiù cornutu di un panere di babaluci*, "having more horns
than a basket full of snails."

Sicilians will usually laugh at my attempts to use their dialect:
they proudly claim that no one who was born off the island can

properly pronounce the double *d* that has taken the place of the Italian double *l*, as in *bedda matre e beramente*, "by the beautiful Mother and verily," a phrase with which a Sicilian protests his sincerity, or in *'adduzzu*, "little rooster," the word Tonino makes me say to prove, to his perpetual amusement, that I am still unable to locate the particular spot between palate and throat from which the tongue must launch the double *d*.

Sicilian has a different grammar as well; it tends, like Latin, to put the verb at the end of the sentence, and it uses its tenses differently from the Italian. The future tense is lacking altogether, so contemplated actions are perforce tinged with an element of constriction—"I have to go" for "I shall go"—as if to underline how rarely the Sicilians have been masters of their own fate.

❧ It is expressions of pity and disgust that we hear most often under the beach umbrellas and during the first visits of the season, pity for the old man, custodian of the big well at the edge of Alcamo Marina, who is murdered in the middle of the road two days after Natalia's return, and disgust for the "scorched earth" policy the dominant Mafia clan is perpetrating. The well belonged to the Rimis, the family of mafiosi who for several generations were the unchallenged masters of Alcamo and have only recently been defeated and put to flight by a new clan. Several of the family's closest associates have been murdered, anyone who attempts to buy or rent any Rimi property is warned off, and it appears that even the threatening telephone calls our friend received may be ascribed to his having performed some professional services for the Rimis, rather than to an exaggerated idea of his income. Now this old man lies in a pool of blood at Alcamo Marina, his only fault that of having administered the sale of water from the Rimis' well and transmitting the proceeds to wherever they are hiding.

The dark stain that persists on the sandy pavement near the well—impossible not to glance at it as one drives by—is one more reason to feel relief as I get in the car after lunch and, turning away from the beach, head south toward Bosco. No cars come careening around the curves toward me now that it is siesta time, and Sicily lies still in the two o'clock heat, its faint shimmering the only movement other than my own. The rich red of the winter earth has dried to old brick, pale around the edges where the dust settles, and the dead grass at the roadside heaves and twitches at the car's passage. The sun has burned off the superfluous and the merely decorative everywhere but in gardens artificially sustained. Elsewhere no grass grows, no flowers, and green is reserved for the productive: the olives, the vineyards, and the fruit orchards, the tomato and the melon vines. A bubble of heat and light in which we are suspended, July deceives us with its languor; it floats on the surface of a giant cauldron that throws up from its steady simmer harvest after harvest: mounds of dark purple eggplants and shiny green peppers, sweet red tomatoes, golden peaches and crimson-streaked nectarines, pears whose thin yellow skins are stretched taut with juice, fat watermelons by the truckload and monumental bunches of Cardinal grapes, the dark red table grapes that are the first to ripen.

Just below Alcamo I turn east onto the highway, passing Vaddinuccio, where we own a piece of land and a small house hidden from sight among fruit trees. Now consigned to the limbo of *novara* until Tonino and Turi decide what to do with this small property whose value lies more in its proximity to the town than in its fertility, Vaddinuccio was until recently our last feudal fetter, its vineyards cultivated in *mezzadria* by Peppino, the sharecropper who planted them.

Peppino's father had worked for Tonino's grandfather, and his eldest brother was the *mezzadro* at Bosco until he retired, shortly after I came to Sicily. Peppino himself tended the vines at Vaddinuccio when he was not working in Germany as a mason, and he repaired the little house to use as a summer cottage for his family, planting vegetables and fruit trees and raising chickens, ducks, and even the odd turkey.

The relationship between the later generations of Simetis and Peppino's family, a most uneasy relationship based on distrust on the one hand and resentment on the other, had been reduced by my time to the unavoidable. The major and most unpleasant encounter came annually on the day in which the grapes were harvested, when my mother-in-law, my children, and I were deposited at Vaddinuccio (the Simeti men being busy elsewhere) to sit and knit and chat while Peppino and his entire tribe picked and toted grapes. Ostensibly we were there to share sociably in the pleasures and rewards of the *vendemmia;* everyone knew, however, that our presence was to insure that nothing untoward was added to or subtracted from the growing pile of grapes that waited, heaped on a heavy canvas tarp, for the truck to come and take them away to be weighed.

The discomfort of that day was somewhat alleviated by my secret delight in the other, in July, when Peppino and his son would appear at Alcamo Marina, their little Fiat 500 a veritable cornucopia on wheels, bursting with the fruits of Vaddinuccio brought in homage to the padrone: bushels of tomatoes; a crate of prickly pears; another of table grapes; a basket of *sbirgi,* a rare and delicious variety of pale green nectarines. And invariably, every year, much to my in-laws' annoyance, this magnificent tribute of fruit was just a little too green to be edible.

The vineyards at Vaddinuccio grew old together with their *mezzadri,* and a few years ago they were torn out and the contract was terminated, thus ending an era whose passing no one mourned, except perhaps for a momentary twinge of regret when we remember the *sbirgi.*

Once off the highway the car bounces and skids along the dusty track, raising in its wake a thick brown cloud that hangs motionless awhile before settling on the hedgerows and turning the dark purple-black of the blackberries to beige. The first of the berries are ripe already and have attracted some children from a nearby farm, who scuffle their bare feet in the silky dust and leap up the bank like startled rabbits at the sound of my engine. At the top of the rise I pass Nino Di Giovanni and his nephew, hard at work in the shadow of their one-room house. The nephew, tall and as thin as a cane, is known to us as *U Prufissuri* from his habit of tiptoeing up the hill, sticking his toothless grin inside the kitchen curtain unannounced, and asking for Tonino—*"U Prufissuri c'è?"* At the moment he is busy with a pitchfork, tossing forkfuls of dried fava beans into the air in the hopes that some slight breeze will carry off the pieces of dried stalk and pod as the rust-brown beans fall heavily to earth, while his uncle is winnowing oats in an enormous sieve suspended horizontally under a tripod of branches.

Down in the valley a trail of dust marks Mr. Amato's passage with the tractor along his melon rows. The first of the melons are already ripening, and in fact there are two fat watermelons sitting on the doormat outside the kitchen as I drive by. I should have thought that so much tilling would release moisture from the soil, but Tonino has explained to me that, on the contrary, each slice of the tiller blade breaks up the capillaries along which the humidity escapes and the fine cloak of dust that settles on the plants prevents the leaves from drying out.

The house itself is still, except for the cat, who drops silently from the mulberry tree to rub against my ankles, and for Happy barking in the courtyard. *U Prufissuri*'s breeze is an illusion: nothing stirs the pool of heat that submerges the house, and it is an effort to wade to the gate, find the key, pull back the iron bar, and push into the courtyard, hotter still, where the walls throb with the sun, and the listless, drooping leaves of the Virginia creeper do not even quiver as the dog does a perfunctory version of her welcoming dance. Constant watering has kept the potted plants and vines alive and green, but underfoot the cobbles are bare and sunbaked, all weeds gone except in the square onto which the hose leaks. The hammock hangs heavily, uninviting, and wasps drone around the faucet, waiting for a drop of water to accumulate.

Corseted by thick stone walls, the house is impervious to heat, and as I pause inside the door to let my eyes accustom themselves to its shadows, the cool air, smelling slightly of damp and of lavender, raises gooseflesh on my bare limbs. Stretched out in the slats of light that filter through the bedroom shutters, I twitch my toe lazily to chase away a fly and reread the same sentence three times. The book propped up on my chest nods in the drowsy air, and outside a cicada drills insistently through the heat.

> When the cardoon flowers, and the loud cicada sings
> perched on a tree, pouring from under his wings
> a flood of shrillest music time and again:
> when summer is ripe, and the heat a burden of pain,
> then are the she-goats fattest, and wine is best,
> and women most fain; but men are languidest,
> for Sirius parches the heads and knees of men
> and burns their bodies with drowth.
>
> Hesiod, "Works and Days," in
> *Oxford Book of Greek Verse in Translation*

If Sicilian men dry up in the summer heat they manage to hide it very well; I do not remember noticing in more youthful days any seasonal letup in the stream of steady and audible admiration that my five feet and ten inches provoked in this short-statured race. At times this was unpleasant—I dreaded meeting the wall-eyed delivery man from the Partinico slaughterhouse who would pause on the sidewalk in front of a butcher's shop, as the blood from the enormous side of beef balanced on his shoulder dripped down onto already much-spattered overalls. Leering askew at me, he would growl as I passed: "What thighs! You make my blood boil!"

But on the whole the Sicilians are more dignified than, let's say, the Romans: they stare and follow and comment, but rarely pinch. It is the persistence that is tiresome, and was even more so twenty years ago, when young and foreign females alone were still a great rarity. Connie Cronin, a very blond American anthropologist who was also working at the Dolci Center, got so fed up with being followed about Palermo on her day off that she finally turned to Vittorio, a young coworker of local origin, for advice on how to discourage her admirers. Vittorio thought about it for a moment, then answered briskly: "It's easy. Just limp."

Vittorio was very resourceful in carrying out his self-appointed role as defender of the honor of his foreign coworkers. He spread the word around the bars and *caffè* of Partinico that I held a black belt in judo, probably a superfluous precaution in what was really a very tranquil village, but he enjoyed telling me about it. That, plus Tonino's early appearance on my horizon, should have more than sufficed, but one day I was stopped just outside my front door in the Via di Benedetto by a well-dressed middle-aged man. I expected an inquiry about an English course I had been asked to give for prospective emigrants, but as soon as he started talking about the very first moment he had seen me, I realized I was in for something else. And in fact he began to follow me about town, to loiter outside my house in the evening, and, if we met by accident in the Corso, to doff his hat in a bow worthy of d'Artagnan, which I was unable to counter with anything more snappy than an embarrassed cringe.

This went on for several weeks until I came home late one evening from a party to find him still standing outside my door, and embarrassment gave way to alarm. Shortly after that I arrived at the office one morning to see him standing in the doorway talking to Vittorio, so later I sought Vittorio out in the room where he worked the mimeograph, to ask him if he could do anything to free me from these unwelcome attentions.

"*Porca miseria! PORCA MISERIA! Ci penso io!*—I'll take care of it!" And he stormed out of the office.

A tiny and very dapper young man with carefully waved hair and a pencil-line moustache, Vittorio was an anthropologist's gold mine, as he had a great capacity for detached analysis of the Sicilian way of life and thought, but at the same time he very much fancied himself to be the epitome of the fiery Latin and was extremely proud of the uncle who had been part of Salvatore Giuliano's band. It was therefore with some misgivings that I awaited his return.

After our lunch break, he came into the room where I was working.

"Mary, it's okay. I've taken care of it."

"That's wonderful, Vittorio, but what *did* you do?"

"Oh, it was easy. I went to him and said, 'Hey, you want to do me a favor? You know the Via di Benedetto?' He pretended he didn't know what I was talking about. 'You know the one I mean,' I said. 'Just forget it. Forget you've ever been there.' "

I never saw the man again.

If it wasn't for the siren call of the siesta, I would be engrossed by the book that is threatening to slide off my stomach and tumble to the floor. I found it quite by chance, attracted by its title, *The Gardens of Adonis*, and have been fascinated to follow the author, a French classical anthropologist named Marcel Detienne, in his

> progressive deciphering of a botanical code whose components range from the myrrh from which Adonis was born to the lettuce which became his death-bed. The structure of this code appears to be strictly based upon a vertical axis passing from the "solar" plants which are hot, dry—even scorched—incorruptible and perfumed to the plants from below which are cold, wet and raw and are closely connected with death and foul smells. In between these two extremes, occupying an intermediate position at what one might call the "right" distance, are those plants which in the Greek view correspond to the normal life of civilized men, in other words the cereals, cultivated plants in which the dry and the wet are balanced and which constitute a specifically human type of food.
>
> From J.-P. Vernant's Introduction to Marcel Detienne,
> *The Gardens of Adonis: Spices in Greek Mythology*

If I am immediately inspired to see in this botanical code the remote origins of my mother-in-law's ideas about *cucuzza* being cold and cabbage hot, Detienne uses the code to refute *The Golden Bough*'s interpretation of the Adonis myth and ritual, in which according to Frazer the *lavureddi*, the little gardens of Adonis that are offered in the churches during Holy Week, are "charms to promote the growth or revival of vegetation." On the contrary, Detienne sees them as part of a very different ritual, one that (I giggle to myself as I read along) would certainly startle the somber, black-shawled Sicilian matrons who carefully tend their *lavureddi* each spring. He claims that the little vases seeded with fennel (aromatic), barley (median), and lettuce (cold and moist) that sprouted and withered rapidly under the fierce heat of Sirius, the Dog Star, were prepared for the Adonie, the festival in which at the end of July the courtesans and concubines of Athens honored, with much wine and licentious behavior, their favorite, Adonis, the lover of Aphrodite. Adonis, like the seedlings, dies young and without progeny, an image of illicit, ephemeral, and sterile love, beyond the bounds of civil society that, protected by Demeter, rests on the twin pillars of monogamous marriage and diligent agriculture.

🌿 Despite a wistful corner of my fancy that would have me otherwise, I know by now that I am prosaically but unshakably a devotee of Demeter, and when the end of the afternoon comes and a breeze lifts off the sea and wafts new energy through the shutters, it is no bawdy revelry for which I gird myself. A far more chaste festival calls me, the Festino of Saint Rosalia, virgin saint and protectress of Palermo. While the countryside dozed in a sunbaked stupor, Palermo has been preparing for the contemporary version of what was once one of the most famous celebrations in all Europe.

Rosalia, legend has it, was the daughter of Sinibaldo, lord of Quisquina and Rose, and cousin to King Roger II. Repelled by the licentiousness and luxury of the Norman court in which she was brought up, at fifteen she withdrew from the world and went to live in a cave on Monte Pellegrino, the sudden, barren mass of rock that raises at the western tip of the Bay of Palermo. She is said to have disappeared in 1159 without leaving a trace, but in 1624, while Palermo was languishing in the grip of the Black Death, she appeared in a dream to a hunter who was napping on the mountainside and revealed to him the whereabouts of the cavern where her bones lay.

The archbishop of Palermo and all the senators proceeded in great pomp to the cave and did indeed find the bones. After six months of careful study (careful, some say, in that care was taken to wait until the plague was waning of its own accord), the bones were proclaimed genuine and brought down in triumph to the city, where they are conserved in a silver urn in the cathedral. The plague abated and by popular acclaim Rosalia became the patroness and protectress of Palermo.

Coins and other relics from the prehistoric, the Punic, and the Greek eras show that Rosalia's grotto, watered by an underground spring, was sacred to the chthonic deities long before it received its definitive consecration as the sanctuary of the virgin hermit. The grotto now forms the nave of a chapel, its roof crisscrossed by rudimentary tin gutters that catch the water dripping from the rocks and dispense it to the faithful. The entrance is hung with ex-votos that testify to the miraculous powers of the saint and her waters, and under the altar is her statue, a young girl reclining in a posture of ecstatic rapture. Her head and hands are carved from white marble, a wreath of golden roses circles her brow, and her body is wrapped in a robe of gold cloth, a gift from the Bourbon King Charles III.

Despite all the gold the shrine is simple, sweet and yet impressive, and it is easy to understand why it captivated Goethe, who visited it in 1787 and in his journal remarked:

The shrine itself is more appropriate to the humility of the saint who took refuge there than the pomp of the festival which is celebrated in honour of her renunciation of the world.

Goethe, *Italian Journey*

Goethe was not in Palermo for the Festino, but like many cultivated Europeans he had read the descriptions of Patrick Brydone, the first Englishman to include Sicily in his grand tour. Brydone's letters home, published in 1773, caused something of a sensation in England and on the continent as well, for they revealed an island about which most Europeans knew absolutely nothing. They also revealed an intelligent, educated, and amenable sightseer, whose good-humored enthusiasm and open-mindedness must have endeared him to his Sicilian hosts as well as to his northern readers.

Brydone's account of the Festino of 1770 is well worth reading for its description of the extraordinary ceremony and the magnificence with which Palermo celebrated its hermit patroness.

Palermo, July 12

About five in the afternoon, the festival began by the triumph of St. Rosalia, who was drawn with great pomp through the centre of the city, from the Marino to the Porto Nuovo. The triumphal car was preceded by a troop of horses, with trumpets and kettledrums, and all the city officers in their gala uniforms. It is indeed a most enormous machine; it measures seventy feet long, thirty wide, and upwards of eighty high, and, as it passed along, overtopped the loftiest houses of Palermo. The form of its underpart is like that of the Roman galleys, but it swells as it advances in height, and the front assumes an oval shape like an amphitheatre, with seats placed in the theatrical manner. This is the great orchestra, which was filled with a numerous band of musicians placed in rows, one above the other: over this orchestra, and a little behind it, there is a large dome supported by six Corinthian columns, and adorned with a number of figures of saints and angels; and on the summit of the dome there is a gigantic silver statue of St. Rosalia. The whole machine is dressed out with orange-trees, flower-pots, and trees of artificial coral. The car stopped every fifty or sixty yards, when the orchestra performed a piece of music, with songs in honor of the saint. It appeared a moving castle, and completely filled the great street from side to side. . . . This vast fabric was drawn by fifty-six huge mules, in two rows, curiously caparisoned, and mounted by twenty-eight postillions, dressed in gold and silver stuffs, with great plumes of ostrich feathers in their hats. Every window and balcony, on both sides of the street, were full of well-dressed people, and the car was followed by many thousands of the lower sort. The triumph was finished in about three hours, and was succeeded by the beautiful illumination of the Marina.

I believe that I have already mentioned that there is a range of arches and pyramids extending from end to end of this noble walk; these are painted, are adorned with artificial flowers, and are entirely covered with lamps, placed so very thick that, at a little distance, the whole appears so many arches and pyramids of flame. . . . There was no break nor imperfection anywhere, the night being so still that not a single lamp was extinguished.

Opposite to the centre of this great line of light, there was a magnificent pavilion erected for the viceroy and his company, which consisted of the whole nobility of Palermo; and in the front of this, at some little distance in the sea, stood the great fire-works, representing the front of a palace, adorned with columns, arches, trophies and every ornament of architecture. . . . In an instant, the whole of the palace was beautifully illuminated . . . and appeared indeed like a piece of enchantment, as it was done altogether instantaneously, and without the appearance of any agent. At the same time the fountains that were represented in the court before the palace began to spout up fire, and made a representation of some of the great *jets d'eau* of Versailles and Marly. As soon as these were extinguished, the court assumed the form of a great parterre, adorned with a variety of palm-trees of fire, interspersed with orange-trees, flower-pots, vases, and other ornaments. On the extinguishing of these, the illumination of the palace was likewise extinguished, and the front of it broke out into the appearance of suns, stars, and wheels of fire, which in a short time reduced it to a perfect ruin. And when all appeared finished, there burst from the centre of the pile a vast explosion of two thousand rockets, bombs, serpents, squibs and devils, which seemed to fill the whole atmosphere: the fall of these made terrible havoc amongst the clothes of the poor people who were not under cover, but afforded admirable entertainment to the nobility who were.

Brydone goes on to describe the illuminations of the Corso, where after the fireworks were over the nobility paraded in their carriages, the ladies dressed in sumptuous gowns and dazzling jewels and "pleasure that sparkled from every eye," and concludes:

> . . . I will own to you that I have never beheld a more delightful sight; and if superstition often produces such effects, I sincerely wish we had a little more of it amongst us. I could have thrown myself down before St. Rosalia, and blessed her for making so many people happy.

The next two days were occupied with horse races, *corse dei barbari*, similar to Alcamo's past pleasure and carried out with equal or even greater confusion and peril to the spectators. A proper Englishman, Brydone took a dim view of these barbarian contests, dismissing them as "by no means to be compared with those in England." But this is the only part of the Festino that he regarded unfavorably, as can be seen from his ecstatic description of the Vesper service in the cathedral:

> At once entering the great gate, we beheld the most splendid scene in the world. The whole church appeared a flame of light, which, reflected from ten thousand bright and shining surfaces, of different colors, and at different angles, produced an effect which, I think, exceeds all the descriptions of enchantment I have ever read. . . . The whole church—walls, roof, pillars, and plaster—were entirely covered over with mirrors, interspersed with gold and silver paper, artificial flowers, &c. . . . and illuminated with twenty thousand wax tapers. . . .

The Festino ended with a procession in which floats prepared by the various confraternities and religious orders were decorated

with statues of saints and angels. Brydone concludes his account
by describing these statues as he saw them the next day,

> returning home in coaches to their respective nunneries. At first we
> took them for ladies in their gala dress, going out to visit the churches,
> which we were told was the custom, and began to pull off our hats
> as they went past. Indeed, we were led into this blunder by some of
> our friends, who carried us out on purpose; and as they saw the
> coaches approach, told us that this is the princess of such a thing—
> there is the duchess of such another thing; and, in short, we had made
> a half-dozen of our best bows (to the no small entertainment of these
> wags) before we discovered the trick. They now insist upon it that
> we are good Catholics, for all this morning we have been bowing to
> saints and angels.

Patrick Brydone, A Tour Through Sicily and Malta

At the height of the baroque era, the splendor of the Festino
was an assertion of Palermo's ascendancy over her rivals, the cities of Catania and Messina, and the visual confirmation of the
power and munificence of the Senate, an assembly of nobles that
traced its authority (mostly illusory) back to the Norman reign
and squandered its energy in squabbling over sumptuary laws and
questions of precedence. Saint Rosalia went into a decline during
the nineteenth century, and even the triumphal cart was abandoned, due in part to the anticlericalism of postunification Italy,
and in part to the new paving of the Corso, which couldn't with-
stand such a massive weight. By popular request it was revived
toward the end of the century, but even so, little remained, according to Pitré, to distinguish Saint Rosalia's Festino from that
of any village saint. Unburdened of the need to advertise an aristocratic power and wealth that was fast waning, the Festino became a popular event that drew enormous crowds from all over
the island. It was a common provision in marriage contracts that
the husband was to bring his bride to Palermo for the Festino
during their first year of marriage, and the provincial yokel who
tastes his first ice cream at the Festino and wraps some up in his

handkerchief to take it home with him was a standard figure of fun. The ice cream vendors did a booming business, as did the *semenza* sellers, who had special carts, used only for the Festino, that were shaped like sailing ships and decorated with tricolor paper flags. Rosalia's triumphant passage smacked more of confusion than of majesty, as buckets of water were thrown on the massive wooden wheels to keep them from overheating and catching fire, so great was the friction produced by the cart's monumental weight, and

> the endless crowd pushed and shoved and elbowed so as not to remain suffocated, especially at the moment when the cart passed by. More than a few people fainted at that instant. . . . It was not uncommon to see an entire balcony railing carried away, when the cart itself got caught on it, and then, as if the sky had fallen, the shouts of the frightened bystanders became deafening, and the pushing a stampede.
>
> Giuseppe Pitrè, *Feste patronali in Sicilia*

In all these years I have never been in Palermo for the Festino, nor have the accounts of what remains of it been very tempting. But now that I have read Brydone, I decide that I must have a look at the recently resurrected triumphal cart, which will follow its former route from the cathedral down the Corso to the Marina, the Palermo waterfront that was sadly reduced by the terrible Allied bombing of forty years ago from aristocratic playground to wasteland, now bordered by crumbling, bomb-split hovels and the shell-pocked facades of the few remaining palaces, carpeted with a thick layer of garbage and illuminated by the flashing lights and tarnished tinsel of a fun fair.

The heat has nailed me to my bed longer than I intended, and it is late by the time I get to Palermo and fight my way through all the traffic jams and detours. The triumphal cart has almost reached the end of the Corso, which is transformed for the occasion into a tunnel of wooden arches curved into flowers and fountains, their painted colors gay even now in the daylight when their myriad light bulbs are spent. I too must push and shove and elbow to catch up with the cart, squeezing between soldiers on liberty for the holiday, baby carriages, *semenza* sellers, and hawkers holding down enormous bunches of balloons and strings of inflated Zorros and Spidermen. Palermo is out in force, laughing and yelling, spitting out *semenza* shells and aiming good-natured blows at the urchins dodging and swerving about its ankles. Bright-colored cottons and silks strain across ample bosoms, and fans beat steadily in the heat, while young girls in very long curls and very short skirts wiggle their bottoms at the lines of young police and carabinieri recruits who clear a passage through the crowd for the guard of honor, cavaliers on horseback and halberd-bearing pages in eighteenth-century dress, shades of lime and chartreuse edged with gold braid, which manages to suggest the hand of an upholsterer rather than a tailor.

The search for oxen having been in vain this year, the cart itself, a scaled-down version only two and a half stories high, is drawn by a shiny new tractor, whose red paint is unsuccessfully disguised by large bunches of red and yellow gladiolas and, on the roof of the cabin, a cushion of yellow carnations in the shape of an eagle, Palermo's symbol. The slightly funereal effect of the flowers is echoed in the cart itself, a vaguely boat-shaped affair of cornices and balustrades, fashioned of plaster (or plastic?) and painted dark gold, around whose stern are seated naked figures, a sort of Medici Chapel on wheels. High near the stern, the sides of the cart curve down toward the prow to encompass the tiered seats where the band is installed, outfitted in shades of lavender and mauve. Over all this towers Rosalia, the Santuzza, dark gold and Amazonesque, clutching in her right hand the red and yellow flag of the city.

The cart creaks to a halt at the end of the Corso, under the baroque arch of the Porta Felice, where the mayor and other dignitaries are waiting. We are given a rousing rendition of the national anthem followed by a few Sicilian folk songs, after which the bandmaster, his rank and his paunch emphasized by a claret-colored cummerbund, eases himself down to shake Mayor Pucci's hand. This appears to signal the end; there is some desultory consultation between police and dignitaries, as if they were not quite sure what to do next, but the crowd has had enough and splits up into many little rivulets that flow into the side streets and alleyways of the Kalsa in search of a plate of snails, of *panelli*, an ice cream cone, or *pani cu' la meusa* with which to end the feast day.

As I drive back out to Alcamo Marina to pick up Natalia, I wonder about the contrast between what I have seen today and the exquisite drawings of the seventeenth- and eighteenth-century carts from which today's has drawn its inspiration. And in all justice I am forced to admit that perhaps the contrast is not so much between past and present as between intention and realization, that probably the ephemeral substance of the Festino has always been more tawdry and distracted than the official plans and the visitors' chronicles would lead us to think, its choreography plagued by mishap and disorder, its message distorted in the transmission and contested in the reception.

❦ Natalia must sleep at Bosco tonight so that we may leave early the next morning for the airport, where we are to meet my niece Hilary and her friend Lisa, who are flying in from New York for a week of Sicilian sun and sea. Two more friends, young men who have been singing at the Spoleto festival, arrive by train shortly afterward, turning Bosco into a house party.

I am always delighted when any of my family comes to visit us. It is hard for me to believe when I look back on my decision to marry Tonino and live abroad permanently that the fact of leaving my family should have merited so little consideration. Youth and cultural bias, I suppose, combined with my own particular circumstances—my father had died before I started college, my mother was living in Italy, and my two sisters and my brother, all of them considerably older than I, were moving about a lot themselves at that point—made marrying in Sicily seem a not unnatural sequel to going away to college. I could so easily have spun off entirely after my mother's death in 1970, yet somehow love, the comfort of a common humus, and the lines cast out to me by my sisters and brother have overcome the centrifuge of time and distance and infrequent visits, bridging the gap of age and experience and pulling me close to the family I so rarely see.

So I rejoice to find my sister in my niece and to hear the quirks and expressions of our family lexicon filtered through her own special enthusiasms. We talk and talk: it startles me to find how Sicilian I have become in twenty years, how much my doubts and uncertainties, my hang-ups and my passions have shifted target, and to find how hard I must struggle to catch up with the English language. (Humor and slang are two merciless thermometers of estrangement; I hate not understanding why a cartoon in *The New Yorker* is funny and was once quite horrified when another niece of mine told me she had had her clothes ripped off in Morocco. I thought she meant they had been torn from her back and imagined her standing forlorn and naked in the Casbah.)

It is also startling—and a relief—to find how easily conversation flows across our common history, even with these kids in their twenties who can't remember the fifties I grew up in and take for granted or even as superfluous so many of the freedoms my generation rebelled for. Nothing, I have discovered, is as difficult to explain to the young as discarded prejudice: Francesco, watching the film *Novecento* on television, is bewildered by the virulence of the anticommunism, while Natalia is quite unable to comprehend why blue jeans might be considered inappropriate for school.

Bosco is filled with life, its mammoth proportions justified at last by the voices and the laughter echoing across the living room, its spaces filled with card games, with sun worshipers stretched out in deck chairs, with long and boisterous meals. This is the image we had in mind when we drew up the plans to rebuild after the earthquake, and if in our youthful inexperience we didn't realize what the underpinnings of such a scene would involve, like the Festino to the Palermitani, it is no less dear to us for being ephemeral and slightly unreal.

Through it all I churn, cooking, chauffeuring, explaining, playing the role of Earth Mother to the hilt. In my desire, deep and heartfelt, that my niece's vacation be a special one and that she share my love for things Sicilian, I can detect a slight and extraneous vein, something of the same anxiety that hit me before Francesco's departure. It is not uncommon, I suspect, for those who are born, like me, much the youngest in a large family, to feel forever obliged to account for themselves, to justify the afterthought and measure up to the august siblings who came before. So perhaps I am overbearing in my eagerness to serve as an interpreter for these young Americans, tiresome in my readiness to answer a casual question with a lecture or in my insistence that they look at this, try that, taste this other.

I trot out Sicily's culinary treats: fresh ricotta, sheep's cheese and salame, olives and olive oil, sweet peppers roasted on the coals and eaten with slices of bread toasted on the fire and rubbed with garlic, oil, and salt. I make mounds of Sicily's favorite summer dishes: *spaghetti alla coppola*, "with a cap on," with fresh tomato sauce and basil topped with dark slices of fried eggplant, or *caponata*, which is eggplant, olives, onions, almonds, and capers stewed in a sweet-and-sour tomato sauce. The quantities of food that disappear, the frequent trips into the *cantina* to refill the wine bottles, the baskets of dark red grapes from the vineyard that empty as rapidly as the bowls of *pere facce bedde*, the little "pretty-faced pears" with bright red cheeks that have ripened near the houses of Zu Natale, the groans of satiated pleasure afterward—all are signs that in this at least I have not exaggerated.

Long mornings at the beach followed by big lunches require ample siestas, so the week flies by with very little time for sight-seeing. On our way into Palermo to take the boys to the train, I decide that our guests must at least see the cathedral at Monreale. Built by William II as an answer to Archbishop Walter of the Mill, the church is a monument to royal authority, a somber and magnificent statement of wealth and divinely granted power. The visitor who comes up from Palermo, his retina dancing with the exuberance of the baroque city and the confusion of the modern, loses some of this effect, perhaps, but for us today, coming from the hot white light, the rusty soil, whitewash, and bare stone of the countryside into the cool penumbra flickering with the million gold tesserae of the mosaics and the Cosmatique inlays that line the walls, the cathedral's message is undiluted, almost overwhelming.

The modern church has unwittingly found a novel antidote to King William's ambitions. A sacristan lies in wait behind the door to cover the bare thighs and plunging necklines of tourists who might otherwise give involuntary offense to the Almighty. He pounces on our two boys, who are wearing shorts, and wraps each of them in a little red cloth like a sarong. But Johnson is six foot six, and his sarong barely reaches to his kneecaps. With his every step it flaps open and a sunburned thigh peeks out fetchingly, to subvert the sacristan's intentions and send the girls and me into fits of giggles that quite dispel any initial sense of awe.

On the last day of the visit, a friend takes us all out in his motorboat along the coast beyond Scopello to a wild and beautiful seascape that can be reached only from the sea, or by following a mule track. Developers had planned to build a road out here, linking Scopello to Capo San Vito and opening the area to the villas that have already contaminated the coves on either side of Scopello itself, but several years ago we marched, four thousand strong, out along the mule track in protest, and now the area is a nature reserve, safe from builders and hunters and scuba divers. The mountains fall down abruptly into the sea, leaving space for only a narrow border of tiny fields, vineyards that scramble up the slopes, clinging olives, plumed tufts of *ampelodisa* grass, and bristling clumps of Sicilian palmetto, the indigenous dwarf palm. High up in the mountain gorges eagles circle and the limpid waters teem with life.

It is an extraordinary day, so hot and so still that the sun has baked a smooth glaze onto the sea, now azure, now turquoise, now ultramarine, and the water is so clear that we need hardly bother with the masks we brought. We skirt the coast, weaving around rocky spurs and into tiny coves and grottoes. As soon as the boat idles to a stop a heavy lid of heat closes over us, agitated only by the beating wings and the mewing cries of the sea swallows who flee their rocky crevices at our approach. The sun scorches the skin and pains the eye; the only relief is the dive into the clear, cool water, to slip along the walls of the grottoes where cushions of purple algae mark the waterline, dotted here and there by red sea tomatoes and broken by the pale beige swirls of a lichenlike weed, to tread water, staring down through crystalline fathoms, past legs bronzed against the turquoise and lazily kicking toes to sand and stones and dark purple sea urchins, where schools of small fish flicker and pause, change direction and glide hastily away as the suggestion of a bigger shadow sends us splashing back to the boat ladder, then up and on to the next cove, the next stop, the next swim.

The girls leave just in time, for the heat that pinned us to the boat deck and drove us into the waters of Scopello becomes unbearable on the shore, scorching the already parched land, charring the forests, and consuming the crops. At night flickering red lines eat their way up the reforested mountainsides that by day are hidden by a dense soup of haze and smoke. At sundown Mr. Amato wanders mournfully among his melons, looking at the shriveled leaves and counting the scarred patches where the sun has branded the fruit, while Tonino patrols the vineyards, badly damaged as well. The grapes that have pushed out from under the leaves are daubed with brown, and gloomy forecasts estimate that 30 percent of the crop may have been lost.

The laymen claim that it is not as bad as a year ago June, when the scirocco fanned the mercury up to 117 degrees in the shade, candles melted in their sconces, the elderly died, and the middle-aged had nervous breakdowns, but the farmers know that this is worse. In June the newborn fruit was swaddled in foliage, while now, at the end of July, all the ample bounty of an abundant year is exposed and defenseless.

Like the drooping, papery leaves of the vineyards, we wait, wilted and motionless under the taut white sky, for the heat to break, but no relief comes and the tension grows. On the morning of the twenty-ninth, the head judge of the investigations office of the court of Palermo, Rocco Chinnici, leaves his home to go to the courthouse. He has brought many mafiosi to trial and is said to be on the verge of unmasking the mysterious "third level," the political and economic interests that instigated the dalla Chiesa murder. Like all the investigating judges in Palermo, he travels with an armed escort; police cars deter traffic at either end of the block, and two armed officers go into the apartment building, coming out a minute later with Chinnici, who greets the apartment house porter standing in the doorway. As the men cross the sidewalk and pass in front of a Fiat 500 parked at the curb, the little car lifts into the air, disintegrating under the force of a hundred kilograms of exploding TNT.

Once again Palermo is shocked by the indiscriminate and disproportionate dimensions that the Mafia's ferocity has assumed. The judge dies instantly, of course, as do his guards and the porter of the building, but it is remarkable that the victims are so few, in view of the violence of the explosion, which destroys the facade of the building, twists shutters and breaks windows up and down the block, and smashes the nearby cars to pulp.

🌿 We end the month by taking Natalia and Martina to see Seneca's *Phaedra*, put on by the National Institute for Antique Drama in the amphitheater at Segesta. The evening is hot and still, with no breeze to lift the actors' veils or carry off their words, and from our seats halfway down the tier of curving stone steps we look out across the stage, empty except for a few gnarled gray branches and some scattered rocks, onto a scenery of mountains and sea. Behind the mountains hangs the sky, pale lavender shot with gold as the play opens, deepening and darkening as the light vanishes and the tragedy unfolds. Crimson and orange, congruent to the incestuous passion of the unhappy queen, coagulate to purple as the messenger recounts the atrocious death, then blacken to a pall for Phaedra's suicide and Theseus' despair.

After the play, we pick our way in silence down the hillside, trusting to the feel of paving underfoot to guide us around the curves. An owl calls somewhere nearby, and a tinkling of bells sounds from the sheepfold. Our footsteps tread out perfume from the wild mint growing at the edge of the asphalt. In the valley below, the floodlit temple beckons, floating in a pool of pure, cool light and summoning us out of the darkness.

Chapter Ten

❧ "*Austu, riustu, capu d'invernu*—August, twice burnt, the beginning of winter." Alcamo's proverb pays tribute to the less obvious side of August, the slight cooling of the air that reawakens energies from their summer stupor and stirs the lymph to a final effort. The Greeks acknowledged August's prophecy by the trees they chose to hold sacred: the nut, the apple, the sorb, and the quince, a harvest of autumn fruit. The Italians, on the other hand, ignore it; like lemmings moving toward the sea, all Italy goes on holiday simultaneously, the factories close down, the hospitals release all but their most serious cases, the cities empty. Long lines of cars wait to board the ferry for the islands, the beaches disappear under a dense cover of towels and umbrellas, and hordes of determined and perspiring hikers assault the mountain trails.

Somewhere in the midst of all this agitation Francesco is making his way homeward. The heat is fierce still, and we wonder how the overcrowded train from Rome will seem after a month in the forests of Nova Scotia. Our worries prove unfounded, however; I see gray tufts floating in the sky one afternoon and search at length for the fire before I realize that they are not smoke but clouds, the first to grace our sky in almost a month. The *tramontana* comes to hurry them along, a brisk skysweeper who manages in a day to brush up a month's accumulation of haze, leaving the horizon clean and new. As we drive in to meet Francesco's train, the morning air is cool and clear and after many weeks' absence from our landscape the mountains have moved close again, within—it seems—arm's reach.

Francesco glows as he descends from the train, his belt loosened to accommodate the effects of American food, his saddlebags and suitcase straining with spiffy American sports clothes, his English flowing colloquially, and his head full of plans for next summer's trip. A few days later, when I say to Pam that Francesco loved such and such in America, he interrupts to correct me.

"I loved *everything* in America."

🌿 The Greeks traveled at the beginning of August too. According to Hesiod, "The best time for making a voyage is during the fifty days that follow the solstice, when summer is drawing to a close," and in Athens this was also the month of the Metageitnia, the festival celebrating Apollo as promoter of neighborly union and therefore the month most favorable for moving house and making new neighbors. Most Sicilian rent contracts still run out in August, and even we, while staying put, promote neighborly union in our own small way by renting out the guesthouse.

The guesthouse occupies what was once the sharecroppers' quarters, one very large room with a hayloft, and the former chapel, whose vaulted ceiling collapsed beyond any restoring in the earthquake. We built it with present visits from America and future generations in mind, but between one visit and the next it sits empty across the courtyard, its two glazed doors eyeing us reproachfully for our wastefulness. Tonino responds by talking of renting and I by pressing my thighs together, unable to overcome the sensation that renting part of Bosco is akin to prostitution.

The problem resolved itself very happily last year when Maria Vica told me she was looking for somewhere peaceful and inexpensive to spend a month together with her mother. They turned out to be perfect tenants, discreet and tactful, yet always available for a chat when the evening breezes bring us out into the courtyard, for an afternoon's trip to see the ex-votos in a rural shrine, or for a brief exchange as, coffee cup in hand, I inspect the plants to see what the night has wrought.

This year a friend comes to visit them, an elderly woman who returned to her native Catania to live after her husband's family palace in Palermo was destroyed by Allied bombs. The palace's library, built up by generations, burst into an explosion of paper that rained back down on the city—yellowed, irreplaceable pages and priceless illuminated parchments that zigzagged gently downward and sent people scurrying after what they took to be Allied propaganda leaflets.

Stout and comfortable in her steel-rimmed spectacles and flowered housedress, she knits and tells us stories of the Sicilian aristocracy, passions and scandals: a senile baron solemnly asking his granddaughter's hand in marriage; the aged *principessa* who was given to making regal apparitions at her balcony, stark naked; the two spinster sisters much sought after for their mastery of the malapropism, who, when complaining of the inefficient central heating, claimed that they couldn't get warm even with two gladiators in their bedroom, and who were heard to announce, while pointing to some porcelain eggcups in a shopwindow, that they had decided to make the Contessina So-and-so a wedding present of those lovely French ovaries.

Tonino, coming home one day, says that he has seen a spectacular Saint Joseph's altar being built in one of Alcamo's back streets. I quickly call across the courtyard, inviting Maria Vica and company to explore with me this unseasonal windfall. Although the directions Tonino has given us are somewhat vague, the sound of hammering leads us through the maze of narrow streets and whitewashed houses, where large bunches of palm fronds decorate the intersections, until we find our path blocked by an enormous wooden stage stretching across the street from house to house and hung with lace tablecloths and swags of velvet. On the upper stage is the altar with the traditional tiers of beautifully molded bread and a table set for three, surrounded by houseplants and huge sheaves of gladioli. The apron of the stage is concealed by a large plush wall hanging printed with a reproduction of Leonardo's *Last Supper*, which in turn serves as the backdrop for a lower level, occupied by a long table with thirteen places set, according to the neighbors standing about, to accommodate Christ and the Apostles.

At the other end of the block some men are at work constructing a lean-to, covered with more palm fronds, which our informants tell us will be the Grotto of Bethlehem, and the ground-floor garage adjoining the stage is filled with trestle tables on which a swarm of aproned women are setting out seemingly endless rows of plates. The *virgineddi* will come at noon the next day, the neighbors say, urging us to return then to see the show. Intrigued by such ambitious scenography, we promise to be back.

Our return the next day finds the noon sun centered mercilessly over the narrow street, into which all the neighborhood has squeezed itself to wait, fanning and mopping its collective brow, until the show begins. Rumor and anticipation agitate the crowd, pulling it this way and that, until at last the sound of music draws us toward the far end of the street. A three-piece band cleaves the crowd to make way for a donkey, led by an elderly *contadino*, which carries a youthful Madonna with a small baby in her arms, while an adolescent Saint Joseph walks beside her, perspiring heavily under his Biblical robes and solemn self-consciousness. No such dignity troubles the twelve young Apostles who follow on the heels of the Holy Family, shoving and giggling and tripping over their long tunics. The procession closes with Christ grown up, a boy of about thirteen quite preoccupied with scratching his chin under the woolly beard tied on with elastic and with trying to find a comfortable position for his crown of thorns.

Once the Holy Family has been installed in the Grotto, the hostess, a handsome and well-dressed young woman in her late thirties, comes forward together with two children to invite the *virgineddi* to come and eat at the altar. Although a loudspeaker hung from a nearby balcony transforms the speeches, which are recited with considerable prompting in rhymed dialect, into a series of squeaks and whistles, the invitation is accepted and the Family moves on, losing on the way the tiny and protesting Christ

Child, who is whisked away to the arms of his mother. His four-year-old substitute appears miraculously and in some distress. He has been suspended by a rope from a balcony just above the corner of the stage and concealed from view by an embroidered bedspread; at the appropriate moment he is slowly lowered, flapping and revolving like a fish on a hook, while the crowd claps and cheers. When at last the participants are all seated in their places, the Holy Family on the higher level, Christ and the Apostles on the lower, the meal is served.

A long line of waiters comes stepping out of the garage, chins up and eyes straight ahead, all the male members of the extended family from elegant youths with modish haircuts and an air of savoir faire to bent-shouldered *contadini* with the white line of the *coppola* across their tanned foreheads. Dressed in red dinner jackets, they carry linen napkins on one arm and serving trays balanced, often precariously, on the other. These minions, one to each saintly personage, are supervised by a rather beautiful and very supercilious professional waiter in white jacket and black tie, who demotes one waiter from the upper stage to the lower because a button is missing from his jacket, assists the host and hostess in serving the Holy Family, and averts his eyes in pained contempt as a gray-haired old peasant with only one eye chases a fried fish around the platter, unable to grasp it between fork and spoon, and finally spears it inelegantly and dumps it onto the plate of his Apostle.

The script as its authors must have seen it in their mind's eye apparently did not take into account the need for a dress rehearsal or the requirements of posterity. The actual projection is not a movie but a slide show: long intervals of confusion, discussion, shifting of position, and arranging of veils, which eventually congeal into tableaux for the benefit of the crowd of photographers, both amateur and professional, who climb up on chairs for a better view and shout out their directions. They are the uncontested protagonists of the morning; at their command all the actors freeze into solemnity until the clicking of the shutters stops, then they melt again, the Apostles tucking into the food, giggling, choking, and getting pounded on the back, while the younger waiters try on the crown of thorns for size, and all the gravity and composure of the host is lost in arguments with the waiter and with his wife.

After the third course we leave, taking with us a sense of loss, and we never learn what grave illness or miraculous delivery has motivated such carryings-on, or for what reason—a factory's closing, an emigrant's return—they have taken place in August, like hothouse fruit ripening out of season, all show and no substance.

Beyond the conversation and the company they offer, my August neighbors across the courtyard are a Greek chorus for which I am most grateful. Their delight in Bosco and their appreciation of the life we share there is a warm bath of approval that restores me after the puzzlement with which my mother-in-law regards me.

"*Si usa?*" is her most frequent comment on my clothes and habits. "Is that what's done?" And with her next breath she may remark on how lucky I am to have such well-brought-up children.

I have often resented the implication that I have so little part to play in fashioning my life. But it is not criticism, I realize now, that leads to these remarks, as much as it is her inability to comprehend the range of alternatives that I believe to be available. The degree to which cultural tradition and historical circumstance have dominated her life is brought home to me now, as we work to clean out for rental the house in Alcamo, which has been empty since we transferred Mrs. Simeti to a nursing home two years ago. Nothing has ever been thrown out, drawers and trunks and packages tied up with string spill out bits of lace, moth-eaten fur collars that fall to pieces as they unfold, notebooks and old shoes, medals and medicines and tired purses, each closet and drawer giving substance to a story that Giovanni Verga might have told.

The remnants of purple velvet and the sheet music belonged to the Baronessina, my mother-in-law's mother, who brought to marriage with a prosperous, middle-class landowner a dowry limited mostly, I suspect, to her aristocratic blood, her delicate health, her convent education, and the glory of her father's patriotic service with Garibaldi. She died quite young, leaving her husband with a son and four daughters, and my mother-in-law's childhood memories are steeped in awed love for such a talented, distinguished woman and in resentment at having been abandoned by her: the sound of her mother playing the piano after the children were in bed; the coach ride to the warmer climate of Palermo where they wintered in a *pensione;* being taken, mute and terrified, to call on the elegant friends of her mother's convent days; her fear of the exotic, yapping lapdog; the "Institute" where the nuns made fun of her timidity and gave her a superficial grounding in academic matters and a very thorough education in needlework. We can trace her progress as we sort through the boxes, from childish attempts at samplers and pincushions, through pillows with classical scenes stitched in openwork, to a vast number of exquisitely embroidered silk and batiste baby bonnets.

Of the four daughters, one died in infancy and one on the eve of her marriage. The father, who is strangely absent from my mother-in-law's memories, must have had premonitions of a changing era, for the son took a course in calligraphy and both surviving daughters attended lessons in dressmaking. The booklets from these lessons are tied up in ribbon, my mother-in-law's name written on each of hers in a different kind of Gothic script, possibly the only practical application of her brother's education, which was rapidly rendered obsolete by the invention of the typewriter.

The father, having thus prepared his children for life, died when my mother-in-law was twenty-one, and she and her sister were whisked into matrimony at four o'clock in the morning. It was 1920, postwar Italy was in a state of great unrest, so the newlyweds went no farther than the house at Finocchio for their honeymoon, and then returned to Alcamo to take up residence in the big house across the Corso from her father's, under the aegis of the Simetis, who stare down at us from the oval frames hanging in the front hall, the wife straight nosed and serious in her high, stiff-necked dress and upswept hairdo, the man dark browed and intimidating, despite his long and beautifully tended whiskers.

For the groom, Sebastiano, it was a case of resuming residence, for he had never strayed far from the stern eye of his father, Don Turiddu Simeti, Cavaliere del Regno, who was one of Alcamo's most respected and substantial citizens, a man of great ability and authority of whom the elder *contadini* (even those more sincere than the shepherd) still speak with awe and affection, a man always ready to lend money when needed without asking interest—a rare thing to judge by the air of wonder with which they say this—and never known to raise his voice in anger.

He once suffered a momentary eclipse, when rumor spread that the gold of the Madonna, of which he and some other town notables had the safekeeping, had been stolen. A crowd of angry *contadini* tried to batter down the door of the Simeti house, and only the intervention of the carabinieri allowed Don Turiddu to make his way to the Matrice and demonstrate that the treasure was safe in its strongbox. That was the last time he set foot in a church alive: convinced that the rumor had been the work of the priest, he became violently anticlerical and repented only on his deathbed, much to the dismay of his grandsons, who with the absolutism of youth took his request for the last rites as a betrayal.

It is not difficult to imagine with what trepidation, if not terror, the young bride regarded her father-in-law. But her guilefulness in getting what she wants and a lively sense of humor even when in pain suggest a spark of stubborn independence that might have found more productive expression had she had backing and encouragement from her husband, a rather handsome young man of shy charm, to judge by the old photograph album in the *sa-*

lotto, whose sensitivity and intelligence were rendered ineffectual by the overindulgence accorded him as an only and somewhat sickly child and, in later years, as a severe diabetic.

My father-in-law couldn't be bothered to finish school, and with neither the training nor the health—and perhaps not even the inclination—to strike out on his own, he lived under the shadow of his father's command for fifty years, administering the property that had come to him as his wife's dowry and watching the simultaneous decline of his father's strength, of his family's fortunes, and of the provincial agrarian economy that had generated them. The only means of reaction available to him was the search for a scapegoat, which as a young man drew him into Mussolini's wake—hence the black neckerchief and the roll of tricolor bunting that Francesco and I mistake for patriotic toilet paper—and in his later years sent his sweet and affectionate nature into storms of suspicion and bitterness over ill-mannered neighbors and thieving *contadini*.

My mother-in-law's position must have been made more difficult in the beginning by her initial inability to produce an heir: miscarriage followed miscarriage, and even when at last she gave birth to male twins, her triumph was short-lived, for the elder baby smothered to death when his wet nurse fell asleep with the child at her breast.

Of eight pregnancies, three children lived to grow up. Stefano, the surviving twin, doubly cosseted and cared for after his brother's death and very much tied to home, left Sicily only once, in 1943, when he was drafted into the tattered remains of the Italian army and took the train to Rome to report. We find in the desk a letter written by his grandfather, asking his friend the *carissimo Generale* to look after the boy, "a child at heart." Stefano arrived at the Rome station, took one look at the confusion of a city from which the Germans were retreating as the Allies advanced, and took the next train home, where he remained, fighting valiantly but ineffectually to stave off the family's decline until he died at the age of forty.

Turi came next, the rebel, who tried many trades before becoming a painter, and financed his whims and his travels, from which stacks of postcards survive, by selling off anything he could get his hands on as scrap metal, so much so that whenever someone in the family wonders as to the whereabouts of some long-missing and forgotten object, another member will inevitably answer that Turi must have sold it.

And finally Tonino, very much the baby, his early years still fairly privileged, closeted in the courtyard at Alcamo to play with the son of the *podestà* and driven in the gig to his private elementary school by his grandfather (Francesco has found in the old man's black fustian riding breeches, high boots, and spurs an inspiration for next year's Carnival), the later years more carefree and makeshift as the harsh postwar period ground down all pretension, and after Don Turiddu's death in 1948, there were the inheritance taxes to be paid. Bits of land and pieces of jewelry were sold off to pay taxes, to keep the younger sons at the university, and to finance the schemes—the spare automobile parts and the oil press—with which Stefano was going to remake the family's fortune.

Surrounded by incompetent men and oblivious youths, my mother-in-law's only strategy for survival was that of economy, a necessity that age distorted into obsession. The signs of her economies are all about us: Stefano's first overcoat carefully made over into an inelegant and embarrassing jacket for Turi; a Carnival dress made from the yellow rayon of a parachute that Turi had rescued from a munitions dump; the wool from worn-out sweaters unraveled and wound neatly into little balls that lurk in the corners of every drawer; half-used tubes of ointment and empty pill bottles; jars of withered olives whose tops the years have soldered tight.

It is slow work to sort it all out, the objects and the memories they evoke. Each scrap of material must be recalled, identified, and narrated before it is tossed on the rubbish heap, the piles of letters reread, the faded sepia faces given a name and a place on the family tree, the hats and the lace veils modeled before the mirror. As I share the children's delight and interest and occasional bewilderment, I regret that they will never have the opportunity to put their hands to the feel and texture of their other heritage. My family possessions, gathered after my mother's death from scattered warehouses rather than some ancestral home, were sorted out and dispersed when Francesco and Natalia were too small to participate, and what little I brought across the ocean— photographs, a school yearbook, a few small figurines, some silver- ware, and a patchwork quilt—has, like a potpourri too long un- covered, lost its perfume in this foreign air.

🌿 Sidetracking and storytelling notwithstanding, we manage to empty out the two front rooms and make space for the masons and the painters before Ferragosto, the mid-August holiday, brings the next wave of visitors. Ferragosto, which falls on the fifteenth, began as a civil holiday, the *feriae augusti* proclaimed by Caesar Augustus in 18 B.C. to celebrate the beginning of "his" month, and was later adopted by the Church to honor the Assumption of the Virgin. As such it was in the past a very important feast day in Sicily, especially at Messina, where civic pride produced an attempt, apparently unsuccessful, to outdo the glories of the Palermo Festino.

Our ubiquitous Englishmen have left us descriptions, the most complete being that of W. H. Smyth, who visited Messina in 1818.

> The most curious feature of the whole spectacle is the Barra itself, representing the supposed assumption of the Blessed Virgin, a mir- acle never thought of until nearly eight hundred years after her death. It is a species of car, about forty feet in height, supported by iron machinery and fancifully decorated. The base represents a sacred tomb, in which is a choir chanting over the body, while the twelve apostles, collected from all parts of the earth, are in attendance, per- sonated by youths of good families, of from twelve to fifteen years of age; and above them is a circle that revolves horizontally with children attached to it representing angels, under a large sun and moon that turn vertically with six infants, as cherubim, suspended at the

ends of the principal rays. In the centre is a mass of clouds support-ing an azure globe with gilt stars, surrounded by other children, in white dresses decorated with various colored ribbons, as seraphim, and above the whole stands the Almighty, in a rich gold brocade, sustaining on his hand with an extended arm, the Virgin, personified by a beautiful little girl in white silk pantaloons studded with gold stars. It need scarcely be added that when this unwieldy machine, with its legion of living angels in rotary motion, is tottering along in procession, attended by nobles, senators, soldiers, priests and monks, in all their varied costumes, amid colors flying, bands playing, guns firing, and the whole populace praying, crying and shouting, a most novel and singular scene is presented.

W. H. Smyth, *Memoir descriptive of the resources, inhabitants and hydrography of Sicily and its Islands*

The pendulum of time has swung back again, and Ferragosto is once more a predominantly civil holiday, in which even those for whom a month of summer vacation is unthinkable—the farm-ers and the shipkeepers, the precariously or the self-employed—close up and go to the beach. Many of the contrasts have now been ironed out by Sicily's sudden wealth, but ten or fifteen years ago one glance at the beach sufficed to distinguish the bronzed and relaxed middle-class habitués from the peasants who frol-icked awkwardly in the water like seals disporting themselves on land, their tans stopping at their shirtsleeves or following the out-line of an undershirt. In the years, not infrequent, in which the sea was rough and the inviting splash and tumble of the waves concealed an undertow, the holiday often ended in tragedy, as some young and inexperienced farmer, placing his faith in an inner tube, would be sucked out to sea to panic and drown.

We prefer to avoid the crowded beach and enjoy the peace of Bosco with our guests from Palermo and with Martina's mother, Carla, come down from Milan for a week; to wind large platefuls of pasta onto our forks and eat fruit straight from the tree, yellow-green figs oozing a drop of golden honey from their bottoms, red grapes and green, and above all prickly pears, bright ovals of fuchsia, chartreuse, and yellow, extracted from their spiny skins and heaped upon a platter. Dearly beloved part of the Sicilian summer, they are very delicate, difficult to gather and easy to bruise.

Michele, his country roots unsevered by thirty years of doctoring in a city hospital, lectures us on how to pick and offer prickly pears. A grape leaf placed in the palm of the hand like a potholder is the best means of holding the fruit without bruising it or getting prickles in your fingers, while with your other hand you cut it from the cactus. If they are to be eaten right away, the pears should be brought to the kitchen in a bucket of water and then skinned, still using the grape leaf to roll back the thick and spiny skin split open by three (no more) cuts of the knife.

If, on the other hand, you are going to make a present of the prickly pears, you must place them gently in a wicker basket lined with grape leaves and cover the top with another layer of leaves that are held in place by a crisscross of thin strips cut from green canes and stuck into the weave of the basket itself. Michele claims that all gifts of fruit should be presented in this way, and that if a peasant neglects to do so, it signifies a lack of respect for the recipient.

Tonino and Turi take advantage of the deserted streets immediately following the holiday to park our van in the Corso outside the Simeti front door and carry down the various pieces of furniture and other odds and ends they have decided to adapt to current use. To Bosco comes my in-laws' bedstead, bars of silvery (nickel-plated?) brass in a severe geometric pattern, six feet high at the head and only slightly lower at the foot. This imposing dinosaur, unable to survive in the cramped habitat of a modern apartment, is to find an adequate resting place in our enormous Bosco bedroom.

The bed has stood unused for years in the big front bedroom at Alcamo, which is high ceilinged and has a balcony that gives onto the Corso and a door communicating directly with the *salotto*, so that visitors could be ushered from the *salotto* directly into the bedroom, where they were received with hushed, concerned appreciation if it was a time of sickness or death, and with proud pomp if the visit was occasioned by a birth. In the latter event, dutiful mother and newborn scion would receive homage ensconced in the matching embroidered linen sheets and the rose-colored, lace-encrusted bedspreads of heavy watered silk that are still carefully preserved in a trunk, one big set for the double bed, one tiny one for the little crib next to it.

My in-laws had long since abandoned the front bedroom and its bed, their aged limbs unable to cope with the distance to the kitchen and the bathroom (black and white Art Deco tiling and massive lavender fixtures, installed just after the war by Don Turiddu for the monumental sum—we found the bill in the desk—of forty-eight lire), and I have been eyeing the bed for a long time. So I am as eager as Natalia and Martina to set it up, Tonino tightening the great bolts with a wrench while the girls and I attack the bars with rags and brass polish and then make the bed, smoothing out with exceptional care the old family bedspread of heavy white piqué edged with tatting. Carla comes upstairs just in time to join me in standing back to admire the final effect.

"I feel as if I ought to lie down on it and die."

I suspect my sister-in-law, who is usually attuned to my reactions, to be rather put off by what she imagines to be a bit of black humor on my part. She has no clue to my sudden discovery that to possess such a bed is to become a matriarch, to take up one's appointed place in the family history. This is a bed for the creating of life and for the leaving of it, and such inevitability weighs heavily on me, accustomed as I am to looking at such cycles from the outside.

Once when Pam and Claudia and I were chatting, one of those long, meandering conversations in which we savor above all the taste of the English tongue, it suddenly came out, I can't remember how, that each of us is secretly horrified by the idea of being buried in her husband's family tomb. It is much the same chill that comes over me now, and this time I recognize it for what it is: it is not so much the Sicilian way of dying that I fear as the loss of my expatriate status. Perhaps being an expatriate is a state of mind before it becomes a choice of habitat, a preference for detachment, for leaving questions unresolved because the visit is too short or the difference in background and upbringing is too great. It would seem that I prefer to remain uncommitted, be it in my bedroom at Bosco or in my final resting place.

The problem of the bed resolves itself a few evenings later, as I undress with sleepy laziness and toss my black lace bra onto the bedpost. With this one careless flick of the wrist I transform the bed from catafalque to movie prop: Marcello Mastroianni stretches out to watch as Sophia Loren peels off her black net stockings, the only ghosts that will trouble my sleep tonight.

❦ At the end of the week Carla departs, taking Martina with her, my mother-in-law returns to her nursing home, and even Maria Vica and her mother leave, their month's vacation over. We wander about the empty house, prey to that peculiar listlessness that comes toward the end of summer, when unaccomplished summer projects pile up against the anticipation of autumn, holding the scales immobile. The children dawdle over summer homework assignments, lost in speculation about new books and new classmates, while I contemplate lists of all that remains to be done before our return to Palermo, the canning, the painting, and the repairing that have been put off from guest to guest. My slips of paper are lifted and shuffled aimlessly by the scirocco that blows in, dust laden, from the south, canceling with one hot breath the two weeks of cool weather that have revived us. Just before the sun sets, bruising the sky an angry yellow, the wind drops and the air grows close and heavy, and as we go to bed the sky crackles and booms in a distant fireworks display. I lie in the dark, listening to the rolls of thunder and watching the lightning throw bars of light through the shutters and across the ceiling. The interval between flash and roll grows shorter and shorter as the voice of the thunder deepens; then the storm passes on, fades and distends, leaving a heavy silence. A wind, mysterious and voiceless, rustles the tired paper of the almond leaves, fanning them in a steady patter, gentle and soporific, which pushes me further and further toward sleep. Just before I sink over the edge, I recognize the sound, almost forgotten, of raindrops.

The garden is quite literally sparkling clean the next morning, beaded with the rainwater that rests like drops of quicksilver in the furry centers of the geranium leaves and in the purple throats of the petunias. The smell of damp earth mingles with the perfume of the lavender, the thyme, and the rosemary, and the plants appear to quiver with new energy as the moisture courses up their stems and spreads out across their leaves. This is the precious water of August—*Acqua d'austu, Ogghiu, meli e mustu*—which will bring oil, apples, and must, swelling the olives and the grapes and, as far as Bosco is concerned, increasing the sorb apples.

It reaches our subconscious roots as well, sending us out early and eagerly into the cool morning air that caresses the skin like a linen sheet, laundered and sun dried and smelling of lavender. If the air is clean, the ground is muddy: this gentle draught was nowhere a surfeit such as would leave puddles on the road, but the plowed earth clings in heavy lumps to our shoes as Natalia and I tramp along the rows of the tomato patch, picking the tomatoes for the sauce we are going to make today.

Making the year's supply of tomato sauce is *the* most important domestic ritual in the Sicilian summer, and each housewife believes in the efficacy of her favorite method with fervor equal to that with which she believes in the efficacy of her favorite saint. There are basically two rival schools of thought: the one favors passing the scalded tomatoes through the tomato mill, then sterilizing the filled and capped bottles in boiling water; the other prefers to heat up the empty bottles, fill them with boiling hot tomato sauce, and then lay them in a nest of woolen blankets, so well wrapped that they will take several days to cool off. Then of course there are many minor variations: some prefer to add a few onions to the cooking tomatoes, some don't cook the tomatoes at all but pass them raw, still others disdain the widespread habit of putting a sprig of sweet basil in each bottle.

Preparations begin early, in the spring actually, when cracked pots and old five-kilo salted sardine tins are seeded with the tiny-leafed basil that is preferred for sauce making; these are assiduously watered into big and brilliant balls of green. Then crate after crate of empty beer and soda bottles are lifted down from the lofts, rinsed out, and left upside down to drain in the July sun for at least two weeks, so as to eliminate the least bead of moisture. At the same time the Wednesday morning street market at Alcamo is crowded with outsize gas burners, huge aluminum and copper cauldrons, gigantic ladles and mammoth colanders.

Sauce making is no small undertaking for the average peasant family, which in one day will put up anywhere from 50 to 150 bottles, or even more if there are married daughters to be supplied, or the padrone to be served. In fact, when I was first in Sicily, the little sauce that sufficed for my in-laws' needs came from bottles prepared by the Pirrellos or by Peppino. (One year the bottles Peppino left in homage in the stairway behind the front door at Alcamo exploded, painting the entire staircase red, and I have often wondered whether it was chance or, like the green fruit, one more act of guerrilla warfare.)

It was therefore not my mother-in-law who initiated me into the rites of sauce making, but Teresa Vivona, Turiddu's wife. When we were first at Bosco, Turiddu had not yet inherited the piece of irrigated land where he now grows their family vegetables, and each summer he would plant tomatoes and other vegetables at Bosco, for their use and ours. As soon as Turiddu announced that a sufficient number of tomatoes had properly ripened, the whole family would arrive at dawn to do the picking and then, when ten or fifteen crates were filled, we would set up our assembly line in the shade of the almond trees. Teresa, Franca, and I hosed down the tomatoes in large plastic buckets and plucked out the star-shaped green stems, which have a bitter taste, while Turiddu ignited the fire under our big copper cauldron, its bottom black from years of smoke, and spread out on old iron bed trestles the enormous sieve he had made by wiring thin young canes together. Gino, Felice, and Francesco carried out tables and strung an extension cord from the kitchen for the electric tomato mill that a thoughtful friend had once given me.

And there we worked, across the morning and on into the early afternoon, stirring and ladling and passing and capping. Teresa was in charge of the cauldron, filling it with tomatoes while she stirred until it was time to ladle them out onto the canes, so as to drain off the incredible amounts of watery juice that these plants had managed to suck up from the dry soil. Felice, still young enough then to be fascinated by *any* form of machine, operated the mill and sent the thick red sauce cascading into a plastic bucket, while I spooned it into the bottles into which Franca had first poked a sprig of basil. Turiddu and Gino capped the bottles and lowered them gently into the big oil drum, each layer covered with straw to keep them from cracking against each other in the boiling water. Francesco and Natalia ran errands for as long as their interest held out, then disappeared, not to show themselves again until all the bottles, filled with sauce and covered with heating water, lay in the oil drum and the last remaining sauce was being ladled out onto big plates of pasta. Our meal was interrupted by frequent trips out to shove the flame-consumed logs farther under the drum and to see if the boiling point had been reached and we could begin to keep an eye on our watches.

After forty-five minutes of boiling the fire was scraped away and the Vivonas went home, leaving the drum and its contents to cool off in the night air. The next day Turiddu came back to lift out the bottles and wipe away the bits of wet straw that clung to them, separating the green glass of mine, formerly filled with my mother-in-law's mineral water, from the sturdier brown of the beer and *gassosa* bottles that Teresa preferred, and I would carry mine into the house and set them in rows on the shelves of the *palmento,* where I could give them a proud glance each time I passed.

I must confess that sauce making lost much of its appeal when the Vivonas no longer came to share it with me, and after two years of solitary efforts that left me flattened for three days afterward, I proceeded to put aside my cornucopia complex and make a hardhearted estimate of our real consumption. It is thus without too much grief that Natalia and I pick, cook, and pass three crates of tomatoes this morning, and when Tonino and Francesco return from commitments elsewhere to do their part, they find some twenty-five bottles of sauce, an adequate yet unostentatious supply, waiting to be loaded into the drum and boiled.

Such self-control is fleeting, however, and the energy saved in cutting down on sauce is consumed in the days that follow in relishes and chutneys and jams and pickles. Figs must be opened like clams and put out to dry in the sun, or pickled in sugar and vinegar; the green tomatoes, whose skins, unaccustomed to all the water that the rain has brought, would split if left to ripen on the vine, must be chopped up in relish and chutney; the purple plums that are bending down the branches of the two young trees in the valley must be boiled into jam; and then there is the pickled watermelon rind, and the bread-and-butter pickles, and the India relish, and all the other American delights to which I rashly have introduced my family and which they now claim they cannot live without. And while one hand stirs the pot, the other must wield a paintbrush, since the winter rains and summer sun that have forged all this bounty have also wreaked havoc on the varnish of the shutters, the doors, and the windows. Tradition decrees that wood is my province, while Tonino must keep the rust at bay on anything—like the outer doors and the latticed grills on the downstairs windows—that is made of iron.

And two hands are not enough, to judge by the neglected flower beds, the letters to be written, the mending untouched, the cartons of books that I might as well have left in Palermo. The list of summer tasks and projects is potentially endless, but one entry, still unaccomplished as the end of August approaches, threatens to discolor everything else with the murky shade of resentment—the trip we had planned to take. Each summer the roots we have put down at Bosco ensnare us further, as each innovation means an appointment with planting or harvesting that we cannot miss, and through the years our travels have shrunk from a month in Burgundy to two weeks in Puglia to five days in Syracuse, and last year none at all.

Why, I wonder as the pickles bubble on the stove, should I have settled on an image of myself as Earth Mother? Why not a tanned and blasé habitué of Sicilian beaches? Or better still, an amateur archeologist, assiduous visitor and chronicler of excavations throughout the island? How is it possible that in twenty years I have managed to go six times to America and only twice to Syracuse?

I think of Syracuse as I spoon the relish into sterilized jars, and of the trip we took two years ago with Gabriella and her family; I think of wandering about Ortygia, the tiny peninsula that has always been the kernel of the city, when it expanded under the Greeks for miles inland, and then when it shrank back again after the barbarian invasions. Until the last war Syracuse ended at the isthmus connecting Ortygia to the mainland, confined to a handful of palaces and churches and dominated by the cathedral, which hides a Doric temple behind its baroque facade. Now the city is expanding once more. Broad streets and modern residential neighborhoods fan out from the isthmus to embrace the early Christian catacombs and the classical monuments of the archeological park, the Greek theaters, the altars, the tombs and sanctuaries, and the Latomie, the quarries that served as prisons for the defeated Athenian army after their fleet was trapped and destroyed in the Syracuse harbor in 413 B.C.

Those who were in the stone quarries were treated badly by the Syracusans at first. There were many of them, and they were crowded together in a narrow pit, where, since there was no roof over their heads, they suffered first from the heat of the sun and the closeness of the air; and then, in contrast, came the cold autumnal nights, and the change in temperature brought disease among them. Lack of space made it necessary for them to do everything on the same spot; and besides there were the bodies all heaped together on top of one another of those who had died from their wounds or from the change of temperature or other such causes, so that the smell was insupportable. At the same time they suffered from hunger and from thirst. During eight months the daily allowance for each man was half a pint of water and a pint of corn. In fact they suffered everything which one could imagine might be suffered by men imprisoned in such a place. For about ten weeks they lived like this all together; then, with the exceptions of the Athenians and any Greeks from Italy or Sicily who had joined the expedition, the rest were sold as slaves. It is hard to give the exact figure, but the whole number of prisoners must have been at least 7,000.

This was the greatest Hellenic action that took place during this war, and, in my opinion, the greatest action that we know of in Hellenic history—to the victors the most brilliant of successes, to the vanquished the most calamitous of defeats; for they were utterly and entirely defeated; their sufferings were on an enormous scale; their losses were, as they say, total; army, navy, everything was destroyed, and, out of many, only few returned. So ended the events in Sicily.

Thucydides, *The Peloponnesian War*

The Latomie are cool and mysterious now, even on an August afternoon, their sheer stone walls throwing shadows on the orange trees and bougainvillea vines that flourish where once the Athenian soldiers huddled in the dust.

The dirty pots and pans sing out my anger at such scanty acquaintance with these places, and as I plunge my hands into the dishwater, I remember diving into the icy pool at the source of the Ciane. Now a river that flows five kilometers to the sea through a dense thicket of yellow flags and wild papyrus, Ciane was once a handmaiden of Persephone who tried to save her mistress from the Lord of the Underworld, and was thus metamorphosed in punishment.

But foremost in my mind is the day we spent at Pantàlica, the prehistoric necropolis carved into the middle of the Iblean Mountains that lie inland from Syracuse. Barren and stony, these hills are bleached and desolate under the August sun, and it is difficult to imagine what can grow in the fields carefully marked off by stone walls, so thick is the litter of remaining stones, so sparse the covering of thistles and dried grass. We drove past miles of these blistered, stone-ringed fields before reaching the narrow, winding valley that the second of Syracuse's rivers, the Anapo, had cut deep into the hills. The sides of the valley that fall in steep cliffs from the barren crest down to the river bottom are honeycombed with tombs, low rectangular doorways leading into small, smooth-walled chambers carved out of the living rock. The precision with which the tombs have been cut and finished belies the difficulties inherent in their position and the crudeness of the stone tools that were employed.

> The inestimable labour with which each and all of the thousands of graves were cut; the devotion which, through hundreds of years, was spent in providing the dead with durable abodes such as the living denied themselves; the severe beauty and power of the rock: invest the scene with an aura of sublime solemnity. Death resides in this immense stone; at the same time it is vibrating with the potency of unquenchable life. Enter any one of the graves; you feel, as nowhere else, that you are in the womb of the Great Mother, from which the dead will be reborn, mysteriously, for another span in the light above.
>
> Günther Zuntz, *Persephone: Three Essays on Religion and Thought in Magna Graecia*

More than five thousand of these tombs riddle the valley walls, the earliest going back to the thirteenth century B.C., when invaders from the mainland pushed the coast-dwellers inland. The corresponding city of the living on the plain above the cliffs underwent sporadic periods of growth as the invaders in turn fled the arrival of the Greek colonists, was abandoned for over a thousand years, then came to life again at the beginning of the fifth century A.D. when barbarian raids sent the citizens of Syracuse, then the western capital of the Byzantine Empire, inland toward Pantàlica, where they took refuge in the tombs of their fore-fathers. We follow the narrow paths that cling to the cliffside and wander through the Byzantine houses and chapels, carved from adjacent tombs that were enlarged and joined to form split-level homes, the large smooth-walled rooms abundantly equipped with niches and alcoves and built-in shelves, the doorways widened into picture windows offering a spectacular view across the valley, and at the threshold a sudden drop to the river below.

All around us is a desert of rock and thistle and dust; below us the floor of the valley is hidden under an inviting canopy of green. The roadbed of a narrow-gauge railway that once passed here still threads its way beside the river, and we can see it emerge from the trees in several places, the tracks and ties removed to leave a perfectly good dirt road that we have been told is well worth following in the car. It takes a good many false turns be-fore we find the right track onto the railway bed, and our sense of adventure grows when we discover that the track tunnels through the rock at times, tiny tunnels for toy trains that barely allow the Simeti van to scrape through. Our friends go first in their car, and it is they who find the place to stop for lunch, a little path that descends to a clearing at the river's edge.

The path leads us down into a different world and a different climate from that which hovers above us on the cliffs, shimmer-ing white and straw-colored in the heat. Here the spring-fed waters of the Anapo, still icy and clear so near their source, refrigerate the air, which trills with birdsong and rustles as the breeze stirs the leaves of the Oriental plane trees that line the banks, brought here by the Greeks, no doubt, who in turn had learned their love of the shade-giving plane from the Persians (Xerxes hung the plane trees of Lydia with golden ornaments as a tribute to their beauty). Here their shade darkens the water as it runs from one shallow pool into the next, jumping down with a silvery splash across moss-covered stones and tugging at the twigs and the tufts of maiden-hair fern that cling to the river's edge. *Capelvenere*, the Italians call it, Venus's hair as she arose from the sea, with a silver sheen underwater, but completely dry as it emerges. The surface of the pools breaks into faint ripples under the darting dance of the water skates, and tiny dragonflies hover, their double wings opaquely black in the shadow, shimmering with iridescence when they catch the light. Farther downstream from where we sit the trees pull back to reveal the sunbaked cliffs, the thirsty mouths of the tombs, and the drone of the cicadas in the thistles, suspended like Tantalus over the liquid song of the river, which here flows gurgling and sparkling over a wide and cobbled bottom. Some cows pasture leisurely in the thick beds of wild mint that grow on the banks, each cropping of their jaws releasing a wave of mint's sweet smell.

Upstream the trees grow closer and the shade is darker; the current swiftens in the narrow channel, and eels, carp, and trout lurk in the shadows of the rocks or flash over small waterfalls. The sound of laughter rings out above the music of the water, and the playing of a flute: possibly the young couple in the Citroën that passed just as we were parking?

> O cicada, drunken with drops of dew, you sing your country music in solitary places; you sit on the topmost leaf beating out the sound of a lyre with your rough legs on your sun-darkened body.
>
> Now sing some new gay song to the tree-nymphs, shrill out an answer to Pan, so that I may escape from love and sink into noontide sleep as I lie beneath this shady plane-tree.
>
> Meleager, "The Cicada," in *The Poems of Meleager of Gadara*

Up with Pan and down with Demeter! Despite such an imposing rallying cry, the most I obtain is one day off, a Saturday we spend with friends in Mazzara del Vallo, the biggest fishing port in Italy, which lies below Tràpani and Marsala. Despite its position on the western coast, this area has always been more Levantine, more Arab than Greek, ever since the Phoenicians set sail from Tyre to colonize the island of Mothya just off the coast of Marsala. In the sixth century B.C. Mothya became a military base for the Carthaginians and a thriving commercial center until it was destroyed by Dionysus of Syracuse, and it was at Mazzara itself that the Arab invasion of Sicily began. The waters around Marsala, and particularly the mud-bottomed lagoon surrounding Mothya, are giving up one treasure after another into the hands of the underwater archeologists: a Punic warship still bearing on its prow the olive branch placed there in vain to bring good fortune at its launching; the fifth-century Greek statue that some say represents an Auriga, others a Phoenician judge; and still more ships and more amphorae, located but yet to be recovered.

But Pan is not interested in the Levantine. Our patron for the day, he moves us, when we have finished swimming in waters chilled by Atlantic currents from Gibraltar and dining on Mazzara's famous fish, into going eastward, to the very edge of Greek Sicily, to see the Cave di Cusa, the quarries from which the stonemasons of Selinunte cut the mammoth columns for their outsize temples. The quarries, dug no deeper than ten or twelve feet into the gray stone, were abandoned abruptly, probably during the siege with which the Carthaginian army responded in 409 B.C. to Segesta's request for aid against her rival city.

It is not difficult to imagine the panic that the news of the Carthaginian landing brought to the quarries: the masons flinging down the compasses with which they traced a circle some twelve feet wide upon the bedrock; the slaves dropping the chisels and hammers with which they chipped away the surrounding stone; the drivers unharnessing the oxen from the sledges loaded with the finished drums ready for the slow trip to Selinunte. The sledges have long since rotted, toppling their burdens onto the ground where they lie askew, indicating the road along which the terrified slaves took flight, and no ladders lean against the drums that stand, a narrow chasm carved about them, still awaiting the final cut that should sever them from the earth. In the place of scaffolding the fig trees grow, and an enormous carob, split and flattened by lightning until its vast branches lie almost horizontal to the ground. Centuries of wind and rain have taken up the interrupted labor of the slaves, chiseling cracks and holes into the face of the stone, filling them with the seeds of the caper plants that trail long ropes of coin-shaped leaves and carving a refuge for the swallows that swoop and cry overhead.

All too short a day, it is as much distraction as we can now afford from our present concern, the grapes that hang in slowly ripening bunches on the vines. No greater hiatus is possible now; we too are suspended on a thin stem of tension, one eye on the weather, the other on the grapes, assessing the benefits of the recent rain, checking for signs of rot, estimating quantity and quality. Tonino comes home with a dreadful story about an acquaintance who has had fifteen acres of trellised vineyards sabotaged. The guy wires were cut so that the whole trellis collapsed, sagging down with all its burden of wire and post and vine, pressing the ripening grapes into the earth as the must trickled away in the dust.

Tonino is visibly shaken as he tells me, "I don't think I could survive something like that."

Chapter Eleven

That as the god inclines his noble head
In each direction, ripening vineyards grow,
Hollow vales and deepened glades fill out.
We shall, then, sing, in native songs, our debt
Of praise to Bacchus, bring on cakes and plates
And lead in by the horns a sacred goat
To stand beside the altar, and proceed
To roast his fertile flesh on hazel spits.

Virgil, *The Georgics*

The ripening grapes on September's sacred vines are not the only sign, as the month begins, of autumn's approach. The rain of ten days has given birth to grass, thin tentative blades poking up sparsely through the dried gray mat of last winter's lawn. The rose hips are reddening now, together with the hawthorn berries and the yellow sorb apples. If I need Natalia, I must shout down the road, for chances are that she is making a sly visit to Nino Di Giovanni's *azzeruola*. The azarole, also called the Mediterranean medlar, is a variety of hawthorn that bears fruit the size of crab apples, with waxy yellow skin and a sharp bittersweet taste that has the power to awaken memories. Sicilians who come to Bosco in September are always excited to find the azarole growing by the side of the road, recalling childhood feasts long since forgotten, while I, with no such memories of my own, am content to think that I am tasting fruit such as the Greeks must have eaten, intense and penetrating flavors undiluted by centuries of hybridizing.

The first days of September also bring us to Palermo for a

foretaste of our imminent return to city life, when we participate in a torchlight procession in memory of General dalla Chiesa and his wife on the anniversary of their death. Tonino and Francesco abandon the cisterns they are scraping out just in time for us to drive over the mountains and join the crowd that is forming in the semidarkness of Via Carini, at the site of the ambush. This morning the authorities held the official commemoration, to which they neglected to invite the dalla Chiesa children, who have been very outspoken in claiming that the island's politicians failed to support the general in his battle against the Mafia, thus allowing him to become an isolated and therefore easy target. This evening's march is unofficial, promoted by a committee of concerned citizens, and it is moving to see the simple but dignified informality with which the long line, headed by the three young dalla Chiesas, takes shape and heads for Via Libertà, then along Via Ruggiero Settimo and down to the prefecture. This is a strange march for Palermo: silence instead of slogans, the only banners the flames of the wax torches wavering in the darkness. Bystanders join in, walk a little way, drop out. According to the newspaper, some five thousand people participate, but from where we are, near the rear, it is impossible to see how far ahead the river of smoking light flows. We must be satisfied with noting the participants nearby, the familiar faces of the politically active Palermitani with whom we have marched a dozen times before mingling with people from the neighborhood or passersby who may never have walked behind a banner or felt before the need to give visible expression to their opinions.

There are some people marching here tonight whose politics and public records would appear to move them in the opposite direction. But their presence, although irritating and even painful, is interesting, since it is in the heterogeneity of this crowd and in the breakdown of old equilibriums that hope, if there is any, lies. There is much in the news these days to indicate the turbulence below the surface: Chinnici, the magistrate who was murdered at the end of July, left a diary that is rumored to contain grave accusations about corruption and Mafia influence in the

Palace of Justice, and another article claims that since the La Torre law went into effect a year ago, allowing the police to investigate the bank records of suspected mafiosi, some eight trillion lire have been withdrawn from the island's bank accounts.

The turbulence is tangible in the streets of the city: the arrogant roar of the motorcycles and the angry honking of the cars, Palermo's customary music, are punctuated by the scream of sirens, as the magistrates rush from home to office and back, their escorts in bulletproof helmets poking their pistols from the squad car windows. For the first time in their history, the Palermitani are respecting No Parking signs, the ones that have appeared on both sides of the block in front of the buildings where these judges live. The siege will grow tighter before it lifts, but so far the city manages to take it in its stride. Pam asks the wife of one of the judges how she can stand a life in which her husband's every move is accompanied by armed escorts.

"You get used to it," she answers. "*Appena sento le sirene, calo la pasta*—As soon as I hear the sirens, I put the pasta on to boil."

Francesco disappears ahead of us, glad for the chance to meet up with city friends; Tonino, Natalia, and I march together, find ourselves walking next to friends, falling behind in the midst of strangers, pointing out acquaintances and trying to put names to familiar faces. As I walk along I count upon my fingers: for the dam on the Belice River, for the nature reserve, for women's lib, against the Mafia, for better schools, against the missiles at Comiso. The best I seem able to do in Sicily is stand up and be counted, remaining—despite the ephemeral solidarity of marching in a crowd—a foreigner, with a useless faggot of notions and skills over my shoulder, tonight incarnate in the box of candles I stuck in my purse as we left Bosco, knowing from past experience that the organizers of such processions never provide enough torches to go around. And in fact at least half of the marchers are torchless, but it appears unthinkable that one should bring one's own. It occurs to me that if this were America as I remember it, the procession would be lit by torches and candles of every size and shape, and that this is a significant difference. Yet I am wrong,

I realize, to think that with my candles and my Americanness I am set apart: possibly I can be no more Sicilian than I am when I march in one of these contemporary processions, these secularized and urbanized versions of the festa, since, as Sciascia says in *La corda pazza*, "it is only at the festa that the Sicilian emerges from his condition of *man alone . . .* to find himself part of an order, a class, a city."

🌿 The flicker of the torches fans into a bigger blaze on the night of the seventh, as the Alcamesi light their bonfires, towering heaps of brush and driftwood, old chairs and splintered doorjambs that have been piled up along the beach at Alcamo Marina or in front of country houses. The flames leap and crackle in the darkness, devouring summer and lighting the way to autumn, although the children who dance about the pyre with manic pleasure may have forgotten that this rite of purification is in honor of the birth of the Virgin Mary.

> In that rare and delicate equinoctial moment, suspended between summer and winter and between light and darkness, she comes to comfort us against the obscurity which, gently still but nonetheless inexorably, spreads its shadows over the earth.
>
> Franco Cardini, *I giorni del sacro: il libro delle feste*

The *vendemmia* is imminent, our own personal *tempus terribile*, for although the ripening of the grapes is a yearly event, we have never managed to impose a routine upon our harvest, which is complicated this year by the presence of a considerable quantity of wine from last year that Tonino does not want to sell off just to make room for the new. In order to accommodate it all, he has borrowed an empty steel cistern from a cousin and summoned a *bottaio* to see if two wooden casks that have stood empty for several years can be reactivated. Our usual *bottaio* has retired and sends as his replacement a man so small and slight as to seem totally unsuited to a trade that requires the bending of iron hoops and the curving of wooden staves.

I realize how wrong I am when I go into the *cantina* later on. The newcomer has disappeared, but there are sounds of scraping coming from inside one of the casks. The little door in the front of the cask has been widened to the size of a small dinner platter, and the *bottaio* has managed to weasel his way inside like a burrowing animal, while a heap of mildewed tartar and sediment is growing on the floor outside the cask. The *bottaio*'s assistant is his complement, a pear-shaped figure who can push where he cannot pass. He smiles at our amazement with vicarious pride such as the proprietor of a freak show might have. He is accustomed to these tricks, but for me it is a relief to see the *bottaio* emerge and then drive off, once he has scraped, quicklimed, and pronounced both casks to be sound, thus dispelling images of Pirandello's *La Giara*, in which a pottery mender climbs into a broken oil jar the better to glue and staple it, only to discover that in order to get out, he must break it into pieces again.

The next day a truck arrives with the borrowed cistern, which it deposits, flat on its back—some twelve feet long and at least four in diameter—just outside the *cantina* door. In a hurry to get it into place, Tonino decides that raising the cistern can be a family undertaking and disregards my incredulity and dire prophecies. So here we are, rolling it into the *cantina* on logs and hoisting it with a series of improvised blocks and tackles. As I pull down on one rope I try not to look at Francesco, who is clinging to the top of another cistern by his toes as he hauls in on a second rope, or to watch as Natalia slips under the suspended cistern to push in the wooden props each time Tonino shoves it a little farther upright.

"This is madness!" I repeat as the great steel cylinder sways above Natalia's head and Francesco leans farther and farther out. "You'll kill us all!" But the ropes hold, the cistern hovers for a moment almost vertical, then tips over and settles squarely onto its four squat feet. We clap and cheer and hug each other, and I notice that Natalia's eyes are sparkling as if we had just raised a Christmas tree.

Not that the preparations end here, however. There are still hours to spend scraping the cisterns and coating machinery and tanks with thick and tarry oenological paint, and wine to be pumped from one cistern to another and the *cantina* to be swept and washed. Natalia and I leave this to the men; other harvests are calling us, the almonds and the "Italia" table grapes. We beat the trees with canes until the almonds fall, their outer layer of fuzzy green fruit split and wizened into a shriveled gray husk that must be pried off before the nuts in their shells are spread out in the sun to dry.

The Italia grapes are a more difficult harvest. A recent discovery for Sicilian agriculture, this tough-skinned variety of table grapes ripens in September, but with the help of a lot of spraying and then of sheets of black plastic that are spread over the trellises to protect them from the rain, the grapes will keep on the vine until December, when they theoretically fetch very high prices. Tonino put in a trellis of Italia grapes about five years ago as an experiment, but we are too reluctant about using pesticides to make a commercial success of it, and we harvest the grapes in September as they ripen.

Harvesting table grapes is a very different matter from harvesting grapes that are destined for the winepress, since each bunch must be handled with the greatest care. Every day Natalia and I head for the valley floor, pushing a wheelbarrow full of empty crates and carrying our various tools: the big shears for cutting the bunches from the vine, nail scissors with which each rotten grape must be severed from its fellows, clean paintbrushes for dusting off any copper sulphate that may still cling to the fruit, and then big sheets of paper to line the crates in which we must painstakingly arrange the grapes so as to display them to their best advantage.

If such attentions are tiresome, at least working conditions are pleasant: a breeze plays under the wide green tent of the trellis and ruffles the leaves overhead, through which filters a pale yellow-green light, a cool and dappled contrast to the glare of the fields around us. The grapes hang down at eye level, enormous dense clusters of golden green, each grape bigger than a quail's egg and swollen with sweetness. Wasps, gathering by the thousands for the *vendemmia*, hover about us as we work, waiting for a grape to fall to earth and split, bleeding the sugary juice from its taut belly, while big brown-and-yellow hornets burrow into the rotten bunches.

Anxious to get the best of the grapes, which are heavily attacked by oidium mold this year, off to the market before the *vendemmia* starts, Tonino sends Cicco and Nito Pirrello down to help me one morning. Cicco and Nito pick the grapes and load them any which way into the crates, which they then bring to me to be cleaned and dusted and packed. They work at their usual relentless rhythm and I race to keep up with them, snipping and dusting and arranging, my juice-stained fingers sticking in the handles of the nail scissors I use to cut off the telltale tufted stems left by the fallen grapes. I have no doubt but that this job is punishment meted out to me for the many times in which as a child I willfully disregarded my mother's requests that I break off grapes by the stem, so as not to "ruin the bunch." It seemed such a picayune preoccupation then, I say to myself as I clip and brush frantically, trapped by the wall of crates the Pirrellos are stacking up around me, in a bucolic version of *Modern Times*.

Every so often Nito, unable to contain his pleasure in some particularly splendid grapes, comes directly to me, cradling the bunch in his rough and callused hands as if it were a baby and, grinning with paternal pride, he lays it gently on my lap.

"I'll take the responsibility for this one!"

When no empty crates are left, they stop picking and help me out, holding the little scissors awkwardly in their thick fingers and scolding each other when one misses a rotten grape. We chat about the third brother, Carlo, who is in the hospital, and then I remember to ask about Cicco's oven.

Tonino came home one day at the beginning of the summer and announced that an era had ended. Cicco Pirrello and his wife had renovated their house and had taken out the wood oven in which Mrs. Pirrello had always baked all the family bread. Tonino seemed quite shocked by such a domestic revolution, and I was curious to know who was the iconoclast in the family and how Mrs. Pirrello felt about giving up a task that must have been so basic to her life and so laden with significance.

"It was her idea," Cicco answered. "She asked me what I thought, seeing as there are only the two of us at home now, and she's getting tired. I told her it was up to her. But an old wolf loses its fur but not its vices. Our daughter's got an oven in the country, and my wife has been going out there every Saturday to bake her bread."

🌿 One more element of distraction intrudes upon our preparations when school reopens. Until a few years ago, the schools started on the first of October, leaving us time to get the grapes in first, but someone in the Ministry of Public Education decided that more was more and pushed the date forward two weeks, even though the provincial offices rarely manage to finish assigning the teachers to their various schools before the middle of November, so that some classes limp along on reduced hours for as much as two months.

Alcamo has resolved the conflict between *vendemmia* and school by not taking the latter very seriously for the first two weeks, during which the attention of both students and teachers is directed elsewhere, but few of the Palermitani have vineyards, so we must attempt to divide ourselves in two. We are up at six in order for me to get the children to their schools in the city by eight-thirty, and then drive out to Bosco again at noon, in time for a long afternoon and evening of homework and farmwork. It is tiring emotionally as well as physically: Francesco and Natalia are vociferously reluctant to drive off and leave their classmates to enjoy the relaxed afternoon gatherings when the pressure of homework has not yet dispelled the pleasure of meeting up with friends again. Even I am ambivalent, for despite the dirt, the noise, and the tension of city traffic, these first uninterrupted mornings in my Palermo study entice my mind toward the writing that awaits me in October.

It is not as if we returned each day to scenes of idyllic rural relaxation. The countryside quivers with suspense, like a race-track just before the starting gun. In the past the decision to begin was individual, welding convenience and tradition to the outcome of lengthy consultations on the state of the grapes and the weather forecasts, but nowadays everybody bursts into frenetic activity at once, the day the gates open at the big *cantine sociali*, the cooperative wineries to which almost all the Alcamo grape growers confer their harvest. At sunrise on that day the pickers fan out through the vineyards, lugging big two-handled plastic buckets behind them as they comb the rows, and the roads teem with tractors and trucks loaded with grapes, the corners of the heavy canvas tarps that hold the juicy harvest flapping in the wind and blunt-tipped pitchforks sticking out on top like hairpins. Lines of cars pile up behind the slow-moving tractors or edge gingerly around decrepit trucks, resurrected for the *vendemmia* but not to the point where their brakes and taillights function. Alcamo changes overnight; the sleepy southern town bustles like a metropolis, and even the shopkeepers and the traffic police simmer with muted excitement.

The caprices of the weather add to the tension: if rain at the end of August was an answer to our prayers, bringing the water without which even the hottest of suns cannot properly ripen the grapes, rain now would be disastrous, for the grapes would rot and the fields would dissolve into muddy traps for the heavily laden tractors. It is hot and cool by turn, and the winds buffet and change and promise no good as we inspect the sky each morning on our way into Palermo. One morning we awake to the scirocco, which dusts the sky to a pale bronze, so that we see the disk of the rising sun as through a smoked glass. And scirocco usually means rain.

The generic pre-*vendemmia* tension is sliding into despair at Bosco. The borrowed cistern has a hole halfway up that spurts out a fine fountain of wine when Tonino tries to fill it, and the machine for processing the red grapes has something undefinable wrong with it. Unable to find anybody with time enough to come out into the country and fix the cistern, Tonino borrows a soldering iron, with which he manages to close the extant hole and to melt five more holes in the process. Tearing his hair, he returns to Alcamo in search of help, leaving the children and me to hose down the *cantina*. We conspire as we scrub, plotting how we shall take the *vendemmia* into our own hands next year, leaving the experimenting and the improvising to Papà, but organizing the routine by ourselves, and not at the last minute, either!

Dusk is falling, and we have almost given up any hope of salvation when Tonino drives up the hill with a passenger, an elderly gnome in a bright red jump suit, thick-lensed glasses, and a beret squaring off his bald head. In the space of fifteen minutes he solders tight the cistern and dismantles the refractory machine, putting a piece in his pocket that he promises to have ready the next morning. He also offers to give Tonino a lesson in soldering.

"On a piece of scrap metal, though," he adds firmly. "Don't you go practicing on the cisterns anymore; I don't want to have to come out and patch them up again."

Supper is late that night but cheerful, and the next afternoon, while Tonino and Francesco put the finishing touches on the *cantina*, Natalia and I start harvesting the red grapes, armed with pruning shears (a safer tool than the *runcuneddu*, the traditional sickle-bladed knife known to harvest fingers as well as grapes) and a stack of plastic buckets. More or less cylindrical and with a handle on either side of the rim, these buckets have a capacity of about two bushels and weigh about thirty kilos when they are full, so that one is grateful, in this case at least, for having progressed from tin to lighter plastic. We each take a bucket and start in at the beginning of a row, cutting the *'ddisa* that ties up the branches of the first vine and pulling them open to get at the fruit, seeking in the tangle of stems and tendrils the umbilical cord that must be severed before the bunch can be lifted out and dropped into the empty bucket where it lands with a resonant thud, a sound that becomes softer and wetter as the bucket fills up. The shape of the vines betrays our whereabouts: ahead of us the branches are gathered about their fat belly of grapes, while those behind us are torn and drooping after their delivery.

Harvesting grapes is hard work: one must bend double to liberate the low-growing bunches from the clutch of the vine, and the bucket, light at first, gets heavier and heavier as you drag it along the row from vine to vine until, full up, you leave it where it stands (feminine prerogative) and start in on another one. The ripe grapes burst in the picking and the sticky must runs down your arms and gets wiped onto your forehead and into clothes and hair, attracting flies and wasps and vinegar gnats that buzz around your temples and wade up and down your bare arms.

But the beginning is seductive: we need to pick only enough to give the machinery a trial run, the afternoon is cooled by a breeze that brushes away the insects, and the dark purple grapes, heaped in the blue plastic buckets until they dangle over the rim, are beautiful. When fifteen buckets, a tractor load, are filled, we whistle for Francesco, who drives down the hill to pick them up. We wait to give him a hand as he hoists each heavy bucket to his shoulder and carries it to the tractor, then we start homeward. As we walk up the hill, the sun setting at our backs turns the eastern mountains to copper and paints a ruddy bloom on the grapes that are bouncing up the hill ahead of us.

Unlike the white grapes, which go directly to the press, red grapes must be whirled through a machine that separates them from their bitter-tasting stems and then left to steep in their own juice for several days until the skins give up their color and their strong tannic taste. The gnome has fixed the separator as promised, and it sucks up our little load and whirls it around in a perforated cylinder so that centrifugal force tears the grapes from the stems and pushes them through the holes. They fall, bruised and dripping, into a basin and are then pumped into a cistern to steep. The first of the grapes are in.

The next day numerous Pirrellos arrive to finish off the red and to harvest a small vineyard of white grapes that have ripened earlier than the others and are beginning to rot. They can work for us only this one day, since they are committed elsewhere, and Tonino fears they will not be able to finish before dark, so after lunch he orders all the family down to help. Although our contribution is modest—a Pirrello picks two rows in the time it takes a Simeti to do one—we manage to finish the plot of white grapes by about five-thirty, which is a perfectly respectable time for stopping, even if there are two more hours of daylight left. Tonino suggests that we start back up to the house, but the Pirrellos will have none of that and insist on beginning another vineyard while the light lasts. Five days will pass before we do any more harvesting, so to start in anew makes no sense except in terms of the Pirrello sense of duty and justice. In the face of such iron morality it hardly seems proper for us to surrender, so I send Natalia off to help Tonino in the *cantina*, and Francesco and I stumble after the Pirrellos, trying to hide our exhaustion. Every bunch of grapes costs now, every bending down reveals a new ache, and we can manage to drag only one bucket between the two of us. There are more empty buckets than can be accommodated, once filled, by the single tractor load agreed upon, and Francesco arranges the extra empties so as to take up as much space as possible. Finally, and none too soon, he announces that no more buckets will fit, and we must stop. There is no room for me in the tractor either, and I stagger up the hill, watching the Pirrellos striding ahead of me. Even Cicco, who is sixty-eight. As Nito heads toward the *cantina* to help Francesco unload, he shakes his head at me.

"That load wasn't full. You shouldn't let yourself be confounded by a couple of buckets of grapes!"

❧ We must wait for the Vivona family to finish harvesting their own grapes before continuing with ours, and just as well, since we ache in every muscle. Only the picking is suspended, however: Nino Di Giovanni has begun to harvest the vineyards that lie beyond the northern limit of our property and to bring the grapes to us for pressing. When Tonino first agreed, three or four years ago, to buy Zu Nino's grapes, it didn't occur to him to reflect that if this old *contadino* was the only person in the neighborhood who didn't confer his grapes to a cooperative, it was probably because he was a very suspicious person. And in fact the weighing of Zu Nino's grapes and the measuring of their sugar content has become a nightmare, a long and complicated ceremony of adjusting to a hairbreadth the brass counterweights on the big scales brought up from the olive press at Finocchio, of peering through, above, and without spectacles at the level of the must meter, of checking and rechecking the figures entered into the notebook. It was worse the first few years, when *U Prufissuri* delivered the grapes in four big canvas bags slung from the packsaddle of his mule, which meant a constant stream of small loads to be processed and argued over; things have speeded up since the mule retired, thanks to the hired services and tractor of Tanu, the next farmer down the hill. Tanu also lightens the atmosphere, since despite a firm and outspoken nostalgia for Mussolini, he is a red-cheeked, round-bellied, cheerful soul, who jollies Nino Di Giovanni along with good-natured chaffing, startles Francesco by shouting bits of Dante at him across the winepress, and informs me happily that with the help of the *Encyclopedia of World History*, which he is buying and reading in weekly installments, he has come to realize that "this damn democracy" is more the fault of the British than of the Americans. He smiles at me benignly, expecting me to be much relieved by this absolution.

At the end of the week the Vivonas arrive, driving out from

Alcamo before dawn as the children and I are preparing to leave
for Palermo. Turiddu at the wheel of our tractor will alternate
with Tanu and his tractor as the grapes are poured into the mouth
of the press and the foaming must flows into the big cement tank
sunk into the *cantina* floor, ready to be measured and pumped into
the casks and the cisterns. The *vendemmia* proper is under way.

🌿 When I call up the *vendemmia* in the mirror of my mind, all
normal perspective is reversed: the must of the distant past flows
in a colorful and turbulent river of vast proportions that dwindles
and fades as it nears the present, shrunken by efficiency and machinery into a paltry trickle. Farthest in the background, but
brightest, are vicarious images, the *vendemmia* of Tonino's childhood, when his whole family came up from Alcamo Marina in
cart and gig for a harvest that lasted more than a month. There
were no cooperative wineries then, and Don Turiddu bought up
most of the *contrada*'s grapes, which arrived in heavy, open-topped
wooden casks, packed in along the dirt tracks on muleback, a steady
stream of dark and long-legged Sicilian mules delivering their
burden of grapes to the *palmenti*. There were seven of these pressing bins in all: two stood under the porch roof in the courtyard,
two in the *cantina* that is now our living room, one that now belongs to the Blundas, one in the corner of the remaining *cantina*,
and finally the *palmento padronale*, the biggest bin, with the beautifully carved stone spout, which still stands in our kitchen and
was reserved for the Simeti grapes.

Each *palmento* was manned by three people, two to load and
empty the bin and one to do the treading. When the mule came
to a stop next to the *palmento*, the driver—a boy if the beast was
steady and the track good—would lean down from his perch high
on the wooden packsaddle, untie the ropes slung around the tall
casks of grapes, and unhook their rope handles from the saddle
as the two loaders, in concerted effort, hoisted them free and

dumped the tightly packed grapes, their juices already flowing, into the *palmento*. With a few strokes of a wooden paddle the treader would heap the grapes into the center of the *palmento* and then, grasping the rope that hung from the ceiling, he began his dance, stomping the pile of grapes down into a thick, flat carpet, circling round to kick them toward the center again, then flattening them out once more with his heavy spiked boots. Over and over he stomped and kicked until the greater part of the must had run out the stone spout and into a large wooden vat that stood on the floor in front of the *palmento*. What remained of pulp and skins, seeds and stems, was shoveled into a corner to make room for a new load, and while the treader began his dance anew, the loaders would pack the skins into the presses. Each *palmento* had its own press, usually an iron *torchio*, a three-legged iron basin with a big iron screw standing in the middle, around which a cage of wooden slats fitted. When the cage was filled with grape skins, a heavy wooden cover was lowered, pressed down by an iron crosspiece that rotated down the screw until it could be tightened no further. Then the press was opened so that the compacted grape skins could be broken up and pressed all over again.

The iron *torchio* was modern compared with the *stringitore* that served the *palmento* in the *cantina*, an enormous wooden screw supported by a heavy wooden structure and turned by a beam more than ten inches in diameter. The must here ran down from tightly woven rush sacks filled with grapes and flowed along the narrow circular trough carved into the big stone base, the one that now serves us as a seat, surrounded by iris in the garden.

When the must spilling from the *palmento* and trickling from the presses had filled the vat, the measuring began. "*In nome di Dio*—in the name of God—one, two . . . ," the measurers filled the *quartare*, flat-bottomed, double-handed copper jugs in the shape of Greek amphorae and sealed with the king's crest to prove their measure was exact, "three . . . four . . . five . . . ," the must was scooped up in the *quartara* and emptied into another vat. Eight *quartare* made a *salma*, five *salme* made a *botte* (about 580 liters). "Fifteen . . . sixteen . . . sixteen and one . . . eighteen . . ."

The man who measured the must took care to avoid the unlucky number, and when he arrived at forty, shouted out the *botte* to the person who was keeping the records, a member of the family if not Don Turiddu himself. The farmer who had produced the grapes would run across from the vat to watch as a notch was cut across a piece of cane that had been split in half, then tied back together again. At the end, when the measuring was finished and the cane untied, the notches could be counted on both halves, the one that Don Turiddu kept and the half he gave to the producer, a receipt less perishable than paper, and easily legible even for the illiterate.

The must, once measured, was poured into a central vat from where it was pumped into the huge casks lining each side of the two *cantine* in double rows. Tonino, when he wasn't carrying messages and running errands, loved to take a turn at pumping, pushing the heavy iron handle back and forth like a road mender on the railway. Everyone worked, even Mrs. Simeti, who supervised the cooking of meals for the harvesters in the Simeti vineyards, and waited, inflexible, at the end of a long day for the women to come in from the fields and join her in saying the rosary in the chapel.

For more than a month the mules came and went. When the casks were full and the first seething stage of fermentation had passed, the family moved back to Alcamo, leaving the young wine to mature quietly until it was ready for sale. Then the mules would come again, this time harnessed to carts that were loaded with big barrels. It took twenty carts to empty one cask and transport the contents to Balestrate to be loaded on ships and carried to the distilleries of the north.

Small wonder, then, that despite all the worry and exhaustion Tonino loves the *vendemmia* so, the present rewards of his own labor informed as they must be in his mind by all the excitement and animation of his childhood memories. Even I am haunted, come September, by the memory of my first *vendemmia*. It was the year of Stefano's death, when we found ourselves unexpectedly running the farm. Tonino's agricultural experience was limited to classroom theory and memories from his youth, while I, who had been to Bosco only once or twice and had never even seen the *vendemmia*, was suddenly floundering in the midst of it, lodged in a falling-down farmhouse with no light or running water where I was expected to cook for a crew of fifteen Sicilian peasants.

I soon learned that the basic rule of such a cuisine is to keep it runny. Whatever I cooked had to be swimming in the sauce or juice or dressing that was required to wash down the thirty kilo loaves of bread that disappeared every day. The tomato, onion, and tuna fish salad that made up the 10:00 a.m. breakfast (picking started at sunrise) floated in very watery vinegar and oil, and the stewed eggplant and potatoes or the egg fritters we ate about 2:00 p.m. were awash in tomato sauce. More sauce had to be prepared for the evening pasta, which was followed by grilled sardines or sausages, or by cheese and salame.

Turi drove in and out from Alcamo, bringing pillowcases bulging with bread and the meager rations with which the elder generation thought it fit to feed the peasants, plus whatever we decided he should buy on the sly. Tonino and I slept at Bosco on cots set up on the second floor, which even then, before the earthquake, trembled at every step. Our sleep was troubled by the hoots of a large beige owl that had flown through a broken window and built a nest in an attic, and we awoke each dawn to find the blankets covered with a light sprinkling of plaster dust.

I was out early, picking the tomatoes for the breakfast salad or for the sauce, peeling potatoes, or chopping onions. The grapes were brought up by muleback to the house and then trucked to a cooperative. The muledriver, who was new to our employ and thrilled me when he addressed Tonino as "Don Antonio," would once a day exchange the grape casks for barrels that he took down to fill at the well, bringing back the water with which I was to cook and wash the dishes.

In my spare moments, which were not many, I would join the harvesters in the vineyards, to pick a grape or two inexpertly and listen to their cheerful banter. What little I then understood of the Sicilian dialect was still much more than they imagined, so my presence in no way inhibited them. Indeed, I was amazed and amused to find that the high price the Sicilians set on virginity was strictly a physical matter: however pure the honor of the young girls in the crew may have been, their chatter was as earthy and unrestricted as that of the men.

Although the setting often seemed unreal to me, the hard work was tangible enough. I was embarrassed to present the food my in-laws sent out and upset by the harvesters' complaints. (I now realize that they probably felt obliged to complain, since they all belonged to Peppino's family.) The stove, a rickety, three-burner affair attached to a canister of bottled gas, was balanced on planks set over two oil drums filled with dry fava beans, and I reached my nadir when Turi, in a hurry to get some beans for the mule, upset the stove: the eggplant stew ended upside down on the dirt floor, a total loss, just as fifteen famished harvesters were gathering. I nearly wept.

But I loved the evenings, when a long table and roughhewn benches were set up in the courtyard, and we ate in the warm glow of oil lanterns. I would look around at the creased and sunburned peasant faces, the women with kerchiefs still tied behind their heads, the men keeping their caps on against the evening damp, and I would listen to them teasing and laughing and making innumerable jokes that had to do with the shape of the sausages. I was so ignorant then that my only terms of reference were Italian movies, and I was proud to think that I had made, and even with a certain grace, the jump from Radcliffe to *Bitter Rice*.

Even that first *vendemmia* of mine has dwindled beyond any recognition: the old exhausted vineyards have been replaced by only half as many new ones, electricity powers the press and pumps the must into shiny steel cisterns, and the Vivonas have long since taken over from Peppino and his family. Their role, too, has shrunk: in the early years the whole Vivona family moved out to sleep in the guesthouse, and I cooked for everyone, whereas now they drive out with baskets of food each morning, and most days only Turiddu, Teresa, and Franca come. The boys participate only on Sundays, giving up their holiday reluctantly and only to spare their mother's health, not, as in former times, because the family would have to live for months on what it could earn during the *vendemmia*. As Felice unloads the grapes from the tractor into the press, he announces to Francesco that he has entered a competition for a job as a municipal street sweeper—900,000 a month and you only work mornings!

My own part in the *vendemmia* has altered as well, reduced to a race to get the children to school, the meals on the table, the sticky, must-stained jeans and T-shirts into the washing machine and out onto the line, the books and clothes packed up for our reentry to city life. It seems ironic and unfair that at the very culmination of a year's work and hopes, my part should be reduced to tertiary service, that I should be excluded from production and its satisfactions. Resentment feeds on my tiredness and mingles with the guilt I feel about the hours of respite I steal each morning, as if, my marriage to Bosco in crisis, I were allowing myself to be seduced into illicit trysts with the books and papers in my Palermo study.

Not that I am far from the country even there: as I sit at my desk I can hear from time to time the porter moving among the pyramids of demijohns in the next room, dispensing wine to our clients, and as my mind wanders or weighs a sentence, I look out the window to a thin wedge of earth, a paring of old agriculture left by the city's advance, in which a few orange trees grow, a medlar, and one much taller almond, together with grass, weeds, and kittens. The almond leaves are limp, ready to let go, and I can just discern the tiny buds on the oranges and the medlar, which will blossom at the end of October. Behind the trees a thick mat of ivy, October's plant, covers a high stone wall that cuts off my view of the city, delimits my place in it, confines my role in it to solitary activity of the mind.

I pass the hours that the children are in school in reading about the Eleusinia and the Thesmophoria, the great festivals with which the Greeks honored Demeter at the close of the agricultural year.

The Mysteries celebrated in late September at Eleusis, where

Demeter first paused in her frantic search for her daughter, were so solemnly surrounded by secrecy that scholars today can only surmise what took place within the sacred precincts of the temple among the initiates who came in procession from Athens and from all over the Hellenic world. I find a dozen accounts, each different, of how Demeter, goddess of grain, her daughter Persephone, the Queen of the Underworld, and Dionysus, god of wine, come together in what the Homeric Hymn calls "the awful mysteries," which appear to have enacted the descent of Persephone into Hades and the holy marriage of Demeter (some say to Dionysus, some say to Zeus), and to have culminated in a moment of mystic contemplation as an ear of ripe wheat, promise of immortality, was held aloft before the celebrants.

The Eleusinian Mysteries were followed, in October, by the Thesmophoria, about which we have more detailed documents. In their original form, these were rites reserved to the legitimate wives of Athenian citizens who came together for three days of fasting and chastity, to mourn the departure of Persephone and the burial of the seed under the earth. A pig was sacrificed and the pieces thrown together with pine cones into the sacred vaults of Demeter, where the rotting flesh of the sacrifice fertilized the seed, thus insuring the fertility of the fields and of the family.

> It is not merely fortuitous that the followers of Demeter Thesmophora take the ritual name of Melisse (Bees), of the insect that symbolizes the conjugal virtues. Emblematic of domesticity, faithful to her husband and mother to legitimate sons, the bee reigns sovereign over the intimate space of the hearth, attending to the conjugal patrimony and never failing to maintain an attitude of reserve and modesty: to her duties as a wife are thus added those of sober and hardworking supervisor, alien to the frivolous chatter in which her sex is wont to indulge.
>
> Marcel Detienne, in M. Detienne and J.-P. Vernant,
> *La cucina del sacrificio in terra greca*

Is *this* where Demeter would lead me? Have I fled definition all these years only to end up as a bee? Revolted by the idea, yet threatened by my revulsion, I thrash about like an uneasy sleeper, tugging at the constrictions of the identity I have constructed for myself here, only to pull it tight at the least breath of change, as though my one great leap of twenty years ago had exhausted all my capacity for elasticity and adaptation.

The children burst in upon my musings and fill the drive back to Bosco with talk of school. Once more I am forced to ponder the ironic fact that the school system should have been at once the channel through which I have most actively participated in Sicilian society and the source of my most bitter regrets about living here. The decision to retire to Bosco and dabble in Demeter is mine to make if I will, but what freedom of choice will Francesco and Natalia have in the third millennium with five years of Latin and Greek and nary a glance at a computer?

We drive over the crest of the hill and draw up to the *cantina* to find Turiddu coming toward us in the tractor, his trailer load of grapes bouncing and jiggling behind him, and it occurs to me, a last thought before I turn my mind to more prosaic matters like pasta, that this year mine is a harvest of mixed blessings.

Epilogue—October 1983

The farmers' work returns to them full circle—
Their year revolves, retracing its own steps.

Virgil, *The Georgics*

❧ The last day of the *vendemmia* is mine. The children have gone off to Palermo with Tonino, whose presence is required at the university, leaving kitchen and *cantina* in my charge. It is my last day at Bosco as well, and the silence of the big house echoes with the comfortable sadness of endings, inventories, and preparations, for tomorrow we shall drive into Palermo to stay. Tonino wants to remain at Bosco for another day or two, to put the *cantina* to rights and to mother the fermenting must, but the children and I will cease our commuting, returning to Bosco only for the weekend. The city awaits us, winter clothes and wool blankets, early persimmons glowing orange amidst pyramids of bright green cauliflowers, smoking tripods of chestnuts roasting at the curbstones, bloodshed and decaying beauty. In the department stores September's display of school supplies has already given way to toys for I Morti, and any day now the bar on the corner will set out the first trays of marzipan fruit and the *pupi di cena* glistening in their sugary colors. But despite the attempts of commerce to accelerate the seasons, the summer will die reluctantly, the heat will linger into autumn, and eager adolescents will wilt under the noonday sun, perspiring heavily in their newly purchased sweaters and boots.

The seasons overlap at Bosco as well. Close to the ground summer is more lush than ever, a last, prolific, rain-encouraged flowering before the petunias and the marigolds disappear under the rising tide of grass and wood sorrel, but this morning the sky above the flower beds is wintry. The *tramontana* has chased summer southward for the moment at least, blowing dark clouds from the north and sending the mercury plummeting. Yesterday's T-shirt is not enough, and I go back upstairs several times to search for additional layers, for stockings and a heavy sweater, and set split peas to cooking on the back of the stove, in answer to a first autumnal craving for hot soup.

Against the gray clouds, the quince bushes rock and sway with each gust of wind, their branches bent into giant wickets by the weight of the fuzzy-skinned fruit slowly ripening toward yellow, and the thicket of musk roses waves its bright red rose hips at me. I wave back lightheartedly: if the quinces are a reminder of work to come, two years of pricking my fingers to harvest the rose hips, of picking out their bristling centers and cooking them, only to end up with half a jar of jelly, was enough for me. "You are where I draw the line!" I answer to their greeting.

The wild roses on the upper road are also heavy with hips, I noticed yesterday as I drove along, and the season has been generous to the hawthorn, the smilax, and the lentisk, which are thick with all sizes and shades of red berries awaiting our last, late, Christmas harvest. The courtyard is lit by the numinous glow of pomegranates, the first two fruits of my gift from the goddess. Sprung from a single stem and swollen with seed, their skin is deep scarlet and ready to split, but I hesitate to pick them, aware that I have no adequate altar on which to offer them.

Heedless of this autumnal scene, the wild lilies have flowered for the first time since Turiddu dug up the bulbs from the Blundas' valley and planted them in the middle of the footpath. These lilies are seductive, almost funereal in their perfume, yet chaste and delicate in dress, pale pink chalices that are borne aloft, six or eight clustered on one long and slender-ankled stem. Unable to find them in any of my wildflower books, I call them lilies as Turiddu does, but suspect them of being a form of amaryllis and harbor a still deeper doubt: were it not hubris to think that Homer could be wrong, I would say that these were Persephone's narcissuses, blooming alone and irresistible at the end of summer, a pale torch to light her way to the Underworld.

I am very arbitrary about how I draw my lines. Having put the rose hips beyond the pale, I spend the morning experimenting with *mostarda* instead of getting on with my packing. *Mostarda* is an etymological curiosity as well as a culinary one, a condiment originally made from must, which lent the name "mustard" to the yellow sauce we spread on hot dogs, and then in turn to the family of plants from whose seeds the modern mustard is derived.

What I am trying to make is the original mustard, a chewy sweet paste made of must and cornstarch, boiled down into a sticky muck into which currants, pine nuts, and almonds are stirred just before it is poured into molds to dry and harden. My mother-in-law used to make it every year and always had a piece ready for the grandchildren when we went to visit her at Finocchio during the olive harvest. Natalia doesn't know what I am talking about when I say I want to make *mostarda*, but as soon as she comes home today and sniffs at the boiling must she will remember her grandmother's *mostarda* spread out to dry on chairs, nose level for her then, in the sun at Finocchio.

Mrs. Simeti's memory has been so eaten away by age that she does not remember ever making *mostarda*. My search for a recipe was finally and unexpectedly rewarded when we were going through drawers at Alcamo this summer and turned up a little notebook filled with a girlish version of my mother-in-law's handwriting. In the front pages she had carefully copied out the lyrics of her favorite songs, "The Soldier's Farewell" and "The Barber of Seville," while the second part is filled with recipes for pastries and puddings and other sweets. Some are transcribed in full, perhaps from ladies' magazines, others are simple lists of ingredients and their quantities, but all are expressed in strange measures that no longer have a place in the metric Italian kitchen: two *soldi*'s worth of butter or milk, a "roll" of ricotta or of *maiorca*, fine white flour milled from a variety of wheat that was once specially grown for pastry making, sugar *onze uno e mezzo*. The recipe for *mostarda* calls for a *quarto* of must, which I am at a loss to interpret until To-nino thinks to ask Nino Di Giovanni. A *quarto* equals 750 grams.

As a first try I don't do too badly. The *mostarda* has a cloudy gray color I later learn could have been avoided by clarifying the must with wood ashes (before next September I must discover the proper measure for wood ashes), and it won't be around long enough for me to find out whether it would have dried to the req-uisite hardness. But I am amused by what I am doing, and the sweet smell of the boiling must, the steady simmer of the split pea soup, and the hospitable converse of the flames in the fire-place keep me company.

I work in fits and starts, one ear attending the sound of the tractor that signals that it is time for me to pull on a windbreaker and go outside to throw the switch on the grape press and start its big brass screw turning. Ours is an old press, its red paint chipped and rusting, and it does a very inefficient job, but what we lose in quantity we gain in quality. The same delicate squeeze without bruise would cost us extra in a more modern machine, so each year we decide affectionately to cope with the eccentric-ities of this one for one more season.

The winepress is very physiological: a conical mouth on the top swallows the grapes and sends them down to the bowels of the machine, where the brass screw rotates within a brass cylin-der that is perforated with slits that let the must run out. The screw pushes the grapes tighter and tighter against a weighted lid, which every few minutes eases up to emit a large cylindrical turd of dry skins, seeds, and stems. These heap up and are eventu-ally trucked off to the distillery to provide rubbing alcohol, while the must drains down into a length of plastic hose and into the *cantina*.

Turiddu maneuvers the tractor so that the trailer is parallel to the press, and standing beside the two machines, he slowly emp-ties the buckets of grapes into the mouth of the press. I climb up on a ladder propped against the other side and help to guide the grapes down into the maw of the beast, plucking out the leaves and stirring the sticky, slithery, sugary mass to break up the tangles that catch in its throat. Despite all Tonino's pessimism, the tiny, fragile beads that embroidered the vines in June have survived the drought and the heat wave, the peronospera mildew and the oidium mold and have grown into small but perfect spheres, pale green burnished to brass by the sun and swollen to translucence by the August rains. The bunches are big and heavy and stiff, their stems held rigid in a corset of tightly clustered grapes.

Turiddu and I are undone by our admiration for the marvel of the grapes and interrupt our work continually to vent our excitement, pointing out a particularly generous bunch or a perfectly ripened load. The differences and difficulties of the past months forgotten, Turiddu glows with good will.

"Ah, signora, when it's like this, you want the *vendemmia* to go on forever."

When the last grape has been unloaded, Turiddu drives off again, the empty buckets clattering and bouncing in the trailer as he puts on speed, racing against the *tramontana* to finish before the rain comes, and I switch off the empty ruminating of the press and set to scrubbing out the big oil drum I used to boil my bottles of tomato sauce in. Tonino intends to press the unmarketable remains of the Italia grapes and boil their juice down into *vino cotto*, a thick, sweet syrup somewhat like molasses, which is used for cooking and also for raising the sugar content of must from poorly ripened grapes. When he told me of this plan a few days ago, I told him he was mad—one more unnecessary complication in an already chaotic and exhausting *vendemmia*—but now, as I crawl in on my hands and knees to reach the bottom of the drum where this afternoon the must will boil, I realize it is not madness that divides us, but a lack of synchronization. Satisfied by a whole summer of harvests, I have been fretting to reduce the *vendemmia* to a well-organized routine, something to be gotten over with so that I can concentrate on the next concern. My need to move on (the old frontier spirit?) clashes with Tonino's need to improvise and experiment, to reinvent the *vendemmia* each year, so as to press out every drop of satisfaction and keep alive the sense of excitement he remembers from his childhood. I do believe he has exaggerated this year—but so have I. My preoccupation with distant decisions and future harvests has deafened me to the message that Demeter whispered to me at Enna last November and closed my mind to the archaic rhythms I profess to seek. I have yet to learn the lesson, to live—and let my children live—each season as it comes, without justification or apology.

Around me as I scrub, the *cantina* breathes and murmurs. The untold thousands of tiny vinegar gnats that move and settle in a dense cloud, blackening everything that has been touched by must, spin off a faint whispering drone, into which their predators, the wasps, weave a fugue of buzz and hum. Like giant muted kettle drums, the massive cylinders of fermenting must gurgle and rumble a soft basso continuo, accompanying the staccato that comes from the far end of the *cantina*, where the big casks, their wood shriveled from disuse slowly swelling in the damp heat of fermentation, ooze drops of must that fall in erratic syncopation into the mosaic of aluminum freezer trays arranged on the floor below.

These trays must be emptied from time to time, and a vigilant eye turned to the fermenting cisterns, which are prone to boiling over in their enthusiasm. No sooner have I set the oil drum upside down to drain than the chugging of the tractors announces Turiddu's return. Once more I take up my station at the press. A weary but grinning Dionysus wreathed by a sweat-stained beret instead of grape leaves, Turiddu picks out an enormous, perfect cluster and holds it aloft before me in a dangling fall of golden grapes.

With this load the vat is full, and I must measure with a stick calibrated in *salme* the depth of the must, its muddy color already hidden by the thick scum of fermentation, then blow aside this froth and take a sample in a plastic tube, into which I drop a mercury-laden glass that measures the density and the sugar content. Once I have added the results of my measuring to the long columns written with a felt-tipped pen on the flank of a steel cistern, I switch on the pump and send the must coursing toward the cask where it will undergo the miraculous metamorphosis from its present murky state, yellow brown and scum covered, into the clear pale gold of wine.

The pulsing throb and suck of the pump adds its voice to the music of the *cantina*, a visceral, volcanic sound that echoes in the cool and chthonic darkness. Easy in my acquired skills, yet still surprised by them, I perform these simple rites with pride and pleasure. The must flows through the pipes, a libation to Demeter and Dionysus, and it is here, surrounded by a tall colonnade of steel cisterns, far from the sacred precincts of Eleusis or the flowering shores of Lake Pergusa, that in honoring the mother, the daughter is revealed to me: Persephone, the eternal expatriate, the goddess of unreconciled contrasts and alternate allegiances, who *chose* to eat the seeds of the pomegranate, that she might enjoy two roles, two worlds.

Author's Note

🌿 I have approached the thorny issue of relating contemporary Sicilian folklore to classical Greek rites with the same blithe ignorance with which I approach my garden, putting in bits and pieces that appeal to me, with little regard for any theoretical framework. This journal has no scholarly pretensions and is not intended for those who debate the question professionally. I hope only to entertain those who know nothing of Sicily and to make their visit here more rewarding.

Sources

BRYDONE, PATRICK. *A Tour Through Sicily and Malta*. Edinburgh, 1840.

CAMPORESI, PIERO. *Alimentazione, folclore, società*. Parma: Pratiche Editrice, 1980.

CARDINI, FRANCO. *I giorni del sacro: il libro delle feste*. Milan: Editoriale Nuove, 1983.

CICERO. *The Verrine Orations*. Volume 2. Translated by H. H. G. Greenwood. Cambridge: Harvard University Press, 1967.

CRONIN, VINCENT. *The Golden Honeycomb*. London: Rupert Hart-Davis, 1959.

Delle cose di Sicilia: testi inediti o rari. Volume 1. Edited by Leonardo Sciascia. Palermo: Sellerio Editore, 1980.

DETIENNE, MARCEL. *The Gardens of Adonis: Spices in Greek Mythology*. Translated by Janet Lloyd. London: Harvester Press, 1977.

DETIENNE, M., AND VERNANT, J.-P. *La cucina del sacrificio in terra greca*. Turin: Editore Boringhieri, 1982.

FINLEY, M. I., AND DENIS MACK SMITH. *A History of Sicily in Three Volumes*. London: Chatto and Windus, 1968.

FRAZER, J. G. *The Golden Bough: A Study in Magic and Religion*. Abridged version. New York: Macmillan, 1957.

GOETHE, J. W. *Italian Journey (1786–1788)*. Translated by W. H. Auden and Elizabeth Mayer. San Francisco: North Point Press, 1982.

GRAVES, ROBERT. *The Greek Myths*. London: Penguin Books, 1955.

HARRISON, JANE ELLEN. *Prolegomena to the Study of Greek Religion*. London: Merlin Press, 1980.

HOMER. *The Homeric Hymns*. Translated by Apostolos N. Athanassakis. Baltimore: Johns Hopkins University Press, 1976.

IRVINE, WILLIAM. *Letters on Sicily*. London, 1813.

LAMPEDUSA, G. TOMASI DI. *The Leopard*. Translated by Archibald Colquhoun. New York: Pantheon, 1960.

———. *Two Stories and a Memory*. Translated by Archibald Colquhoun. New York: Pantheon, 1962.

Sources

LAWRENCE, D. H. *Sea and Sardinia*. London: Penguin Books, 1981.

MELEAGER. *The Poems of Meleager of Gadara*. Translated by Richard Aldington. London: Egoist Press, 1920.

NORWICH, JOHN JULIUS. *The Kingdom in the Sun*. London: Allen Lane, 1970.

OVID. *The Metamorphoses*. Translated by Arthur Golding. London: William Seres, 1967.

The Oxford Book of Greek Verse in Translation. Edited by Higham and Bowra. Oxford: Oxford University Press, 1938.

PINDAR. *The Odes of Pindar*. Translated by R. Lattimore. Chicago: University of Chicago Press, 1976.

PITRÈ, GIUSEPPE. *Biblioteca della tradizioni popolari siciliani*. Palermo, 1870–1913. Facsimile edition, 1978. *(La famiglia, la casa, la vita del popolo siciliano; Feste patronali in Sicilia; Spettacoli e feste popolari siciliani; Usi e constumi, credenze e pregiudizi del popolo siciliano)*

PONTORNO, MELO. Article in *Il Giornale di Sicilia*. 4 April 1983.

SCIASCIA, LEONARDO. *La corda pazza: scrittori e cose della Sicilia*. Turin: Einaudi, 1982.

———. *Il giorno della civetta*. Turin: Einaudi, 1961.

SMYTH, W. H. *Memoir descriptive of the resources, inhabitants and hydrography of Sicily and its Islands interspersed with antiquarian and other notices*. London, 1820.

STRUTT, ARTHUR JOHN. *A Pedestrian Tour in Calabria and Sicily*. London: T. C. Newby, 1841.

THUCYDIDES. *The Peloponnesian War*. Translated by Rex Warner. London: Penguin Books, 1959.

VIRGIL. *The Georgics*. Books 1 and 2. Translated by S. P. Bovie. Chicago: University of Chicago Press, 1956.

ZUNTZ, GÜNTHER. *Persephone: Three Essays on Religion and Thought in Magna Graecia*. Oxford: Clarendon Press, 1971.

Where I have quoted from texts in Italian, I have used my own translations.

Sicilian literature offers a particularly rich and rewarding introduction to the island, and besides the works of Lampedusa and Sciascia, those of Giovanni Verga, Elio Vittorini, Federico De Roberto, and Luigi Pirandello are available in English translation.

Index